Jane Austen

Jane Austen is one of England's most enduringly popular authors, renowned for her subtle observations of the provincial middle classes of late eighteenth- and early nineteenth-century England.

This guide to Austen's much-loved work offers:

- an accessible introduction to the contexts and many interpretations of Austen's texts, including film adaptations, from publication to the present;
- an introduction to key critical texts and perspectives on Austen's life and work, situated within a broader critical history;
- cross-references between sections of the guide, in order to suggest links between texts, contexts and criticism;
- suggestions for further reading.

Part of the *Routledge Guides to Literature* series, this volume is essential reading for all those beginning detailed study of Jane Austen and seeking not only a guide to her works but also a way through the wealth of contextual and critical material that surrounds them.

Robert P. Irvine is a lecturer in English Literature at the University of Edinburgh.

Routledge Guides to Literature*

Editorial Advisory Board: Richard Bradford (University of Ulster at Coleraine), Jan Jedrzejewski (University of Ulster at Coleraine), Duncan Wu (St. Catherine's College, University of Oxford)

Routledge Guides to Literature offer clear introductions to the most widely studied authors and literary texts. Each book engages with texts, contexts and criticism, highlighting the range of critical views and contextual factors that need to be taken into consideration in advanced studies of literary works. The series encourages informed but independent readings of texts by ranging as widely as possible across the contextual and critical issues relevant to the works examined and highlighting areas of debate as well as those of critical consensus. Alongside general guides to texts and authors, the series includes 'sourcebooks', which allow access to reprinted contextual and critical materials as well as annotated extracts of primary text.

Available in this series

* Some books in this series were originally published in the Routledge Literary Sourcebooks series, edited by Duncan Wu, or the Complete Critical Guide to English Literature series, edited by Richard Bradford and Jan Jedrzejewski.

Jane Austen

Robert P. Irvine

LONDON AND NEW YORK

First published 2005
by Routledge
2 Park Square, Milton Park, Abingdon, Oxon OX14 4RN

Simultaneously published in the USA and Canada
by Routledge
270 Madison Ave, New York, NY 10016

Routledge is an imprint of the Taylor & Francis Group

Typeset in Sabon and Gill Sans by RefineCatch Limited, Bungay, Suffolk
Printed and bound in Great Britain by
TJ International Ltd, Padstow, Cornwall

British Library Cataloguing in Publication Data
A catalogue record for this book is available from the British Library.

Library of Congress Cataloging in Publication Data
Irvine, Robert P., 1965–
    Jane Austen / Robert P. Irvine.
        p.   cm.
    Includes bibliographical references and index.
    1. Austen, Jane, 1775–1817—Criticism and interpretation.   2. Women
and literature—England—History—19th century.   3. Love stories,
English— History and criticism.   4. Middle class in literature.   I. Title.
    PR4037 .I785 2005
    823'.7—dc22   2004015162

ISBN 0–415–31434–8 (hbk)
ISBN 0–415–31435–6 (pbk)

Contents

3: Criticism   91

4: Austen on screen   148

Acknowledgements

Thanks are due to my editor Liz Thompson, and to series editors Richard Bradford and Jan Jedrzejewski, for their patience, and to them and their referees for their very helpful comments on the first draft. Thanks also to Broadview Press for permission to reproduce material from my introduction to their 2002 edition of *Pride and Prejudice*. The Department of English Literature, University of Edinburgh, were good enough to give me sabbatical leave to get started on this book. Thanks also to Vicky Millar and Jake Heskia, for the loan of the flat and a shoulder to cry on; and to Penny Fielding, for even more generous accommodation and tolerance in this book's final stages.

Abbreviations and referencing

Page references in this text take three forms, depending on the type of text being referred to. A page number in square brackets in bold thus: [see p. 12] refers you to another part of this volume; plain numerals in round brackets thus: (Johnson 1988: 12) or, in later references, just (12) refer you to a secondary work, listed alphabetically in one of the bibliographies at the end of the volume; while upper- and lower-case roman and arabic numerals thus: (I.ii.34) refer you to volume, chapter and page numbers in the most recent Penguin Classics editions of Austen's novels (2003: also in the bibliography). These volume numbers, and the accompanying non-continuous chapter numbers, are those of the original editions of the novels, which appeared in two or three separate volumes. As well as Penguin, World's Classics and Broadview editions use these original divisions to mark the text.

Introduction

Jane Austen is one of very few writers to be well known to thousands of people who have never read any of her books. She is one of a few writers to have been taken, like Shakespeare, to represent something enduring about her nation. As such, she can be invoked in public debate in Britain in ways that have little to do with what she actually wrote or the context in which she wrote it. She is therefore one of the few writers from the past of whom an understanding is necessary to allow the modern reader to make a more informed contribution to contemporary discussions of class, gender and nationality.

Part 1 of this book attempts to summarise both the political and the social context in which Austen wrote, and the particular literary resources that were available to her as a woman novelist at the end of the eighteenth and beginning of the nineteenth centuries. Part 2 then explores the six novels that she published, or prepared for publication, in her lifetime. Part 3 then discusses the various ways in which those novels have been discussed by academic literary critics in the past sixty years or so. Finally, Part 4 introduces the reader to the ongoing critical discussion of film and television adaptations of Austen's work.

The aim of this book is to give readers a map with which they can navigate through Austen's works, their historical, social and literary context and the critical discussion that they and their film versions have generated. Or rather, it offers four maps, each cross-referenced to the others. Newcomers to Austen might most usefully begin with the section of Part 2 on the novel that they are currently reading. That section will direct them to Part 1, where the social or political issues raised are discussed at greater length; or they could use the references at the end of that section to guide them to criticism outlined in Parts 3 and 4 on particular aspects of that novel that have caught their attention. Those readers already familiar with some of Austen's novels might find it more useful to turn directly to Parts 1, 3 or 4, to fill in any gaps in their understanding of Austen's historical period, or to discover the problems currently being debated in academic criticism of her novels and their screen adaptations.

Life and contexts

Introduction

Part 1 puts Jane Austen's career as a novelist in the context of the historical development of English society, of the novel and of the place of women in relation to both, in the century or so until her death. It appears to spend comparatively little time on the details of her life, for which you should turn to any of the cited biographies. But it assumes that her life and career as a novelist as summarised here are interesting precisely because they were shaped by and reflect the particular forces and assumptions that characterised her age, her class and her nation. These are the forces and assumptions that we will see being acted out and questioned in her novels in Part 2. After outlining Austen's biography Part 1 will accordingly move from the general to the particular: from English society in general to the place of women in that society, to the place of women writers, and finally women novelists in particular; and from the eighteenth and early nineteenth centuries in general to the decades after 1770, and then specifically the aftermath of the French Revolution and of the wars with France, in which Austen actually wrote her fiction.

For a clear outline of how the events of Austen's life correspond to those of political and literary history, please consult the Chronology at the end of this book [see pp. 161–5].

Austen's life

Jane Austen was born on 16 December 1775 at Steventon in Hampshire, in the south-east of England. Her father, the Reverend George Austen, was Rector of Steventon church. Both his family background and that of his wife Cassandra (*née* Leigh) were in the rural landowning classes, but his father was a mere surgeon (a much cruder and less prestigious profession than it would later become), while Cassandra's lineage ranged much higher. Paying posts in the Church of England, known as church 'livings', were at this time in the gift of the landowners on whose estates the parishes lay. The Steventon estate was owned by George Austen's wealthy second cousin, Thomas Knight, who two years before Austen's birth had also granted George the living of nearby Deane.

But the income from these two positions only came to about £200 a year. To put this in perspective, a skilled worker such as a carpenter or blacksmith could earn around £100 a year at this time, and the 'gentry', smaller landowners such as Knight, could collect between £1,000 and £5,000 annually in rents and other income from their estates (Spring 1983: 58). In *Sense and Sensibility*, Edward Ferrars' living of £200 a year is regarded as too little to support a wife (III.iv.270; cited in Spring 1983: 62). Yet Jane was George Austen's seventh child, and another arrived three years later. He supported this large family with additional income from one of the farms on Knight's estate, and by boarding and tutoring local boys. Revd Austen also tutored his own sons, but Jane and her sister Cassandra, three years her senior, were educated at first by their mother, in reading, writing and religion at the very least. The girls continued their education for two years at boarding schools, first at Oxford and Southampton in 1783, and then from 1785 to 1786 in Reading. At such establishments they studied needlework, English, French and Italian, and possibly music and drawing. These were the conventional 'accomplishments' expected of young ladies of their rank, although they also seem to have covered some history (Fergus 1991: 34–7; Honan 1997: 31–4, 37) [see pp. 24–5]. Their brothers' education, on the other hand, would have centred on the Latin language and its literature. Acquiring a knowledge of these subjects was something of a rite of passage into the masculine ruling class and a requirement for entry to Oxford or Cambridge universities and thus to the church. This was the path taken by James, the eldest, and Henry, the fourth son, who were supported financially at St John's College, Oxford, by their father, but also subsidised by the college as descendants of its founders through their mother's higher-ranking side of the family. In contrast, the two youngest boys, Frank and Charles, were packed off to the Royal Naval Academy at Portsmouth at around twelve years of age to begin careers as midshipmen.

We know that Jane Austen began writing at an early age as three volumes of stories and verses survive that were composed in her teens. This material was written between 1787 or 1788 and 1792 for the entertainment of family and friends and with the family's full encouragement. The second volume includes an impressive short fiction in letters called 'Love and Friendship', and the third culminates in the already sophisticated short novel, 'Catherine, or the Bower'. In 1794 Austen wrote another that survives in a later copy as 'Lady Susan'. And in 1795 and 1796 she wrote 'Elinor and Marianne' and 'First Impressions', the novels that, much later and after some revision, appeared at the start of her career as a published author as *Sense and Sensibility* (1811) and *Pride and Prejudice* (1813) respectively. The reason for the long gap between the writing and publication of these novels we shall discuss below. In 1797 George Austen submitted the manuscript of 'First Impressions' to London publishers Cadell & Davies who rejected it without even looking it over, but this disappointment did not stop his daughter immediately beginning the revision of 'Elinor and Marianne' that would turn it into *Sense and Sensibility*. By 1799 she had completed another novel, 'Susan', which would be published after her death as *Northanger Abbey* (1817).

In 1801 Austen's father retired, and his son James, who was already looking after Deane as its curate, took over the duties of Steventon as well. The income from the parish remained George's for his lifetime, and he took his wife and daughters with him to Bath, then a fashionable resort to which many professionals chose to retire at the end of their careers, quite independently of their hope of any good effects from the supposedly healing waters of the spa. The Austens had several practical reasons for the move, but biographers often speculate that they may also have wanted to increase Jane and Cassandra's chances of meeting potential husbands (Halperin 1984: 124; Tomalin 2000: 174; Spence 2003: 132). In 1795–6 Jane had slipped into a serious relationship with Tom Lefroy, another family friend, but his relatives made sure this did not get as far as a proposal of marriage from a very young and penniless man. It was not at Bath, however, but on a visit to James at Steventon in 1802 that the eldest son of a wealthy local landowning family called Bigg-Wither, old friends and neighbours of the Austens, proposed to Jane and was accepted. The following morning she withdrew her acceptance. This vacillation is usually read as being between the substantial financial comfort that marriage to Bigg-Wither offered Jane, and her realisation that she could never love him, between material self-interest and romantic principle, although Bigg-Wither seems to have been a man very hard to like, let alone love (Halperin 1984: 134–5; Honan 1997: 193–7; Nokes 1997: 251–3).

It was also while living at Bath that Jane first succeeded in selling a novel, 'Susan', receiving £10 for the manuscript from the publishing firm Crosby & Co. This was not a great sum even then, but probably a typical payment for a two-volume novel from an unknown writer: Frances Burney (1752–1840), the most financially successful female novelist of the period and much better connected than Austen in London publishing circles, received only £20 for the manuscript of her first, three-volume, novel, *Evelina* (1778) (Turner 1992: 114). But although advertised, 'Susan' was not published, and having sold the manuscript outright Austen could do nothing about this. Austen's publishing options will be discussed later [see pp. 13–16]. George Austen died quite suddenly in Bath in 1805, and with him went the £600 a year that was his income from various sources at this time. Mrs Austen, Jane and Cassandra hung on in Bath for another year or so, living now on Mrs Austen's private income of £210 a year, supplemented with remittances from the more prosperous of her sons. In 1806, the Austen women moved in with sailor Frank, his wife Mary and their little daughter, in Southampton. In 1809 Mrs Austen's second son Edward, who had been adopted as heir by Thomas Knight (the son of George Austen's cousin and patron of the same name), invited them to settle at Chawton Cottage, back on the Hampshire estate on which the two girls had grown up. They jumped at the chance (Honan 1997: 250). Jane was to live at Chawton for the rest of her life, and it was here that she not only revised *Sense and Sensibility, Pride and Prejudice* and (eventually) *Northanger Abbey* for publication, but also wrote three new novels, *Mansfield Park* (in 1811–13, published 1814), *Emma* (in 1814–15, published 1815) and *Persuasion* (in 1815–16, published posthumously in 1817); and began a fourth, 'Sanditon', in 1817. In May 1817 she took lodgings in Winchester to be near the physician who was treating her for an illness, probably a glandular disorder called Addison's disease, which had been progressively weakening her for a year; but the treatment was to no avail and she died there on 18 July 1817. She was forty-one years old.

It is striking, in this brief sketch of Austen's career, that the steady development of her output as a novelist seems to have been suspended when she left Hampshire in 1801, only to be energetically resumed on her return there in 1809. An aborted novel, 'The Watsons', seems to be the only prose fiction that she began between those dates. Biographers often suggest that Austen's creativity depended on the rural surroundings, both natural and social, in which she had grown up, and that her unhappiness in town prevented her from writing (Lascelles 1995: 29; Tomalin 2000: 169; Shields 2001: 73). It is, however, at least possible that the public entertainments available in Bath and Southampton not only allowed little time for writing but removed the necessity for story-telling initially conceived as family entertainment, without Austen being particularly unhappy about this (Nokes 1997: 342, 350–1). In addition, Austen spent a large proportion of this period staying with friends all over the south of England as well as moving house several times, and the very unsettled nature of this existence militates against a project demanding as much time as writing a long novel (Fergus 1991: 104–6). It is certainly possible to see Austen's time in Bath and Southampton as valuable to her writing in the new experiences that it offered her (Honan 1997: 228–30; Shields 2001: 108). Her brother Henry, in the 'Biographical Notice of the Author' which he attached to the posthumously published *Northanger Abbey* and *Persuasion*, claims that 'some' of her novels were 'the gradual performance of her previous life' and were withheld from publication 'till time and many perusals had satisfied her' of their real worth (Austen 1998: 270–1). Henry presumably refers not just to *Northanger Abbey* but to *Sense and Sensibility* and *Pride and Prejudice* as well. His portrayal of an author suffering 'an invincible distrust of her own judgement' (270) in this way may be designed to fit in with the feminine modesty and self-effacement demanded of female writers [see pp. 8, 12–13]. But his comment also suggests that Austen continued to revise her work even when not composing new material. The immediate aftermath of her father's death, when she abandoned 'The Watsons', may be the only real interruption in this ongoing creative activity (Honan 1997: 215).

Yet the timing of Austen's second, and more determined, effort to get her work published remains odd. The wives and daughters of poorly paid clergymen were always in a financially insecure position, dependent on an income that, unlike an income from an estate or from capital investments, abruptly ceased on his death, and they were unlikely to be able to save enough in his lifetime to live off the interest afterwards. In this event, many turned to the only other 'investment' they could fall back on, namely their education, often unusually good for women, by becoming professional writers (Davidoff and Hall 1987: 125; Lovell 1987: 42; Turner 1992: 63). Of the three Austen women in Bath, Jane was the only one with absolutely no private resources to contribute to their household, Cassandra having a small private income of her own (Halperin 1984: 145–6). Yet her first visible move towards resuming her career as a published novelist, an angry letter to the publisher Crosby demanding that he either publish or return 'Susan', is not made until April 1809, *after* the move to Chawton had been decided on and thus a return to more comfortable circumstances already assured (Le Faye 1995: 174–5).

Austen's England: hierarchy, modernity and gender

The England in which Jane Austen lived and worked was, on the one hand, structured by a long-established political and social order and, on the other, undergoing rapid and accelerating social and economic change. The political and social institutions of the nation were still those of the period historians sometimes, for convenience, refer to as 'the long eighteenth century'. This is the period beginning with the so-called 'Glorious Revolution' in 1688, when a group of English lords forced the Catholic King James II into exile and replaced him with his Protestant sister Mary and her Dutch husband William, Prince of Orange. The revolution established a constitution which, by the Bill of Rights of 1689, abolished the arbitrary exercise of power by the monarch and gave real legislative and executive power to the Houses of Parliament: the hereditary House of Lords and, primarily, the elected House of Commons. The revolution brought to a close the political and religious wars of the seventeenth century in England and is called 'Glorious' because it was, in England, peaceful, although it was not so in Ireland and Scotland. The 'long eighteenth century' can most usefully be taken to end in 1832, when the first of the nineteenth century's Reform Bills was finally, after a long struggle, passed by parliament. This slightly extended and greatly rationalised the qualifications for voting in elections for the Commons. For example, wealthy property owners in the expanding industrial towns were allowed to vote for the first time after 1832.

For the political settlement of 1688–9 was not a democratic one. The aristocracy, the titled nobility, the great landowning families of 'quality' or 'rank', simply inherited political power, with their most senior males sitting in the House of Lords. But the right to vote for members of the House of Commons was also very restricted, mostly to the (male) gentry, those who held property in the form of country estates. There were only a few hundred aristocratic families in England in this period, but over 10,000 gentry families (Vickery 1998: 14), out of a total population that by 1801 was over nine million (Plumb 1950: 144). English society in the long eighteenth century can thus be divided politically into three groups: aristocracy, gentry and everyone else. This last group included the vast majority of the population with no property who did manual work for a living: tenant farmers and rural labourers, and the increasing numbers of factory workers and miners, who had no vote in anything. But among those with no vote was also a very varied section of society often referred to at the time as the 'middling sort' (Hunt 1996: 15). In the towns and cities this included an expanding urban middle class whose property took the form of stakes in manufacturing companies or trading concerns, and who were actively engaged in commerce. In both town and country, it included those living off interest paid on capital investments, often those who had retired from their own enterprises; and lawyers, churchmen and officers in the armed services.

Jane Austen's immediate family belonged to the rural version of this professional group, earning its living mainly in the church and the military. But it retained close ties to the gentry. Mobility between gentry and the rural professional classes was normal, as only the eldest son of a landowning family inherited the estate (by a law known as 'primogeniture'), and the army and the church were common destinations for younger sons. An understanding of precisely where one stood in the social hierarchy was important to anyone in England in this period: the Austens stood below gentry families like the Knights or the Bigg-Withers but, because George was university-educated, above any kind of merchant. Yet social identity remained defined more by one's local or family connections with those above or below one in this hierarchy, from whom one could ask favours or to whom one could grant them, rather than by one's solidarity with others on the same social level as oneself. How far a man might get in the army, or in government, was determined by the extent to which these 'connections' with the power to do so pushed positions his way. This is called 'patronage'. So, for example, George Austen, the orphaned son of a country surgeon, is taken up by an uncle who paves his way towards a scholarship to Oxford. He is then given his two church livings by a second cousin, Thomas Knight (Spring 1983: 62–3; Honan 1997: 14–15). We will discuss patronage in Austen's fiction in the case of *Pride and Prejudice* and *Mansfield Park* [see pp. 58, 63–4]. It is because people tended to identify themselves within these local networks that using the term 'class' to describe the 'middling sort' is a bit anachronistic in Austen's period (Martin 1998; though see also McMaster 1997). 'Class' identities, later in the nineteenth century, group people by the source of their income (labour, capital or land). As such, class is something shared by people in the same economic situation all across the nation, and indeed the world. But class was beginning to emerge as a type of social organisation in Austen's lifetime: 'At some point between the French Revolution and the Great Reform Act [of 1832], the vertical antagonisms and horizontal solidarities of class emerged on a national scale and overlay the vertical bonds and horizontal rivalries of connection and interest' (Perkin 1969: 177). Accordingly, many discussions of Austen's novels centre on her treatment of class [see pp. 114–15, 121–4].

Indeed England in the long eighteenth century, while it remained a quite rigidly hierarchical society, also saw the emergence of a range of characteristically modern institutions, of which class can be seen as one. A limited monarchy with a sovereign parliament allowed the emergence of a recognisably modern state system. The state was centred no longer on the person of a king or queen commanding the loyalty of aristocrats, but rather on a bureaucracy mostly concerned with the raising and distribution of revenue, especially to the increasingly important and professional armed forces. Trade with Britain's colonies in North America, the Caribbean and India, including the Atlantic trade in African slaves [see pp. 134–8] made Britain rich. This trade made possible, and was in turn financed by, a new system of stake-holding capitalism, with trading companies owned by groups of investors. Investors soon included many landowners as well as members of the urban commercial and professional classes. The eighteenth century is Britain's first great capitalist age, and expanded and raised to new prominence a class of people whose wealth consisted in company stocks or government bonds, that is in (recently acquired) money (they are often referred to as the 'moneyed' classes), as opposed to those whose property consisted mainly of (inherited) land (the 'landed' gentry and aristocracy).

Capital, generated and invested more or less independently of government control, in turn made possible and necessary the emergence of another modern institution. This is a public culture of information exchange, often referred to as the 'public sphere' after its discussion under this name in the 1960s by Jürgen Habermas (1989). The emergence of this public sphere was perhaps driven at first by the need of investors to know what was going on in the business world, but it also provided a space outside parliament in which government policy, social practice and contemporary ideas and issues generally could be freely debated.

This space was constituted on the one hand by the coffee-houses and salons (semi-public meeting spaces in the town houses of wealthy families) of London and a few other cities, but also by the rapidly expanding world of print and its regular daily, weekly or monthly journals. Such spaces and such publications made possible a rational criticism of society that is part of what we call the 'Enlightenment' of this period. Existing social practices and institutions, rather than being taken as authoritative merely because they were inherited from the past, were to be examined and explained in order that they might be improved, on the basis of whatever consensus could be reached in the public sphere.

Jane Austen, then, was writing within a society that was both hierarchical and modernising. But her relation to both social hierarchy and social change was shaped by the fact of her gender. There are, broadly speaking, two types of story that social and cultural historians tell about the changing place of women in English society in the long eighteenth century. One of these describes an increasing separation between the types of activity open to men and those open to women. As agriculture became more and more a capitalist industry, and as trade and manufacture expanded, these activities no longer took place, at least partly, in the homes of the farmers and tradespeople. The wives and daughters of prosperous farmers, merchants and artisans became 'physically isolated' from the world of public business (Hill 1989: 51) and thus lost the prestige and authority that came from contributing to family finances and the local economy. At the same time, the very prosperity of the family enterprises removed the need for them to work in the first place. A division opened up among the 'middling sort' between a public world of work, now exclusively male, and a private world of the home and of leisure to which the women were confined. And through this domesticity of their women, the middling sort could claim a share in the culture of their social superiors in the gentry, whose women of course had never worked. This share in gentry culture is referred to as 'gentility' (Davidoff 1995: 181), making the menfolk of the middling sort 'gentlemen' (Barrell 1983: 31–40) and thus distancing them from their poorer parents or grandparents. 'For a middle-class woman of the early nineteenth century, gentility was coming to be defined by a special form of femininity which ran directly counter to acting as a visibly independent economic agent' (Davidoff and Hall 1987: 315). It is argued that capitalism thus narrowed the sphere in which women could enjoy authority and responsibility to the world of the home, and principally to domestic economy and childcare. The wealthier such women were, the more they could delegate such tasks to servants, and the more they were left in lives of pointless leisure (Stone and Stone 1977: 396).

This 'domestic thesis' (Klein 1995: 97) or theory of emerging 'separate spheres' for men and women (Davidoff and Hall 1987: 33) can, however, be challenged on several grounds. For one thing it tends to identify publicly performed economic activity with the 'public sphere' as such. Women of the 'middling sort' may not have worked as much as their mothers or grandmothers, but that does not mean they were excluded from all forms of public life. Other forms of public activity may have remained, or become, open to them: institutionalised charitable work or the organisation of local assemblies and other social events (Vickery 1998: 10, 240–1). The home itself was not necessarily entirely 'private', remaining an important site of business negotiation where hospitality performed a crucial role in cementing economic relationships (Vickery 1998: 9, 195–6). Further, much of the evidence for the 'domestic thesis' is drawn from 'advice' or 'conduct' literature, which counselled young women of the propertied classes on the behaviour required of them as daughters and in courtship: how to behave in public, what to look for in a potential husband, how to respond to his advances and so on. Famous examples include James Fordyce, *Sermons to Young Women* (1766: the book from which Mr Collins tries to read in chapter xiv of *Pride and Prejudice*); John Gregory's *A Father's Legacy to his Daughters* (1774); and Thomas Gisborne, *An Enquiry into the Duties of the Female Sex* (1798). In particular, these books emphasise the necessity for young women always to appear subordinate to the needs of men, and not to express their own needs or desires; a feminine self-effacement often referred to as 'modesty' [**p. 126**]. However, such literature by its very nature describes not how young women of the middle ranks behaved, but how somebody thought they ought to behave (Vickery 1998: 5–7). The private writing of propertied women themselves in this period does not always suggest a perception or resentment of an increasing exclusion from the public world. Women in the long eighteenth century remained economically and legally subordinate to men, but this was hardly a recent development, and may not have been made noticeably worse by the expansion of capitalism in the organisation of the economy.

The second story that social and cultural historians tell about the changing status of English women in the long eighteenth century starts from rather different premises. The 'domestic thesis' often involves the assumption that a culture of feminine domesticity was a 'middle-class' invention, and indeed a way in which the new moneyed classes, excluded from political power by not possessing land, could assert their moral and cultural superiority over the landed classes who monopolised state politics (Davidoff and Hall 1987: 30). For the 'privacy' of the middle-class woman made her different not just from the working woman of the labouring classes but also from the aristocratic woman who showed off her beauty and, through her clothes and jewels, her husband's wealth and power in the public assemblies, theatres and pleasure gardens of London. It can, however, be argued that what is striking about property-owning English society in the long eighteenth century was precisely the absence of any major class divide along the boundary between moneyed and landed groups. Instead, one can trace the emergence of a new set of social rules and values that are shared by the moneyed and the landed. This happened partly by the middling sort imitating the gentry, an imitation referred to as 'gentility' above. But the gentry too gave up some of its distinctive ways in favour of a middle-class way of life.

These new rules and values are usually referred to as 'polite' and were formulated and propagated above all through the rapidly expanding public culture of print. The most influential publications were the daily papers written almost entirely by two Oxford-educated occasional poets, playwrights and MPs, Joseph

Addison (1672–1719) and Richard Steele (1672–1729): the *Tatler* (1709–11), the *Spectator* (1711–12 and 1714: the most important of the three); and the *Guardian* (1713). These three journals usually consisted of a single daily essay which discussed, for example, appropriate topics of conversation in various social contexts; standards of dress; standards of taste in literature, the theatre, the opera and so on; morality; and general observations on English society of the time. These discussions often took the form of debates between fictional characters representing various types or classes of men in that society. In the *Spectator*, for example, we meet the established landowner Sir Roger de Coverley, the city merchant Sir Andrew Freeport, the army officer Captain Sentry and so on. Though appearing as individual sheets of paper, these essays were collected and republished in book form throughout the eighteenth century, thus acquiring a lasting influence well beyond the immediate context of their original production.

One striking aspect of these essays is their strict avoidance of taking sides in party politics, in a period when political debate was fiercely partisan, along lines still largely defined by attitudes to the conflicts of the previous century. But this avoidance of party politics itself reveals the profoundly political nature of Addison and Steele's project. On the one hand, to speak or write in any way that tended to divide property-owning people from one another along the inherited fault-lines of rank, party or religion was to step outside the standards of the polite; on the other hand, polite standards were clearly not available to the mass of the population, the 'vulgar' majority, who owned no property and had neither the money, leisure nor literacy to read the books, buy the clothes or frequent the social spaces discussed in these journals. Polite standards of behaviour, polite reading, were to define as a group the *propertied* classes irrespective of the nature of that property, establishing a set of cultural norms that could be shared by the new, moneyed classes and the old elites alike. They are sometimes referred to as rules of 'propriety', a word with etymological links to 'property': such standards of conduct were *proper* for, or *belonged* to, this specific group of people. To conform to these standards, the merchant classes must abandon the 'vulgar' speech and interests that link them with their quite probably propertyless ancestors: various Protestant fundamentalisms, a frame of reference restricted to the narrow specialist knowledge of their particular trade, and the suspicion of the arts that went with these. But the landed classes must similarly abandon the arrogance, exhibitionism, violence, drunkenness and sexual promiscuity that accompany taken-for-granted inherited power. 'Polite' standards of writing, speech and behaviour allowed this new group of property owners to be integrated *socially* within the established order, although they remained excluded from it *politically*. Thus we can see that the establishment of polite manners clearly has a very distinct political role in the defence of the new economic and political order that had made the public sphere possible in the first place; and not despite but because of the avoidance of party politics in polite discourse (Klein 1993: 108–9). This social integration of the moneyed and the landed is often imagined as a conversation, conducted according to rules of 'civility'. One of its effects is to standardise a particular type of English as the 'correct' one, a national norm which will distinguish the polite from the vulgar (Barrell 1983: 134–57). Some critics have seen Austen as playing an important role in this standardisation, and it will be discussed in Part 2 in the case of *Northanger Abbey* [see pp. 45–6, 145].

But we must also keep in mind that this civility is being propagated as an ideal by Addison and Steele and others through the medium of print. Reading is how this common culture is mostly produced, and writing will be 'polite' if it promotes this political project while not appearing to be political.

In this polite culture, women were granted a central role. Propertied women were, as we have seen, expected not to work and, as women, were also ostensibly excluded from political activity. The conversation of women is therefore imagined as excluding these topics: in the company of women, as a result, men were less likely to slip either into the vulgar details of their professional, trade or farming interests, or into heated partisan political argument. Either of these areas would exclude one group or other of potential participants, and thus prevent polite conversation from doing its job of consolidating property owners as a group. The absence of these topics from the conversation of Austen's characters is thus not accidental, but represents their (and her) adherence to a specific and socially crucial code of behaviour. The presence of women in social spaces was supposed to be an important way of disciplining the conversation and behaviour of the men in correspondence with polite norms (Klein 1993: 105).

> Had our Species no Females in it, Men would be quite different Creatures from what they are at present; their Endeavours to please the opposite Sex, polishes and refines them out of those Manners which are most natural to them. . . . In a word, Man would not only be unhappy, but a rude unfinished Creature, were he conversant with none but those of his own Make.
>
> ([Addison,] *Spectator*, 433, 17 July 1712; Bond 1965: V, 21)

At the same time, conversation with men would improve the depth and rationality of the topics available to women: each gender is imagined as improving the capacities of the other (Klein 1993: 110–12; Cohen 1996: 29–30).

The ideal type of femininity produced by the new economic order might thus be seen not as confined to a private sphere, isolated from a wider social context, following the 'domestic thesis'; rather, it might be personified as a woman who deploys her private, feminine virtues in various public spaces for the moral and social improvement of men. This is still very different from the public sexuality of the aristocratic woman mentioned above, but the polite lady is an ideal that the moneyed middling sort can share with the gentry who constitute the vast majority of landowners. A common culture shared by the middling sort and the gentry, across the class divide usually assumed by the 'separate spheres' thesis, seems to be exactly what we see explored in Austen's novels. Only a character from the lower fringes of the aristocracy, like Mr Darcy in *Pride and Prejudice*, finds integration in this culture difficult [see p. 57]. The aristocratic woman remained defined by her ability to provide her husband with male heirs, and to display his wealth and power to others on public occasions through her own beauty and the expense of the clothes and jewellery that he can afford to dress her in. That is, the identity of the aristocratic (or 'fashionable' or 'elegant') woman was constructed around her physical being, either as a mother or as an object of public sexual display. The polite feminine ideal is instead defined by her inner, mental and emotional, qualities rather than her outer, physical, ones. These give her resources

that she can deploy within the home, for example in the moral and social education of her children: her task here is to produce continuity in the family's values
rather than simply in its blood-line. But she can also carry these private virtues
into a public world, for example to 'polish' male manners in polite company. The
identity of the polite woman, just as much as that of the aristocratic woman,
remained defined in relation to men, but in different ways. In Addison's formulation above, the polite woman does not need to *do* anything, she merely has to be
capable of being pleased: it is the man who actively 'endeavours' to do so.

However, the role that Addison describes as a passive one could be turned into
a very active one by women themselves. Such a role does at least demand that
men recognise the rationality and intelligence of women, and as such grants a
new legitimacy to women's contribution not just to polite conversation but to
the wider conversation among the literate which was the world of books and
periodicals. It is to the specific place of the female writer in the long eighteenth
century that we must now turn.

Austen's profession: writing, publicity and the market

We have outlined two stories about the fate of middle-ranking English women
in the long eighteenth century: on the one hand, their increasing exclusion from
the world of work and the loss of influence and status that went with it; on the
other hand, their increasing centrality to a polite culture encompassing both the
middling sort and the gentry. Accounts of the opportunities available for female
authors in the long eighteenth century vary according to which of these stories is
given most credence.

On the one hand, as we hinted at the end of the previous section, a polite
culture that granted women the power to improve men through their conversation could also grant this power to their writing. To see how this might be
imagined we can turn to *Pamela* (1740–1), the first novel by Samuel Richardson
(1689–1761), a writer who was an enormous influence on Austen. *Pamela* can be
read as, among other things, a parable of the morally and socially improving
effects of women's writing on men. It is an epistolary novel: that is, it consists
entirely of letters. Almost all of them in this case are written by Pamela Andrews,
a servant-girl in a gentry household, to her parents. One of the reasons why
Pamela is so important in English and indeed European cultural history is simply
that it grants to a lower-class woman not only a narrative voice in which to
describe her own life, but also a moral authority, vested in that voice. The reader
is invited to trust Pamela's judgement of what is happening to her. The letter form,
and the intimacy of the relationship with those to whom the letters are addressed,
seem to guarantee the truth of apparently unedited thoughts and feelings, committed spontaneously and transparently to paper. What Pamela describes are the
increasingly violent sexual advances of her master, Mr B, up to and including
kidnapping, imprisonment and attempted rape. And those thoughts and feelings
express a pure sexual and social virtue, bravely resisting the assaults from a
corrupt social order. So far, the inward, private nature of Pamela's virtue allows

her only a passive role in the novel. She does, however, eventually achieve a remarkable effect on Mr B, causing him to repent of his ways and offer her marriage, which she, convinced of the authenticity of this transformation, accepts. But she achieves this in a very particular way: inadvertently, and through her writing. Mr B steals her letters, reads them, and discovers the inner, subjective truth of a woman he had previously treated as a sexual object. Mr B, that is, is morally transformed by becoming a reader, and a reader of a text written by a woman, the same text as the one we are reading when we read the novel *Pamela*.

Pamela herself is of course the creation of a male writer, and she is as idealised a version of private femininity as that set up in the *Spectator*. Nevertheless, she represents an important precedent, a model for the acceptance of the moral authority of women writers by men. Feminine words in the form of writing, just as much as in polite conversation, have the capacity to improve and to civilise the vulgar male. But note also that this feminine writing gets its moral authority in large part from the very privacy of the letters in which they are written. Writing, produced in an enclosed private space, and read in an enclosed private space, is thus the means whereby a female writer can provide a *public* moral critique of her society (of, for example, the arrogance of inherited power, or masculine sexual aggression) without compromising the feminine privacy which gives it moral authority in the first place. Austen constructs a private space for her heroines without using the first-person letter format used by Richardson, as we will see in *Sense and Sensibility* [see pp. 52–3]. It is through Richardson that modernity, in the shape of polite culture, can be seen to open up new opportunities for the woman writer (Todd 1986: 110; Spencer 1986: 89).

Indeed, capitalism itself, in its transformation of the publishing industry, can be understood as making possible new careers in writing for women. Writing was one of the few profitable occupations which women could undertake at home, 'without apparently posing a threat to their respectability' of the kind posed by being a singer or an actress, for example (Turner 1992: 65, 69). Working for money does not seem to have been seen as necessarily 'vulgar' for women until much later and it is most likely that the vast majority of women writers were writing for money (Turner 1992: 60–1). And new types of relation between author and publisher facilitated the production of public print by the private lady.

There were three ways of getting a work published in Austen's period (three that need to concern us here, in any case), each with its own particular benefits and dangers. Perhaps the oldest established was publication by subscription. This required the collection of names of people who committed themselves to purchasing the work when it came out, paying either in advance or on delivery. They were rewarded for their support by having their names printed at the start of the work. The advantage of this system was that it removed the element of financial risk to either author or 'bookseller' (as publishers at the time were called). If a spirit of emulation set in among wealthy potential subscribers, it could generate a substantial sum. However, it required the author to be either already well known, or to have a patron whose taste could be trusted by others. Early in the eighteenth century, the poet Alexander Pope, London-based and well con- nected in aristocratic and political circles, had been able to secure the subscription of some of the wealthiest and most influential figures in the kingdom for his translations from the Greek of Homer's epics *The Iliad* (1715–20) and *The*

Odyssey (1725–6). This enormous task made Pope a profit of nearly £10,000, enough at the time to set him up financially for life.

Subscription was in effect an extension into the literary world of the patronage system which governed careers in politics and the professions [see pp. 5–6]. But later in the century the demand for books was much greater. This demand could not possibly be met by any system that depended on personal contacts to underwrite book production. By Austen's time, book production was overwhelmingly a market venture, with capital invested in the production of a commodity in the hope of profit from its sale in an unpredictable marketplace.

The speculative alternatives to subscription were essentially twofold, depending on who was to take the financial risk. First, the author could simply sell the manuscript with its copyright to a bookseller in exchange for a once-only payment, usually made within the year. The author retained no rights over the fate of her book once this payment was received, but then the bookseller took all the financial risk. If the book sold poorly, the bookseller bore the loss; if it sold unexpectedly well, perhaps allowing the bookseller to risk a second edition, all the profit was his. The other method was publication on commission. Here the risk was all the author's. She had to cover the cost of printing the book and advertising it, and allow the bookseller a 10 per cent commission on each copy sold. After that, however, any and all remaining profit was the author's; conversely, if the book sold poorly, the author would have to make up any shortfall from her own funds.

The stakes in choosing between these options were particularly high for female authors. The reason for this points to one of the problems attached to the type of authority that polite culture offered women writers: many women writers later in the eighteenth century, in their private correspondence and in prefaces to their work, express misgivings about the extent to which publishing put them as individuals in the public eye. They seem anxious about the extent to which being an authoress, despite the privacy of the act of writing itself, is in fact like being an actress or a singer after all. Having one's name widely known in any capacity other than as daughter, wife or widow was already to attract the attention of men who were strangers to the family circle, and was thus a breach of feminine modesty. Women writers therefore felt themselves constantly on the brink of crossing the division between public and private on which their authority was based. To this extent it appears that the 'separate spheres' thesis may have much to tell us about the conditions of women's writing in the long eighteenth century. It may exaggerate the extent to which women of the middling sort *necessarily* found themselves excluded from public life, but the counter-examples offered by historians tend to be exercising power within local and provincial contexts, where their family affiliations and personal characters would be well known to all, guaranteeing their respectability. These are indeed the contexts within which Austen's characters mostly live, but her own dealing with the impersonal world of London and its publishing business meant leaving such contexts behind.

Accordingly, a woman author might prefer to remain completely anonymous, and thus protect herself from the damage her reputation might suffer from appearing in public as described above. Publishing by subscription of course demanded publicity, and lots of it. In this respect the capitalist development of a mass market for books, with the attendant depersonalisation of the relation between writer and reader, made it possible for the woman writer to publish her work without herself becoming the object of public attention. In effect, she becomes able to keep her private identity separate from an authorial identity implicit in the book, a commodity that she puts up for sale. It has indeed been argued that the idea of the woman author and the idea of a literary marketplace develop in relation to one another in the long eighteenth century (Gallagher 1994: xvii–xix).

Sale of copyright was perhaps the most attractive option in this regard: it allowed for minimal dealings with the bookseller, with none of the haggling over the price of the paper to be used or the extent of advertising that might be necessary in publication by commission (Fergus 1991: 15). Using a male go-between was necessary in any case where there were legally binding contracts to sign, as women did not exist as autonomous agents in the eyes of the law, but only as adjuncts to their male relatives. In a sale of copyright it was thus comparatively easy to get a male relative also to do all the negotiation necessary on one's behalf, preserving the author's anonymity. Frances Burney had sold her first two novels, *Evelina* and *Cecilia* (1782), outright in this way. The famous quote below comes from a letter to her male mentor, Samuel Crisp, and it is at least in part telling him what she knows he wants to hear. Therefore, the desire that Burney expresses for anonymity here should not be taken as the whole story, but it is evidence of how women authors were *expected* to feel about entry into the literary marketplace. This was written during the height of *Evelina*'s success: the 'pamphlet' she refers to was a satire on the painter Joshua Reynolds, a family friend.

> —just as I received your Letter, I had had information that my name had got into print,—&, what was yet worse, was printed in a new Pamphlet.
>   I cannot tell you, &, if I could, you would, perhaps, not believe me, how greatly I was shocked, mortified, grieved & confounded at this intelligence: I had always dreaded as a real Evil my Name's getting into *Print*,—but to be lug'd into a Pamphlet!—
>   . . .
>   . . . —Yet, after all, I feel very forcibly that I *am* not—that I *have* not been—& that I never *shall* be formed or fitted for any business with the *Public*. . . . I would a thousand Times rather forfeit my character as a *Writer*, than risk ridicule or censure as a *Female*. I have never set my Heart on Fame, & therefore would not if I *could* purchase it at the expense of all my own ideas of propriety.
>   (*c.* January 1779; Troide 1994: 211–12)

On the other hand, the danger of selling copyright is nowhere better exemplified than in Austen's own experience with 'Susan', the novel eventually published as *Northanger Abbey*. As we noted above [see pp. 2–3], she gained £10 for 'Susan' from a bookseller who then advertised it but did not publish it. Austen's only option was to buy back the copyright of her own novel, and it was only after she had made money from her other novels, and the finances of her immediate family had recovered their equilibrium, that she felt able to do this (her brother Henry seems to have negotiated the purchase of 'Susan' at some point after the success of *Emma* in 1815). So when she came to seek publication for *Sense and*

Sensibility in 1811, probably using Henry as go-between, she did so on commission. Because he would make little profit from this arrangement, the bookseller Thomas Egerton took his time and made the book from expensive materials, and set the price at a fairly low 15 shillings. It sold well over two editions, and made Austen £140. Before the extent of its sales became clear, however, Austen agreed to sell Egerton the copyright of *Pride and Prejudice* for £110. Egerton then moved fast, cut corners with the paper and binding, upped the price to 18 shillings, and made a handsome profit on two editions. Jan Fergus calculates that if Austen had published *Pride and Prejudice* on commission at the same price, she would have turned a profit of about £475 (Fergus 1991: 140); that is, over twice her father's annual income from his two church livings [see pp. 1–2]. Austen would publish two more novels in her lifetime, *Mansfield Park* and *Emma*, and both of them would be published on commission.

After *Sense and Sensibility* ('By a Lady'), all of Austen's novels announce themselves to be 'By the Author of "Sense and Sensibility" ' or 'By the Author of "Sense and Sensibility" and "Pride and Prejudice" ' and so on. However, it seems that as her career progressed, and her identity as an author became established, the successful woman author in this period tended to become less anxious about anonymity, and more ready to use the public identity that her works had established for her as a marketing tool. Burney achieved wide acclaim for her first two novels, and her authorship was well known in the literary circles of London of which she had always been a part, as her father too was a (non-fiction) author. An otherwise disastrous period as a lady in waiting to the queen then gave her connections at the highest level. As a result, in 1796 she could publish her third novel, *Camilla*, by subscription, taking £1,000 from subscribers, and *then* sell the copyright for a further £1,000 (and one should note that, judging from the letters, *Camilla* is very much in Austen's mind and those of her correspondents as she begins her career as a novelist). Austen, hidden away in Hampshire, does occasionally worry about appearing as a 'Literary Lion', or what we would now call a celebrity. She writes to her sister Cassandra concerning one of the latter's acquaintances:

> I should like to see Miss Burdett very well, but that I am rather frightened by hearing that she wishes to be introduced to *me*. If I *am* a wild Beast, I cannot help it. It is not my own fault.
>
> (24 May 1813; Le Faye 1995: 212–13)

And yet later that same year she writes in much more robust terms regarding the inevitable loss of anonymity that came with success. She had written to her brother Frank asking permission to use the names of his old ships for those on which William Price, Fanny's brother in *Mansfield Park*, was to serve. Frank seems to have worried that this might give the curious a clue to the identity of the author. She replies, referring to *Mansfield Park* as her third novel, and to the recently published *Pride and Prejudice*:

> I was previously aware of what I sh^d be laying myself open to—but the truth is that the Secret has spread so far as to be scarcely the Shadow of a secret now—& that I beleive [*sic*] whenever the 3^d appears, I shall not

even attempt to tell Lies about it.—I shall rather try to make all the
Money than all the Mystery I can of it.—People shall pay for their
Knowledge if I can make them.—Henry heard P. & P. warmly praised in
Scotland, by Lady Rob[t] Kerr and another Lady;—& what does he do in
the warmth of his Brotherly vanity & Love, but immediately tell them
who wrote it!—A Thing once set going in that way—one knows how
it spreads!—and he, dear Creature, has set it going more than once. . . .
I am trying to harden myself.—After all, what a trifle it is in all its
Bearings, to the really important points of one's existence even in this
World!

(25 September 1813; Le Faye 1995: 231)

When Austen came to publish *Emma*, illness prevented Henry from maintaining his usual role as her representative in negotiations with her booksellers,
but she took over the correspondence with John Murray without any apparent
embarrassment (Le Faye 1995: 295). The court, in the form of its librarian, then
contacted her directly to say that it would be acceptable for her to dedicate the
novel to the Prince Regent (the future George IV, now acting monarch during
the mental illness of his father). In the eighteenth century such a dedication may
have come in exchange for patronage of some kind, financial support or at least
help in finding subscriptions. Now it amounted to a mere command, and the
only possible advantage it offered Austen was some extra leverage in getting the
printers to hurry up in producing proof pages for her to check (Le Faye 1995:
297); the only advantage, that is, other than the dubious honour of recognition
from a debauched princeling for whom Austen, like many in Britain at the time,
felt nothing but contempt. The unexpected ghost of patronage that looms up in
this episode serves to emphasise by contrast the freedom of anonymity that the
modern book market otherwise offered.

But if modernity, with its capitalist market mechanisms and accompanying
polite culture, thus offered a new authority to women writers and new opportunities to turn that authority to financial advantage, it can be seen as offering them
only at a price. The price was a new restriction on the subject matter that women
can include within their works. For just as polite conversation was meant to be
improving to the extent that certain topics, unsuitable for mixed company, were
excluded, so texts by women authors would be respectable so long as they
concentrated on the matters of education, morality, courtship and domestic life
over which women had been granted special, but circumscribed, authority
(Spencer 1986: 14, 20–1; Shevelow 1989: 14–15; Ballaster 1992: 196–211). Once
again, it seems that the opportunities for public writing opened up to women by
early capitalist society can only be understood in relation to a feminine 'separate
sphere' of private life which they were supposed to write *about*. 'During the
eighteenth century, as upper- and middle-class Englishwomen increasingly began
to participate in the public realm of print culture, the representational practices of
that culture were steadily enclosing them within the private sphere of the home'
(Shevelow 1989: 1).

To understand more directly how this shaped Austen's writing, it is necessary to
turn now to the genre of writing that women dominated by the time of her
education, and in which she wrote herself: the novel.

Austen in literary history 1

The novel and criticism

The emergence of the novel as a distinct genre in the eighteenth century, including its slow rise in literary status, is itself linked to the emergence of 'polite' standards of language and conduct and the social alliance that those standards facilitated. Popular prose narrative in late seventeenth-century England comes in many forms: the criminal's racy eve-of-execution confession of their exploits, the puritan religious autobiography, and long romances translated from the French, among others. The last-named genre centres on idealised but doomed courtly love, between impossibly beautiful victim-heroines and impossibly brave warrior-heroes, generating wildly improbable series of events. As such it can be seen as embodying aristocratic values, in describing a masculinity defined in terms of a capacity for violence, and a femininity defined in terms of physical beauty, for example. The novel largely defines itself in opposition to the romance, by describing a world of particularised people and places and everyday social trans-actions in a recognisably contemporary setting. But in doing so it must avoid the vulgarity of the criminal confession, or the dangerous religious fundamentalism of the puritan autobiography. In finding a middle ground between 'low' genres of cheap prose narrative and the aristocratic idealisation of the romance, the novel can be seen as itself an example of the compromise that constitutes polite culture. Of the early English novelists, Aphra Behn (1640–89) criticises the conventions of romance but at the same time continues its focus on aristocratic passion; Daniel Defoe (1660–1731) never fully escapes the origins of his tales in religious con-version narratives on the one hand, and the confessions of thieves, whores and pirates on the other.

Women writers had always dominated the novel: unlike the genres of writing inherited from Greek and Latin antiquity (epic, pastoral, satire, tragic and comic drama, and so on), it did not require a classical education for its production, and since very, very few women even from the propertied classes received a classical education, the novel was available to them as those other genres were not (see Spencer 1986: 6–7). Perhaps a majority of readers of novels in the eighteenth century were also female. This was certainly imagined to be the case, and many propertied women had, as we have noted, plenty of leisure time in which to read. But the involvement of women in both the production and the consumption of novels was one more reason why the genre had a very low status in the literary hierarchy. Richardson purged the novel of Behn's erotic and party-political explicitness, and of Defoe's interest in the criminal, to establish it as a polite form, but this was not enough to entirely redeem it from these low associations.

Female authors' dominance of the novel is particularly marked in the last decades of the eighteenth century, and in this period they developed a range of types of novel. All of them contrast the private thoughts and feelings of a (usually young) woman with a public world of masculine power. The most important precedents for Austen's own novels are those written by Frances Burney. Burney's narratives, such as *Evelina* (1778), *Cecilia* (1782) and *Camilla* (1796), centre on the social education of a young woman obliged to leave home to experience the confusing public spaces of London or Bath. She survives its various (often traumatic) sexual and financial dangers with her virtue intact, and is rewarded with marriage to the hero, from whom various misunderstandings have separated her for most of the novel, but who has been able to instruct her in how to cope with this strange metropolitan world. That is, he is her mentor as well as her lover. The reader's emotional identification with the heroine is here put to didactic use [see p. 126]: that is, the reader can *learn* of the dangers to which young women are exposed in modern social life and how best to survive them. In this respect, Burney's fiction shares a focus with the conduct books mentioned above [see p. 8]. Such novels are often referred to as 'domestic' fiction, not for their setting, but for the values they inculcate: the world of fashionable public display is corrupting, home is the place where both hero and heroine's virtues can be properly fostered; but home is the place to which they retreat at the end of the novel, not the scene of the testing of those virtues that makes up most of the narrative [see p. 113]. *Belinda*, the 1801 novel by Irish author Maria Edgeworth, is another good example of this type. But the novels of Burney, Edgeworth and, after them, Austen, are also more broadly understood as 'realistic' fiction, in distinction from the 'romantic' fiction of the Gothic novelists [see pp. 97–8]. For a thorough discussion of the issues surrounding realism as they appear in Austen, see Shaw (1999).

The Gothic novel is most associated with Ann Radcliffe (1764–1823), author of, among others, *The Castles of Athlin and Dunbayne* (1789), *The Romance of the Forest* (1791), *The Mysteries of Udolpho* (1794) and *The Italian* (1797). The traumas endured by Radcliffe's heroines are not very far removed from those suffered by Richardson's (abduction, imprisonment, attempted seduction, rape or forced marriage) but transposed to historically and geographically exotic locations and spiced with the suggestion of supernatural terrors as well as human ones. Although written in a third-person narrative voice, this usually adopts the heroine's ignorant and terrified perspective on events to evoke a heightened emotional identification and response from the reader. Neither the historical nor the cultural distance of the setting is allowed to get in the way of this identifica-tion: the heroine is to all intents and purposes a genteel eighteenth-century young English lady, submitted to outrageous ordeals by a demonic sixteenth-century aristocrat. The effect of this identification on young female readers caused some concern among their fathers. 'Modesty', the wife or daughter's subordination of her needs to those of her husband or father, was a quality that young ladies were supposed to cultivate, and that required a reflexive disciplining of the emotions [see pp. 126–7]. The indulgence of the emotions encouraged by Gothic reading appeared to run counter to this. Such anxieties about the effects of uncontrolled female reading occur well before Radcliffe: similar complaints were made earlier in the eighteenth century regarding the French romances whose version of love, absolute, passionate, and self-destructive, might give young ladies very false expectations of their inevitable fate in the marriage market [see pp. 22–3].

However, if the novel as a genre was dominated by women writers in the late eighteenth century, a new set of literary institutions also arose in this period which were dominated by men. Throughout the eighteenth century, more and more books of all kinds were being produced for a wealthy readership that was only slowly expanding, but which had an increasing amount of leisure time in which to read. This growth of print culture resulted in the emergence of a new type of critical activity, already visible in the essays on reading and literature in the *Spectator*, which advises this expanding reading public on questions of literary value. This criticism appeared in two types of social institution. One was the periodical journal. The monthly *Gentleman's Magazine*, for example, founded in 1731, began as a compendium of all kinds of news, but soon included critical essays and a record of the month's publications alongside its parliamentary reports. The *Monthly Review*, founded in 1749, became even more specialised by 1780, and by 1790 was attempting to review every new publication each month: by the end of the century it had a print-run of 5,000, the largest in this field. The *Critical Review* (founded in 1756) did a similar job on a slightly smaller scale. And there was room in the market for more idiosyncratic periodicals like the twice-weekly *Rambler* (1750–2), edited and mostly written by Samuel Johnson (1709–84), at this point a journalist and poet, later celebrated as the creator of the first comprehensive English dictionary. The *Rambler* occasionally included contributions from Richardson, and from Elizabeth Carter and Hester Chapone, aristocratic and classically educated women in the same London literary circle as Johnson and Richardson. The *Rambler* set itself a quite explicitly moral task in its essays, the improvement of its readers, but all of these journals were attempting to exert authority over what was accepted as good literature and what was dismissed as bad, establishing a hierarchy of literary values. Despite frequent contributions from female writers, these were male-owned and male-edited enterprises, and shaped the context within which female-authored novels would be received.

The other new institution inaugurated in the eighteenth century is literary criticism as an academic discipline. In 1762 Hugh Blair (1718–1800) became the first 'Professor of Rhetoric and Belles Lettres' at the University of Edinburgh, and Adam Smith (1723–90) gave lectures on the same subject at the University of Glasgow around the same time. Blair's published essays on literary criticism gained wide circulation and high prestige. If the periodicals were designed to tell a new generation of middle-ranking readers which books it was worth spending money on (that is, which would give them suitable material for polite conversation with their social superiors), Blair's and Smith's courses might be seen as designed to supply a new generation of propertied Scottish men with the cultural reference-points, and a written version of 'Standard English', which would allow them to be integrated into the power structures of the only recently United Kingdom (Scotland entered a parliamentary union with England in 1707). But the audience for these lectures was in the first instance exclusively male: women were not admitted to university in Scotland any more than in England. The institutionalisation of literary criticism, in universities and periodicals alike, tended to confirm literary authority as ultimately masculine.

Political economy, sentiment and marriage

My account of the Gothic novel above suggested that the emotional lives of young ladies were perceived to need supervision by the men responsible for them. However, this was not because Enlightenment culture regarded the emotions in general as dangerous disturbers of dispassionate rationality, as is sometimes supposed. Rather, a new importance was attached to 'feelings' or 'sentiments' in the discussion of social organisation, both in general theories of society and in debate about specific social issues. To see why this should be, one should remember that, in order to imagine a type of social identity that could include both landed and moneyed classes, polite culture had to imagine a type of identity divorced from economic activity, not only for women, but also for men. In the second half of the eighteenth century, there is accordingly a marked gap between two dominant languages in which human society is described. One is the language of 'political economy', describing humans as essentially self-interested economic agents in competition with each other for various goods, and explaining how their rational choices eventually produce the economic structures and institutions of capitalism. The other is the language of 'sentiment', describing humans as essentially irrational, emotional or 'sentimental', and explaining how society is in fact held together by their instinctive emotional attachments to each other. Critical studies of Austen have understood her work in its relation to both of these discourses [see pp. 116, 119–21]. The Enlightenment in Britain, because of its roots in the scientific discoveries of Isaac Newton's generation, is often imagined as the triumph of reason over inherited or traditional beliefs, that is, over beliefs *felt* to be true without having been examined and justified in the light of reason. However, the essential feature of the British Enlightenment is not the valorisation of reason over emotion. It is rather their splitting apart and allocation to two separate roles in human life: reason to the pursuit of individual self-interest, emotion to the bonding together of society despite this.

The most celebrated of the political economists was Adam Smith, already mentioned at the end of the previous section. His most celebrated work, *The Wealth of Nations* (1776), imagines the economic world as one of negotiation and contract between economically motivated individuals whose only interest in each other is as the rational means to a selfish end. Such theories can be read as justification for processes already long under way, but reaching a climax in the second half of the eighteenth century. Agricultural 'improvement', the rationalisation of peasant lands into larger farms that were more profitable for landlords, was systematically driving people off their land, into beggary or wage labour, building, for example, Britain's canal network, or in the new factories of the first, water-powered, Industrial Revolution. Such 'improvement' had been going on for a couple of centuries in England. But it accelerated through the eighteenth century as landowners struggled to keep their incomes level with their moneyed compatriots, and either they or their tenants found capital available to invest in new buildings, tools and methods, and appropriated traditionally communal grazing land through 'Enclosure Acts'. In wage labour, of course, the employer has no responsibility to the worker other than a day's wage for a day's work: if the worker is no longer required, the employer has no further responsibility to him or her. From this perspective, the type of society that preceded the commercial order began to look like one in which economic relations between master and servant, landlord and tenant, were also and at the same time authentic emotional bonds: where the landlord was genuinely concerned for the tenant's welfare, rather than seeing him as merely a source of income, and where the tenant regarded the landlord with loyalty and gratitude rather than resentment. One should be sceptical about whether any such society had ever existed, but if it had, it was pretty much gone by the time Austen started writing. The rural England that is the setting for her novels is not a 'pre-modern' countryside in any way, but itself a product of modernity, and the agriculture that supports her gentry families is a capitalist agriculture (Lovell 1977: 118–20; Aers 1981: 126–7; Spring 1983: 63–5; Honan 1997: 260). It was not the idyll that it can appear to later readers, but a scene of considerable economic and human distress [see p. 115].

If economic production was being rationalised, ethical relations with others were understood in contrast as a matter of feeling, of instinctual and unexamined emotion. According to the model of human nature developed by thinkers such as Smith or his friend David Hume (1711–76, author of the *Treatise of Human Nature*, 1739–40), ethical concern for the sufferings of others is produced by our tendency to spontaneously put ourselves in their place, to feel what they are feeling (Mullan 1988: 18–26). To see you in pain gives me pain, for example, and thus prompts me to act to alleviate that pain, even though I have no narrowly self-interested reason for doing so. We know the right thing to do, not because we can find reasons for it, but because our feelings tell us. One could argue that epistolary fiction in Richardson's hands is an invitation to identify with the suffering of the writer-character in this way. This kind of ethics, defined in terms of emotional identification, is often referred to as 'sympathetic' or 'sentimental'. The latter term did not at first carry any of the disparaging connotations that it does now. Rather, 'sentiment' is a quasi-technical term meaning 'emotion', so that Smith's 1759 work on ethics can be called *The Theory of Moral Sentiments*.

For Hume and Smith, a problem remained regarding how to turn our sympathetic identification with *particular* individuals (friends and family, most obviously) into a wider readiness to take into account the *general* good of society as a whole. An important genre of novel developed which exploited the dramatic potential of this gap, usually referred to as the sentimental novel or the novel of 'sensibility'. In a novel like Henry Mackenzie's *Man of Feeling* (1771), the hero encounters various victims of a modern Britain characterised by selfishness, hypocrisy and greed, but can do little for them other than share their pain and shed sympathetic tears. 'Sensibility' can usefully represent a version of sentiment that emphasises the intense particularity of emotional attachment, the absolute commitment of 'the heart' to one other sympathetic soul. In the novel of sensibility, the hero and heroine can only find genuine sympathetic union in each other. The very acuteness of their feelings actually unfits them for survival in the outside world, and indeed even tends to get in the way of a lasting relationship through marriage. Their passion for each other, often figured in their shared passion for other works of sentimental fiction, is almost too refined to find expression within established social institutions, other, that is, than the novel itself. Apart from their letters to each other, tears figure largely as an alternative outlet. Frances Brooke's *The History of Lady Julia Mandeville* (1763), to give another example, offers a hero who is besotted with Julia, but cannot believe that either she or her family will countenance marriage due to his poverty, and in extreme despair he gets himself killed in a duel. In fact Julia and her father were quite happy to listen to his proposals, and the hero is only doomed by his hair-trigger readiness to read the smallest gesture as a sign of rejection. Such stories can be read as cutting both ways: as a condemnation of a social order in which spontaneous feeling cannot be fostered and channelled in socially productive ways, but also as a warning against the potentially fatal effects of the self-indulgent cultivation of extreme emotion.

We have so far been examining the rise of feeling or 'sentiment' as a theme in theory and in fiction. But it has also been argued that the emotions are given an increased authority in more practical matters in this period. For example, it has been argued that the eighteenth century sees a rise in the idea of 'companionate' or 'affective' marriage: that is, marriage motivated by the emotional attachment between husband and wife (Stone and Stone 1977: 325–36). For the landed classes generally, and particularly for the aristocracy, marriage had traditionally been, at least in part, a means to a political or economic end. Marriage was a means of uniting, not so much two individuals, as the estates that were attached to them, and the income and political influence that went with those estates. A woman could not own property, unless as a widow she inherited that of her late husband. Daughters were, legally speaking, themselves the property of their fathers, wives the property of their husbands. Marriage, under such circumstances, might be thought of as an exchange of property between men, of which the bride and her dowry were merely part. In fact, the bride's family retained an interest in her after marriage, as its honour remained at stake in her person: and the marriage contract usually allowed for an amount of property being held in trust by her male relatives (wealth 'settled' on her), generating an income on which she could fall back in the event of the marriage breaking down. Young aristocrats might expect to have a veto over candidates whom they considered particularly unsuitable; but the higher in the ranks of the landowning classes they found themselves, the more there was at stake politically and economically in a marriage, and thus the more the interests of the two families, rather than the feelings of the two people involved, were what ultimately determined the suitability of the match. I say 'families', and traditionally this would indeed have been a matter for discussion among an extended group of elders. However, changes in the laws surrounding the inheritance of property had gradually placed more and more power in the hands of the *fathers* alone. Much land came with a legal document called a 'Strict Entail', determining who would inherit which parts of a property on the death of the present owner, and this for several generations into the future. But since the sixteenth century lawyers had found ways round these documents, so that a landowner was free to decide who among his children would inherit what [see pp. 58–9]. The possibilities of reward and punishment that this offered the fathers of families gave them huge power over the behaviour of their children. A society that imagines authority in general as modelled on the authority of a father over his family is what we call a 'patriarchy' (so the king is imagined as the father of his nation, the divinity is God the Father, and so on); in these legal respects, England at the start of the eighteenth century was probably a more patriarchal society than it had ever been before.

However, it has been argued that by the end of the century it was expected that young people would in the first instance select from those available on the basis of mutual attraction (although a wealthy family might still exert a veto over particular candidates for marriage: Stone and Stone 1977: 272). It is suggested that a young woman's feelings, in particular, had been granted an authority in questions of 'the heart' that they had never had before. This idea of 'companionate' marriage incorporated Addison's idea of a mutually 'improving' relation between the sexes [see pp. 10–11]: the 'feeling' in question is at least as much a matter of sympathy, of a meeting of minds, complementary habits of thought, conversation and manners, as it is to do with sexual desire.

The thesis of an eighteenth-century rise of 'companionate marriage' has been criticised on two fronts. On the one hand, it has been argued that the change identified is effectively restricted to the aristocracy, those who had a lot at stake politically in the cementing of connections between families (Trumbach 1978: 120–2). Motives for marriage among the gentry and the middling sort had always been and remained a matter of personal feeling tempered with varying degrees of avarice and snobbery. On the other hand the 'companionate marriage' thesis, like the 'separate spheres' thesis, can seem to rely too much for its evidence on printed, and especially literary, accounts of how things ought to be, and thus may identify the rise of an imaginative ideal rather than a change in the way that people actually behaved (Gillis 1985: 5). But as an ideal, it shows traces of the political imperatives of the eighteenth-century social settlement. If marriage was the principal way of consolidating the economic power of families, the wealthiest landowners and the wealthiest merchants might marry off their children only among themselves, to the exclusion of the gentry and the less prosperous 'middling sort'. This would open up a new division in the politically precious unity of the propertied classes generally. If personal attraction were allowed its head, however, one might rely on a greater degree of intermixing. We can thus see that a new importance attached to 'feeling' serves the interests of the new commercial order. An attempt in 1753 to introduce a new Marriage Act narrowing the definition of what could count as legally binding marriage, giving families more time and power to intervene between the parties, encountered opposition in the House of Commons on just this account. Here is Robert Nugent, MP for St Mawes in Cornwall, speaking against this Bill:

> An old miser, even of the lowest birth, is generally ambitious of having his only daughter married to a lord, and a guardian has generally some selfish view, or some interest to serve, by getting his rich ward married to the eldest son of some duke, marquiss [sic], or earl; so that when a young commoner makes his addresses to a rich heiress, he has no friend but his superior merit, and that little deity called love.... Therefore I may prophesy, that if this Bill passes into a law, no commoner will ever marry a rich heiress, unless his father be a minister of state, nor will a peer's eldest son marry the daughter of a commoner, unless she be a rich heiress....
>
> Riches is the blood of the body politic: it must be made to circulate: if you allow it to stagnate, or if too much of it be thrown into any own part, it will destroy the body politic, as the same cause often does the body natural: if this Bill passes, our quality and rich families will daily accumulate riches by marrying only one another...
>   (Hansard 1813: columns 14–16)

The Bill was passed the following year, but it does not seem to have stopped landed heiresses marrying merchants' sons, or rich commercial families marrying their daughters into the gentry. And the propagation of these very convenient alliances was guaranteed by what Nugent calls 'love'. Marriage as an institution was still in the service of a political and economic order, but this new order demanded that it appear to be based on something else, namely on the natural feeling of attraction between two autonomous individuals.

In theory, in fiction and arguably in social practice as well, 'feeling' has a new centrality to the social order of eighteenth-century England. To some extent, this coincides with, and shares the limitations of, the new moral authority of the domestic woman. Because economic activity in this period was imagined as the selfish pursuit of profit, with human relationships reduced to mutually beneficial contracts, the world of the home and the family tended to be correspondingly imagined as a refuge for authentic, spontaneous human bonds. And as men are in charge of the commercial world, women are in charge of the ethical space of the home. One should note that in granting this moral importance to women, polite culture is not overthrowing the ancient equation (going back at least to classical Greece) of reason with masculinity and emotion with femininity: rather it is re-evaluating the social importance of feeling, and femininity along with it. Hence the domestic woman is imagined as responsible for the emotional and ethical education of the family's children, and for providing a space in which her husband can rediscover his sentimental human essence after a day of hard-nosed bargaining in the marketplace. In doing so, she is cultivating, in the domestic sphere, authentic emotional attachments between people that are no longer possible in society at large.

Female education

Whether companionate marriage was a new ideal or not, it meant that, in between belonging to her father and belonging to her husband, a young woman from a propertied family had one real opportunity to exert control over the course of her life: in the choice of a marriage partner. But for many young women from propertied but less prosperous backgrounds, with no property of their own and little to expect through inheritance, and with very restricted access to paid employment, marrying a wealthier man could also be an urgent financial necessity. Pressure to make what was called a 'good' marriage could in any case be oppressive, all the more so as it was almost all that was expected of her. Her education, for example, was very unlikely to go beyond the 'accomplishments' likely to improve her chances of sale in what must be called a marriage 'market'. These 'accomplishments' were in one way the middle class's mental equivalents to the fine clothes and jewels of the aristocratic woman: a means of displaying the status of the father or the husband, rather than reflecting any qualities essential to the woman. The bourgeois bride's expensive education was there to show off to the father's or husband's (male) friends and associates. So young ladies were typically taught singing, drawing, dancing and modern languages. As we have seen, ancient Greek and Latin and their literatures, the traditional mainstay of a boy's education, were dispensed only to a tiny and usually very wealthy minority of girls in the eighteenth century; philosophy, history and religion likewise (see Austen's comments on this in her letter to James Clarke of 11 December 1815; Le Faye 1995: 305–6). In short, young women were given the skills necessary to rise in the judgement of men, and thus to secure a husband, rather than to exercise rational or moral judgement themselves (for a thorough discussion of Austen and female education, see Horowitz 1991). It must be emphasised that the authority granted women in moral and domestic matters did not automatically produce a demand for the education of their reasoning or intellectual skills, grounded as that authority was in their being creatures of feeling rather than intellect.

There had been protests against this restriction of young women's horizons, and the masculine caricature of women as intellectually inferior to men on which it was based, since at least the seventeenth century. In 1694 Mary Astell published *A Serious Proposal to the Ladies for the Advancement of their True and Greatest Interest*, suggesting a college in which aristocratic young women would be educated primarily in religion, in order to give them some means of resisting the pressures upon them on their return to society. In *Reflections upon Marriage* (1700) Astell protested against the absolute authority that the institution currently gave husbands over their wives. Later in the century, the historian Catherine Macaulay (1731–91) would develop similar ideas, published in 1790 in her *Letters on Education*. These are already what we would now call 'feminist' texts, but by far the most influential representative of this tradition is Mary Wollstonecraft (1759–97). Wollstonecraft's *A Vindication of the Rights of Woman* (1792) argues powerfully that women are not inherently inferior to men. The idea that they are is a mere inherited prejudice, which does not stand up to rational examination: this overturning of 'prejudice' by the force of 'reason' is what makes Wollstonecraft a specifically *Enlightenment* feminist. A rational examination reveals the real cause of the retarded state of many women's minds to be not their sex but their poor education. In part this examination involves a critique of the idea that women's moral authority lies in the realm of feeling, of the 'heart': any real moral virtue, for Wollstonecraft, must deploy reason as well as feeling, and women cannot be truly good while they are mere creatures of sentiment. But it also involves a critique of a whole range of social institutions which depend upon arbitrary (that is, rationally unjustifiable) power: aristocracy, inherited property, the church and so on. The arbitrary authority enjoyed by men over women is one important instance of arbitrary authority in general, and the reformation of the condition of women will involve a wide-ranging programme of social reform. The *Vindication* includes lengthy discussions of those 'enlightened' men, such as the conduct book writers Gregory and Fordyce mentioned above [see p. 8], who when they come to discuss the role of women in society abandon their critical reason, assume the inherent inferiority and vulnerability of the female sex, and look for nothing more than ways in which society might manage this inferiority and vulnerability, instead of asking how they can be eradicated. Several critics have explored the extent to which Austen shares an agenda with Wollstonecraft [see pp. 126–33].

There was one other effect of the conjunction of feeling, domesticity and feminine moral authority in the last decades of the eighteenth century, however. This is the new legitimacy given to women's role as 'patriots'. Smith and Hume worried about how, indeed if, the particular emotional ties that bound individuals could guarantee the cohesion of society as a whole, despite the different political and economic interests of the various ranks. One way of allaying this anxiety was to imagine society as a *national* community, while redefining 'national' in a very particular way. Instead of thinking of the nation as a political unit, carried on through time by statesmen and the institutions in which they worked, the nation began to be imagined in terms of a set of 'manners', customs and traditions. This 'national character' (Guest 2000: 69) was imagined as outside institutionalised politics and shared by the people of the nation despite their different political allegiances and economic interests. Lifting the idea of the nation above politics in this way opened up new ways in which women could act and speak in national terms without trespassing on the masculine preserve of party politics. Women's public role as patriots has often been seen as a product of the political crisis following the French Revolution (see below). Women had, however, been participating in various types of political activity from early in the eighteenth century (Wilson 1996: 48–53; 2002: 40–1). The rise of the culture of sentiment and domesticity gave new legitimacy to this participation, recast in specifically patriotic terms, particularly during and after the American Revolution (Colley 1992: 252, 263; Guest 2000: 195). Women of the middling sort could argue that in monitoring the nation's morals, and fostering the emotional ties that held it together, they were simply replicating on the national stage the role that they already performed within the family. The family, rather than crown or parliament, could then be seen as the source of the nation's unity. The private realm of the family, because of its role in producing moral virtue, could also be imagined as producing civic virtue more generally (Guest 2000: 236). And as the genre of the private realm, the woman-authored novel can thus be seen as taking on the role of representing the nation as a whole through its depiction of private families [see pp. 141–2].

Austen in literary history 2

Romanticism

The emergence of these new definitions of national and personal identity in terms of feeling also found expression in new types of artistic production. For example, the poetry of the early decades of the eighteenth century had mostly taken 'neo-classical' form: that is, it modelled itself on the types of poetry produced in ancient Greece and Rome. Pope's translations of Homer, mentioned above [see pp. 12–13], are a case in point. It thus placed itself in a tradition that was not specific to England or the English language, but shared with all of Europe. Increasingly, however, poets, including women poets, began to write as the inheritors of a 'national' literary tradition, encompassing Geoffrey Chaucer from the fourteenth century and, especially, Edmund Spenser, William Shakespeare and John Milton from the late sixteenth and seventeenth centuries. So the 'Spenserian' stanza and the sonnet form used by Shakespeare, types of verse unknown to the classical Greeks and Romans, were revived by James Thomson (1700–48) in the Spenserian Castle of Indolence (1748) and by Charlotte Smith (1749–1806) in Elegiac Sonnets (1784) respectively. New interest was taken in the ballads of the rural poor as another embodiment of a continuous national artistic tradition, collected and published in books such as Thomas Percy's Reliques of Ancient Poetry (1765). This national tradition is in general understood as being rooted in a specifically English natural landscape, imagined as remaining the same through hundreds of years, which can thereby embody an English national character that remains the same whatever accidents of history (political revolutions, economic change) happen in the meantime. If the new version of the nation raised it above party politics, this new version of poetry raised the nation above history altogether. (In Parts III and IV we will discuss Austen's relation to the national in various contexts [see pp. 142–7, 153–6, 158–60].)

This is one of the strands in eighteenth-century English culture that is drawn on by those poets, writing in Austen's lifetime, who are now grouped as 'the English Romantics': William Blake (1757–1827), William Wordsworth (1770–1850), Samuel Taylor Coleridge (1772–1834), Lord Byron (1788–1824), Percy Shelley (1792–1822) and John Keats (1795–1821). The other, major, contrast that can be made between the Romantics and the poets of Pope's generation (sometimes called the 'Augustans') might best be phrased in terms of their relation to religion, on the one hand, and social reality, on the other. For Pope, poetry remained tied up with the political and social world in which the poet moved: its concern was to satirise or praise human life by its own moral standards. Religion was a thing apart, the ultimate source of those moral standards, but not, in the main, a proper subject for something as worldly as poetry. The Romantic generation on the other hand wrote in a culture shaped by the Enlightenment. The Enlightenment had thrown the authority of religion into question, by explaining the world in terms of material cause and effect. This is sometimes called the Enlightenment's 'demystification' of the world. The Romantics understand poetry as a way of re-mystifying the world. That is, poetry is for them a way of seeing a transcendent power, something like the hidden but all-pervasive power of God, in the material world itself. This does not mean that this power is actually in the world: the point is, poetry *sees* it there. Where Pope and his allies were concerned to defend common moral standards in society, the Romantics are intensely interested in the subjectivity of experience. That is, they are interested in exactly how much the individual mind (especially the poet's mind) brings to experience, as distinct from an objective world producing experience in us from 'out there'. The titles of two book-length studies of Romanticism by M.H. Abrams, *The Mirror and the Lamp* (1953) and *Natural Supernaturalism* (1971), offer a way of summing this up. Where the neo-classical poet holds a mirror up to the world, and reflects a truth that is independent of him, the Romantic poet holds up (or just *is*) a lamp, shedding a light on the world that would not be there without him. Romanticism is a 'natural supernaturalism' because it finds a non-material power and meaning, like the supernatural power of a religion, in the natural world itself.

Some immediate problems present themselves in relating Austen to all this. First of all, the Romantics are all poets. Second, they are all men. Third, Austen did not know she was living in 'the age of the Romantics' because these six poets were only grouped under this name decades after she died. What is more, literary critics have been calling into question the usefulness of the term 'Romanticism' for some time now. By defining a movement, 'Romanticism', in terms of these poets alone, and then defining an entire period in terms of that movement, criticism had tended to marginalise any number of other writers who might not fit into this model. This is especially true of women writers. Anne Mellor has argued that the male Romantic poets, by their interest in subjective experience, 'effectively stole from women their primary cultural authority as the experts in delicate tender feelings' that women writers had been granted by the new value given to domesticity and sensibility [see pp. 5–10] (Mellor 1993: 23). In consequence, female poets from this period were, until very recently, completely forgotten. Today, 'Romantic' remains an adjective in common use by literary critics. But rather than identifying a set of literary qualities that may or may not be exhibited by any writer in this period, it usually simply refers to the period itself: the period, that is, defined in terms of non-literary features, usually social or political. In particular, 'Romantic' often now means 'written between the French Revolution of 1789 [see pp. 29–36] and the First Reform Bill [see p. 5]'. It is only thus that it is really possible to speak of 'the Romantic novel', for example in chapter 7 of Marilyn Butler's *Romantics, Rebels and Reactionaries* (1981: 155–77).

In fact, until fairly recently, literary critics have tended to place Austen in 'the Romantic period' negatively: that is, she is seen as drawing on the neo-classical or 'Augustan' traditions that the Romantics claimed to be rejecting. Q.D. Leavis, in her influential book *Fiction and the Reading Public* (first published in 1932), placed Austen at the end of a period in English life blessed with a developed common culture which consisted in an ongoing conversation about the properly moral life (Leavis 2000). *Jane Austen and her Predecessors* by Frank W. Bradbrook (1966) similarly sees her as the descendant above all of neo-classical poet and moralist Samuel Johnson, the propagator of the distinctive moral vocabulary that Leavis praises. For other accounts of the tradition on which Austen can be seen to draw, see Moler (1968) and Harris (1989). None of these studies, it should be noted, find Austen's primary influences among writers alive at the same time as her: rather, she stands alone as the triumphant culmination of a tradition. In fact, if her novels are seen as being suspicious of subjective judgement made independently of social convention, then she can be seen as an anti-Romantic writer. Tony Tanner, for example, makes a contrast between Blake's cult of 'energy' as 'eternal Delight' and Austen's 'suspicion of energy' that 'increased in her later work' (Tanner 1986: 141).

However, it is possible to see Austen as taking part in the cultural shifts that characterise her era and that were also acted out by the Romantic poets. For example, their location of poetry in something like the place of religion makes a new claim for the autonomy of their writing from more humdrum moral, social and political concerns. Thus they set their work apart from other less elevated types of writing, as 'literature' in a new, restricted sense. Austen too can be seen to be reaching for something like this high status for her own work (Morgan 1980: 17; Siskin 1998: 198–206; Tuite 2002: 80–1).

In fact, one can see Austen developing as a writer from the older, eighteenth-century modes to newer, Romantic ones. The satire and parody of the Gothic and sensibility in *Northanger Abbey* and *Sense and Sensibility* mock human absurdity in a way not too far from Swift and Pope. But Austen's last published novel, *Persuasion*, embodies a distinctly Romantic 'responsiveness to nature, with its inevitable tone of emotional perspective not objectively part of the view' (Morgan 1980: 172). Recently William Galperin has suggested that we view Austen (and indeed Burney too) as 'romantics', both to highlight the particular interest shown in their writing in individual agency and social change, an interest that they share with the 'big six' poets, and also to expand our sense of the cultural context in which all these writers are understood (Galperin 1998: 378). Indeed, the very awareness of its historical 'moment as distinct, both aesthetically and ideologically', from the eighteenth century that we can see in a novel like *Northanger Abbey* may be what it has in common with the poetry of Wordsworth, for example (Galperin 2000: 36). And the most striking of the factors that made their historical moment distinct was the French Revolution of 1789.

The effects of the French Revolution and the war with France

In the summer of 1789 the catastrophic finances of the French state forced King Louis XVI to call a meeting of his parliament, the Estates General. This consisted of three 'estates': the nobility, the clergy and a Third Estate nominally representing everyone else. The Third Estate might be loosely compared to the British House of Commons, but had none of its power to force measures on either monarch or nobility. On 17 June, however, the Third Estate declared itself a 'National Assembly', representing the nation as a whole. Louis then ordered the dissolution of the Estates General. As an absolutist monarch, he could decide to do so quite arbitrarily, but on this occasion he was simply ignored. Over the following weeks Louis brought troops to Paris, adding to the anger of a population already suffering from food shortages. On 14 July, violence flared between citizens and soldiers; the state prison, the Bastille, was stormed by the mob to seize its supply of arms and ammunition, and the city was lost to royal control. Louis was forced to back down; in June 1791 he took the desperate step of deciding to flee his own realm, with his family. They made for the border with the Austrian Netherlands, now Belgium, as his wife, Marie Antoinette, was a daughter of the Austrian imperial family. But they were captured and returned to Paris, increasingly feared and despised. Louis was forced to accept a Declaration of the Rights of Man and Citizen, and the privileges of the nobility were abolished. In the summer of 1792, the threat of invasion by Austria and Prussia allowed the Jacobins, the fundamentalist republican party in the Assembly led by Maximilien de Robespierre, to seize power. On 21 September, a republic was declared, and on 21 January 1793 Louis was guillotined. The most terrible bloodshed was still to come, however, as the Jacobins, fanatical and paranoid, accelerated the elimination of their enemies (aristocrats, priests, army officers, members of rival parties), imagined enemies ('Austrian spies', 'economic saboteurs') and eventually each other, sending tens of thousands to the guillotine. The killing (the 'Terror') reached its height in the summer of 1794, but in July the National Congress of the Republic finally turned on Robespierre and his allies and they too were unceremoniously decapitated. The National Congress continued to rule until 1799, when an army officer called Napoleon Bonaparte seized power in a coup.

Many in Britain at first welcomed the 1789 revolution in France, seeing it as a repetition of their own establishment of constitutional monarchy in 1688–9. However, the Jacobins' much more thoroughgoing attempt to reform society (the abolition of the aristocracy, of religion, the establishment of a more 'rational' ten-month calendar, and so on), the role played in events by the urban poor (particularly in Paris), and the spiralling violence of it all, dampened the enthusiasm as events unfolded. In addition, on 17 September 1792 the National Convention promised the assistance of the French Republic to 'all those wishing to recover their liberty': the rights of man that had been declared were universal, not specific to the French, and so France had a duty to export them where opportunity arose. The United Kingdom had been at war with France on and off throughout the eighteenth century, over the balance of power on the continent and, increasingly, over colonial possessions overseas. But the war that was declared by France on 1 February 1793, whatever the immediate diplomatic occasion for it, had a new, ideological appearance. It seemed to be a war not between rival states, but between rival systems and philosophies of government. The war was to continue, with two brief pauses, for twenty-two years, that is for most of Austen's adult life.

The great panorama of a two-decades-long global conflict might seem diametrically opposed to the tight focus on family and small-town life that we find in Austen's novels. And yet in several senses these events were very close to Austen (see Roberts 1979 for her personal experience of them). Most obviously, she had two brothers in the navy, and for many years the navy was Britain's only means of directly waging war in the European theatre. The war with France meant the real danger of a violent death for either or both Frank and Charles, and Austen must have been familiar with their tales of battle and the more mundane hardships of life at sea (Honan 1997: 160, 206, 223–4). In thus knowing intimately about events in the wider world through close relationships with her brothers, Austen, one might note, may have been typical of women in this period (Davidoff and Hall 1987: 349–50). For Frank and Charles the war also represented a means of getting rich, as prize money for the capture of enemy ships was shared out, and of getting promotion (the prospect for William in *Mansfield Park*, and achieved by Captain Wentworth in *Persuasion*). But the Terror, too, touched Austen personally. Her cousin and friend, Eliza Hancock, would end up married to Henry, Austen's favourite brother, but before that, in 1781, she had married a French army officer, Jean François de Feuillide. Captain de Feuillide was guillotined in February 1794.

In some ways, the effect of the French Revolution on English society was to reveal contradictions and tensions that had always existed in the post-1688 settlement. To recap: the increasing, and increasingly wealthy, commercial classes had won a place for themselves within what remained an essentially aristocratic political order, by representing their values and ideals (domesticity and the domestic woman, for example) as an aspect of human nature, and thus as universal. The polite culture that embodied those values was capable of including both moneyed and landed classes; but those who had no property of any kind were never intended for inclusion. But if those values represented 'human nature', why not? The rhetoric of universal 'nature', so useful for the purposes of finding common ground among the propertied, could just as well be taken up by the propertyless masses, and used to demand recognition from the 'polite' classes as a whole. Of course, the original claims of the new commercial order were made, and could only be made, through the medium of print, as we have seen. The poor had in the past been crippled in making any claims on the new society by their general illiteracy. But the poor could find allies among disaffected elements of the lower middle classes who might speak or, more to the point, write for them. The 'Dissenters' constituted one such disaffected group: members of the various Protestant churches outside the Church of England, and thus excluded from civic office and political power. In any case, literacy levels among the poor had been steadily rising.

A campaign for parliamentary reform, including universal male suffrage, had gained some temporary momentum in the preceding decade. Events in France at first gave it a new impetus, and it increasingly drew its members from the propertyless artisan and labouring classes; organisations such as the Society for Constitutional Information and the London Corresponding Society were able to hold together a network of groups throughout the country through written correspondence. Despite the boost given by the French Revolution, the demands of these 'Radicals' still tended to be expressed in terms of reclaiming the traditional rights of Englishmen, rather than the abstract rights of the new French constitution and Thomas Paine's republican manifesto *The Rights of Man* (1791, 1792). But however moderate, these demands now appeared to the government as subversive of the entire constitution, fostered by proto-revolutionaries in league with a foreign and hostile government. A French invasion was a very real threat: the republic formed a huge army through universal conscription, the *levée en masse*, and inflicted a series of remarkable defeats on the Austrians and Prussians. Sympathisers with any aspect of electoral reform were thus liable to be branded 'Jacobins'. A 'National Convention' of the Friends of the People in Edinburgh at the end of 1792, drawing delegates from all across the UK, led to three of its leading members being found guilty of treason and transported to Australia for fourteen years: two of them died within a year of arrival there. In May 1794 the British government introduced detention without trial and arrested the leaders of the London Corresponding Society among others. Trials acquitted all charged with treason, but some served time in prison on other charges. Naval and militia mutinies and mass public meetings to protest at food shortages in 1795 fed the government's paranoia, and prompted repressive measures against seditious speech and writing, and against public meetings of over fifty without the permission of a magistrate. Defying a magistrate enforcing these restrictions was punishable by death. In 1798 an actual and bloody uprising took place on the territory of the British crown, in Ireland, led by the Jacobin-inspired United Irishmen: the French managed eventually to land troops in support, but too late to prevent the rebellion being crushed by the British.

However, print culture, rather than the law courts or the battlefield, was the ground on which the ideological battle against revolutionary ideas was fought in Britain. This was partly because of the success of *The Rights of Man*, which sold between 100,000 and 200,000 copies in two years after publication, and was circulated and discussed widely through the radical societies. The most resonant anti-revolutionary statement, to which Paine's book was a reply, was Edmund Burke's *Reflections on the Revolution in France* ([1790] 1968). Burke's argument against the revolutionaries is one of the classic statements of political conservatism, and several critics have seen Austen's writing as reflecting his views [see pp. 116–19]. It argues that a successful state, like a successful estate or a successful family, is one that engages the emotions, the instinctive loyalty, of its subjects. Without such loyalty, any social grouping, the nation included, is simply a collection of self-interested individuals, only prepared to give up their autonomy if they get something of equal value in return. But the intelligence of any one individual is a weak and chancy thing, as like as not to identify that individual's true interests incorrectly. The constitution of the country represents a deeper and more reliable wisdom, developed over centuries. It is because of its long continuity and evolution that we naturally feel for it the respect and loyalty that we feel for parents. To abolish the state because its practices appear irrational, and then draw up new institutions on the basis of abstract principles (as the French were doing), would lead to disaster, for those institutions, commanding no *instinctive* respect, could always be subjected to further rational criticism; and so society would descend into the chaos of perpetual revolution.

One might note that in some ways Burke's *Reflections* takes the language of feeling, developed in order to explain the moral separation of private life from the world of public political and economic relationships, and uses it to explain the political world as well. Burke is suspicious of the political economists' description of the *difference* of modernity from what went before, and imagines instead a continuity between family and state, and between the feelings that bind contemporary English society and those of the 'feudal' past:

> You will observe, that from Magna Charta [of 1215] to the Declaration of Right [of 1689], it has been the uniform policy of our constitution to claim and assert our liberties, as an *entailed inheritance* derived to us from our forefathers. ... In this choice of inheritance we have given to our frame of polity the image of a relation in blood; binding up the constitution of our country with our dearest domestic ties; adopting our fundamental laws into the bosom of our family affections; keeping inseparable, and cherishing with the warmth of all their combined and mutually reflected charities, our state, our hearths, our sepulchres, and our altars.
>
> (Burke 1968: 119–20)

This explicitly political appropriation of the rhetoric of domesticity in Burke is one example of a general shift in the culture in the aftermath of the French Revolution. The English social settlement of the eighteenth century, the absorption of the moneyed classes into an elite 'polite' culture while maintaining their exclusion from political power, had depended on the suppression of explicit party politics from that culture. But the publications of the Radicals in general, and the success of Paine in particular, revealed that there was now a readership outside those classes keen to consume such material. The boundaries of print culture, that is, no longer simply coincided with the boundaries of the polite classes. In this way, the French Revolution forced the explicit discussion of political matters back into the centre of print culture. The public sphere could no longer be taken for granted as the means of maintaining a capitalist–aristocratic alliance, but had become the place where the dominance of that alliance could be challenged.

This produced a shift in the nature of those periodical journals, crucial for shaping the reception of new books throughout this period, that we discussed above [see pp. 18–19]. New journals tended to be explicitly partisan as their predecessors were not. The clearest early examples of this are the *Monthly Magazine* (1796–1825), supporting Paine, and the *Anti-Jacobin Review* (from 1797–8), a journal set up explicitly to counter the *Monthly Magazine* and to find out and condemn, with much satire, other publications' treasonable complicity with French republicanism.

But here too the revolution crisis threw into relief existing political fault-lines: some of the longest-established titles, such as the *Monthly Review* and *Critical Review*, were run by Dissenters, whose non-allegiance to the Anglican state church had always made them suspect and who were indeed inclined to be sympathetic to the revolutionaries (Butler 1993: 130). So self-proclaimed Anglican journals such as the *British Critic* (from 1792) were launched to challenge them on this front as well. This fragmentation of the market for reviews also led to an altogether new type of journal being produced. The Whig party (best thought of as the more reform-minded of the two main parties in parliament: it is often hard to tell it apart from the other one, the Tories) was out of government for the foreseeable future as a result of its early enthusiasm for the revolution, a politically difficult position once Britain was at war with France. So four young and ambitious Whigs diverted their energies into a new periodical, the *Edinburgh Review*, which would keep the Whig perspective alive at a cultural level while it remained excluded from office. It would accordingly address a primarily male and propertied or professional readership, those with some social or political influence; and it would appear only four times a year, attempting not (as the earlier monthlies had attempted) to review everything, but only those books deemed serious or important enough to merit lengthy discussion. The *Edinburgh Review* was founded in 1802; in 1809, John Murray, a London publisher, began the *Quarterly Review*, a Tory journal taking the same form and aiming for a similar elite readership, in partnership with the most successful poet of the time, Walter Scott [see p. 37], and one of the leading Tories, George Canning, later Prime Minister. The result of both these developments (the increasingly partisan identification of the monthlies, and the appearance of much more prestigious quarterlies) was to fragment what had been a fairly unified 'polite readership' into (albeit overlapping) groups based on class and party (Klancher 1987). Literary authority (the right to interpret, categorise and judge works) no longer simply resided with the journals as a genre, but was contested between individual titles.

One can see Burke's political appropriation of the rhetoric of domesticity in the *Reflections*, noted above, as an early indication of this explicit politicisation of the public sphere. The various types of writing, the various discourses, that had emerged as part of a polite culture which suppressed political polemic, were now being used for explicitly party-political purposes, and this included the discourse of domesticity and the family as well as the critical discourse of the periodical reviews. But the new political meanings attached to the discourse of domesticity involved women writers, and their precarious moral authority, in this explicitly political struggle. Wollstonecraft, who demanded equality of education for women, was a defender of the French Revolution; poor women had played a leading part in the street violence of that revolution, in the storming of the Bastille and on the various occasions when the royal family were besieged in their palaces by the Paris mob. In fact the French Republic turned out to be at least as restrictive of women's role in society as the old regime; but from the perspective of anti-revolutionary feeling in Britain, the revolution seemed to have involved, and to have authorised elsewhere, a breakdown in the distinction between proper masculine and feminine roles (for more on the politics of writing after the French Revolution see pp. 117–18). This makes it possible for anti-revolutionary writers to place the defence of a separate feminine domestic realm at the heart of their campaign against Jacobin ideas. The defence of this realm must necessarily fall to women: thus anti-revolutionary women authors were able to claim for themselves a crucial role in this most political struggle, even while insisting that a woman's place is in the home. Of course the separation of the domestic sphere from the political and economic spheres had always been itself politically driven, as we have seen. But now the domestic sphere was quite explicitly politicised, as part of the explicit repoliticisation of the culture in the 1790s that we have already observed. Now, what was at stake in the domestic virtue of private women was not just a compromise between the middling sort and the gentry; it was national survival itself. The domestic ideal developed in novels and conduct books earlier in the century was thus appropriated in the 1790s as the core of the national values which would save Britain from *moral* defeat by the republican French, as its army and navy would save Britain from military defeat. Such claims, and the paradoxical status of the woman writer who makes them, can be seen in this passage from Hannah More's 1799 text, *Strictures on the Modern System of Female Education*. Addressing, as the title goes on to specify, only women 'of rank and fortune', More describes her task thus:

> In this moment of alarm and peril, I would call on them with a 'warning voice,' which would stir up every latent principle in their minds, and kindle every slumbering energy in their hearts; I would call on them to come forward, and contribute their full and fair proportion towards the saving of their country. But I would call on them to come forward, without departing from the refinement of their character, without derogating from the dignity of their rank, without blemishing the delicacy of their sex: I would call them to the best and most appropriate exertion of their power, to raise the depressed tone of public morals, and to awaken the drowsy spirit of religious principle.
>
> (More 1799: 4–5)

In the same paragraph, More insists on the difference between masculine and feminine modes of public agency ('I am not sounding an alarm to female warriors, or exciting female politicians; I hardly know which of the two is the most disgusting and unnatural character' she writes a few paragraphs later) and places herself in the very masculine public role of prophet of impending doom (the 'warning voice' of the first line is a quotation from the first line of Book IV of John Milton's epic poem *Paradise Lost*, 1667, and is that heard by St John in the Book of Revelation, and longed for by the poet himself). One should also note that the address only to wealthy women admits the fragmentation of the reading public that we have already described: More also wrote ballads, short fiction, bible stories and religious tracts for a poorer readership, produced cheaply and priced accordingly. More's patriotism calls for national unanimity while her publishing strategies admit the division of the nation on class lines.

These paradoxes are versions of the paradoxes we have already seen both permitting and restricting women's writing earlier in the eighteenth century. But the implication of feminine virtue in national defence had two further effects. First, by insisting on the political importance of the private behaviour of wealthy women, it placed new importance on women's education. For More, the acquisition of 'accomplishments' is obviously not a good training for this national role. Young women must learn to be self-effacing and subordinate, but they must also learn the principles and strength of mind to resist 'seduction' by Jacobin ideas. Because of the perceived breakdown of properly differentiated gender roles in the French Revolution and its English defenders noted above, More and other anti-revolutionary writers characteristically imagine the ideological threat from France in sexual terms. This sexualisation of the threat from France gave new importance to a woman's 'modesty', her not giving expression to her own sexual desire. It was assisted by the tacit acknowledgement of 'sensibility' as a figure for sexual passion. Jean-Jacques Rousseau (1712–78) was famous both as a novelist of sensibility (in *Julie*, 1761) and as the philosophical inspiration of the Jacobins (in such works as the *Discourse on the Origin of Inequality*, 1755, and *On the Social Contract*, 1762). Sensibility had figured as an emotional commitment that could not be accommodated in wider social institutions [see pp. 21–2]: now those institutions were under threat, sensibility was bound to appear as an accessory to revolution. For More and others, only Christianity could be relied on to help woman resist the Jacobin saboteur in her own breast; that meant young women must be given a rigorous training in their religion. More and Wollstonecraft are diametrically opposed in their politics, but both share a new emphasis on the moral and political importance of women's education. They disagree on what that education ought to be, but share a contempt for the triviality of the education generally on offer to girls at the time.

Second, the penalties for transgressing the rules of propriety became much more intimidating for women writers. For a propertied woman *not* to conform to the ideal of domestic propriety was no longer just to sacrifice the chance of a good marriage, but to give implicit aid and succour to the godless enemy. The anti-revolutionary periodical press was ready to enforce this equation given the opportunity. In the case of Wollstonecraft it got its opportunity after her death, when her husband William Godwin (1756–1836), himself a leading political thinker sympathetic to the Jacobins, wrote a tactlessly candid memoir of her, revealing her two sexual relationships before her marriage and the illegitimate child produced by one of them. Published in 1798, it turned Wollstonecraft into the touchstone for the argument of the *Anti-Jacobin Review* and its allies that radical politics and female sexual promiscuity went hand in hand. It became impossible for a woman writer to advance Wollstonecraft's arguments without risking such personal charges being levelled at her. The increased political importance that the revolution crisis offered women writers was at the price of increased surveillance by the institutions of patriarchal culture, including other women writers in the service of those institutions, like More.

The 1790s and early 1800s see the emergence of a whole school of anti-revolutionary women writers (Kelly 1993; Keane 2000). The novel itself becomes a means of defending the status quo against radical ideas in the hands of Elizabeth Hamilton (*Memoirs of Modern Philosophers*, 1800), Jane West (*The Infidel*

Father, 1802) and More herself (*Cœlebs in Search of a Wife*, 1809). It may seem odd that women writers, given all the restrictions placed on them by a patriarchal society, should be so ready to write in its defence. But one must remember that these were overwhelmingly women of the middle rank, and the authority, however circumscribed, that they enjoyed in domestic and ethical matters had been granted by the very social settlement that now seemed under threat. Austen is often read in relation to anti-Jacobin women writers [see pp. 127–30]. For now I wish only to observe that Austen's references to them in her letters tend to be less than enthusiastic. Here she comments to Cassandra on the reception of *Sense and Sensibility* as reported by Mary, her brother James's wife: 'Mary heard before she left home, that it was very much admired at Cheltenham, & that it was given to Miss Hamilton. It is pleasant to have such a respectable Writer named' (6–7 November 1813; Le Faye 1995: 252). Miss Hamilton is a 'respectable' writer, not a *good* one, and 'pleasant' hardly suggests delight at recognition by this former star in the reactionary firmament (and remember Austen is a comparatively unknown writer at this point). Four years earlier, she is quite scathing about More: after mistranscribing the title of *Cœlebs in Search of a Wife* from Cassandra's letter, she comments:

> the knowledge of the truth does the book no service;—the only merit it could have, was in the name of Caleb, which has an honest, unpretending sound; but in Coelebs, there is pedantry and affectation.—Is it written only to Classical Scholars?
>
> (30 January 1809; Le Faye 1995: 172)

This amounts to an accusation that More is transgressing the very gender boundaries that she is writing to defend. It is also possible that Austen is making an implicit comparison with a much better novel, Godwin's *Caleb Williams* of 1794. This is a philosophical novel of the type closely associated with the radical politics of the 'English Jacobins': politics that may oblige Austen to pretend not to have read it.

Politics and the novel after 1814

In fact by 1809 much of the heat had gone out of the ideological struggle in Britain occasioned by the French Revolution. The rise of Napoleon, who crowned himself emperor in 1804, made the war waged by the British look much more familiar to most of the home population. It now appeared as one more effort to contain the power of a French Empire on the continent of Europe, rather than as an ideological crusade, and a distinction is usually made between the 'Revolutionary War' before Napoleon's accession to power and the 'Napoleonic War' afterwards. On the continent itself, however, Napoleon continued to be seen by significant proportions of the countries he conquered as a liberator from the tyranny of the old royal dynasties: the huge army with which he invaded Russia in 1812 included republican recruits from all over Europe. The vast majority of those recruits did not come back, thanks largely to the Russian winter, and France, for the first time in twenty years of war, began to crumble in the face of its united enemies: Britain, Prussia, Russia and Austria. In 1814 Paris fell to these allies and Napoleon was forced to abdicate and sent into exile: he escaped and marshalled his armies once more the following year only to be decisively defeated at Waterloo. In the meantime, the allies convened the Congress of Vienna, which set about the restoration of the old European order, including all the absolutist monarchies that most Britons had once regarded with horror, but with which the UK had allied itself in order to defeat France.

The year 1814 also saw a turning point in the history of the novel. A novel called *Waverley*, set against the Jacobite rebellion of 1745, when a mostly Scottish army tried to put the son of James II back on the throne, was a massive success. Its author was Walter Scott, who had been the most successful epic poet of his generation until Byron published *Childe Harold's Pilgrimage* in 1812. The novel was published anonymously: as an established poet writing in a prestigious genre, as a professional man of letters with connections at the highest social levels, Scott had no need for any more attention. But the handling in the novel of public matters, of state politics and military history, albeit within the conventional frame of a young man's education, falling in love and getting married, marked this out as a distinctly *masculine* type of fiction. And in any case, a sharp-eyed observer of the literary scene could make a shrewd guess at more than the gender of the author:

> Walter Scott has no business to write novels, especially good ones.—It is not fair.—He has Fame and Profit enough as a Poet, and should not be taking the bread out of other people's mouths.—I do not like him, & do not mean to like Waverley if I can help it—but I fear I must.
>
> (To Anna Austen, 28 September 1814; Le Faye 1995: 277)

The continuing success of further novels by Scott in a similar vein (another five by 1817), and in particular the accolades of the reviews, including the crucial *Edinburgh* and (unsurprisingly) the *Quarterly*, changed the status of the novel more decisively than anything since Richardson. It could now be accepted by propertied men as a serious genre, no longer restricted to the feminine concerns of personal feelings and family ties, but with the potential to contribute to ongoing public debates in matters historical and political (Ferris 1991: 79–94).

In some ways, Austen benefited briefly from the admiration of the men behind this literary revolution. With *Emma* she was able to turn to the prestige machine that was Scott, John Murray and the *Quarterly Review*: Murray published it, and Scott gave it a lengthy and positive (if rather condescending) review in the *Quarterly*, including a paragraph each on her first two novels as well. But her cautious response to this praise, in a letter to Murray, perhaps suggests a discomfort with the patronage, now on lines of gender rather than rank, that it seems to involve:

> I return you the Quarterly Reveiw [*sic*] with many Thanks. The Authoress of *Emma* has no reason I think to complain of her treatment in it—except in the total omission of Mansfield Park.—I cannot but be sorry that so clever a Man as the Reviewer of *Emma*, should consider it as unworthy of being noticed.
>
> (1 April 1816; Le Faye 1995: 313)

In any case, *Emma* was the last novel she published in her lifetime. Scott's success, while it made the novel as a genre more central to the culture, also enforced a new gender division: there was now one sort of novel dealing with serious masculine concerns, and another by and for women. Both could be good, but it was clear which one was the more important. One of the lasting effects of this division of novelistic responsibilities has been the tendency to read Austen's fiction as if it had nothing to say about public politics, despite the crucial role played by women writers in the politics of British reaction to the French Revolution that we have been examining, and to which we will return.

Certainly, Britain's part in the triumph of the old order on the continent did not mean the end of the campaign for reform at home. On the contrary, the end of the war meant that campaign could be renewed without the accusation of treason being levelled at the campaigners. Peace also brought severe economic depression and greater social unrest. Even before the war was over, the 'Luddite' movement protested violently against the loss of jobs that resulted from the increasing mechanisation of traditional industries (Sales 1994: 63). In 1817, the year of Austen's death, the UK government once more introduced detention without trial and acted against democratic societies, but the old order was doomed by economic and social developments. A merchant class might be co-opted into the old regime without being granted the vote, but the new breed of industrial entrepreneurs had economic interests that clashed with their landed rulers and demanded expression within parliament. The constitutional settlement of 1688–9 had survived the threat of political revolution, but it could not survive the Industrial Revolution. Roger Sales argues forcefully in *Jane Austen and Representations of Regency England* (1994) that it is in this context of political crisis in England that Austen's work, and in particular the last three novels written entirely in the 1810s, should be understood, and not the revolution controversy of the 1790s. Austen's fiction is written in the last decades of the old social order, and it is already an order in crisis. As such her fiction negotiates many of the problems of that social order, problems accentuated, but not created, by the French Revolution and its aftermath.

2

Works

Introduction

The discussions of Austen's six major completed novels in Part 2 are intended to introduce you to some of the ways in which these works can be understood within the various contexts, literary and historical, outlined in Part 1. But there is not space enough here to discuss all the issues raised in each individual novel. So, instead, this part examines particular issues in the case of each novel which could equally well be discussed in the case of the others.

These six novels are commonly considered in two groups, for example in the very useful *Cambridge Companion to Jane Austen* (Copeland and McMaster: 1997). The first three, *Northanger Abbey, Sense and Sensibility* and *Pride and Prejudice*, were all finished in an early form in the 1790s, although extensively revised before their publication. *Mansfield Park; Emma* and *Persuasion* were written in rapid succession after the successful publication of *Sense and Sensibility* in 1811. These three later novels are usually seen as more mature and accomplished works. *Northanger Abbey* and *Sense and Sensibility* in particular are often understood as early experiments, starting from a negative movement of parody or satire of other types of writing (the Gothic novel and the cult of sensibility) while also reaching towards the more positive achievement of the later novels. *Pride and Prejudice*, on the other hand, though begun very early in Austen's career, seems a perfectly realised work in its own right; yet it is often seen as lacking the high moral seriousness of vision that begins with *Mansfield Park*. Perhaps because of this, *Pride and Prejudice* remains Austen's most popular novel, and *Mansfield Park* the hardest for modern readers to appreciate. *Emma* on the other hand is commonly seen as the peak of Austen's achievement as a novelist. In relation to *Emma, Persuasion* can appear as a move in new directions: darker, more pessimistic, readier to admit the value of passion and romance cut loose from the demands of society, it is often seen as anticipating the approach of later women novelists and in particular the Brontë sisters. In fact the inwardness of *Persuasion*, its greater concern with the thoughts and feelings of its heroine compared with the social situations in which she moves, is made possible by a mastery of narrative technique that Austen had been developing throughout her career, in particular the use of free indirect discourse, which we will address in our discussion of *Emma* below.

Northanger Abbey is discussed here in terms of the politics of language: that is, what kinds of language have more authority than other kinds, and specifically the gendering of language that gives male speakers more authority than female speakers. This novel is usually read as a satire on Gothic novel conventions, a subversion of them in the name of 'realism'. Yet the discussion of *Northanger Abbey* here will show that Austen is also concerned to defend novelistic conventions in general, against a language that claims to be based in 'common life' but is in fact just as dependent on convention. The discussion of *Sense and Sensibility* will contrast two versions of the self: the self constructed in dialogue with the favoured other, and the private self engaged in scrutiny of its own workings. The Dashwood sisters begin and end the novel in the former state, but in between Elinor exhibits a private consciousness that ultimately gives her power, not partnership, in her relationship with Marianne. *Pride and Prejudice* will be read as an account of the social compromise between landed ruling class and merchant capitalists that we saw as the core of the British social settlement in the eighteenth century. But the romance of Darcy and Elizabeth Bennet also acts out the alliance between local and national ruling groups; and finds a place for women in ensuring national cultural continuity, in spite of the entail that stops them from legally inheriting the estate.

Expanding on this latter point, *Mansfield Park* will be read as a story about feminine agency: that is, about how women can bring about change despite being denied the political, economic or religious means to do so. Fanny Price gains this power from the moral authority of the same kind of inward-looking, self-examining consciousness that we saw in Elinor in *Sense and Sensibility*. Not just a sister, but a whole country estate, is now in need of reform. The discussion of *Emma* will return to questions of language, but this time will understand the language of the private feminine self in opposition to that of a whole community. Free indirect discourse is not just the means of conveying individual thought here, as in *Mansfield Park*, but instead represents a network of speakers and their vocabulary and assumptions. The heroine's relation to this community moves from ironic distance to a grudging acceptance of its social breadth. Finally, *Persuasion* narrows in on more personal and exclusive relationships, sometimes maternal, and on triangular relationships involving seeing and being overheard, suggesting a loss of confidence in language to function clearly and simply as the medium for human relationships.

Northanger Abbey

In 1798–9 Austen completed a novel entitled 'Susan'. By this time she had already completed early versions of *Pride and Prejudice* and *Sense and Sensibility*. 'Susan' was then revised in the following years before the manuscript, with its copyright, was sold to the publisher Crosby & Co. for £10 in 1803. This method of sale gave the author no further control over her book's publication [see pp. 13–15], and Crosby, after advertising the work, for some reason chose neither to publish it nor, when Austen complained about this in 1809, to permit her to publish it elsewhere: her only option was to buy the manuscript back for the original price. This Austen eventually did, in 1816, changing the name of her heroine and the novel to 'Catherine', but it was only after her death in 1817 that her sister Cassandra arranged with John Murray for its publication as *Northanger Abbey*, in two volumes of a four-volume set with *Persuasion*. *Northanger Abbey* is thus not her earliest completed work, and was among the last to be published, but as the first to be *sold* it is usually taken first in any discussion of Austen's major novels.

The story is basically as follows. Catherine Morland is taken to the fashionable resort town of Bath by her neighbours Mr and Mrs Allen where she meets two groups of friends: Henry Tilney and his sister Eleanor, and brother and sister John and Isabella Thorpe. Catherine and Isabella become best friends, although Catherine is drawn to the charming Henry rather than the brutish John. Henry's father, General Tilney, invites Catherine to stay with them at Northanger Abbey. This seems a generous gesture, but it turns out that John Thorpe has told the General that Catherine is rich, and for this reason he is eager that his son should marry her. Catherine experiences Northanger through the conventions of the Gothic novels that she has been reading with Isabella, casting the General as the villain who has murdered his wife. When the General finds out that Catherine is not a rich heiress he throws her out of his house; but Henry follows her home despite his father's anger, proposes and is accepted.

Northanger Abbey is a novel which begins by telling the reader that its heroine is not the heroine of a novel. The first chapter tells us a lot about what she is not: she is not prodigiously clever as a child, not strikingly pretty as an adolescent; not at all wicked, but not very well behaved either. The reader, it is assumed, will expect a young woman at the centre of a novel to be very good, very intelligent and very beautiful. Starting from such expectations, the reader is bound to find Catherine Morland a 'strange, unaccountable character!' (I.i.16). Only at the start of the second chapter does the narrator offer an extended *positive* description of Catherine. These passages are also marked, however, by the narrator's expressions of surprise that such an unheroic heroine should be possible: she and her circumstances are 'remarkable', 'extraordinary'. They thus constitute an extended exercise in irony, since the reader is intended to take these terms to mean the opposite of their literal sense: what is called 'extraordinary' is in fact perfectly ordinary in 'common life' (I.ii.20), and only unaccountable to a sense of what *ought* to happen in a novel. The irony here depends, that is, on a reader who recognises a gap between the world as it is represented in novels and something called 'common life' (I will return to the problematic idea of 'common life').

One way of reading *Northanger Abbey* begins by taking the target of Austen's irony here to be one quite specific genre of novel: the Gothic romance of, especially, Ann Radcliffe and her many imitators [**see p. 18**]. Such a reading takes its cue from two other aspects of the novel. When Catherine first meets Isabella Thorpe she is reading Radcliffe's *The Mysteries of Udolpho*, and Isabella too is a voracious reader of Gothic fiction: this shared interest is fundamental to their 'very warm attachment', and the narrator reverts to irony at the start of I.vi to imply that this basis marks their friendship as, among other things, unoriginal and unreasonable. There are suggestions that such novels are also intrinsically damaging to their readers: Catherine suffers from 'a raised, restless, and frightened imagination over the pages of Udolpho' at I.vii.50.

But the serious charge against the Gothic novel here is that its largely young and inexperienced female readership will take the dangers and horrors it portrays as representations of the real world rather than as a set of novelistic conventions; they will accordingly misread their actual circumstances in accordance with those conventions and fail to understand the 'common life' around them. The effect of undisciplined reading on young women was a recurring concern in the eighteenth century for just this reason. We have already seen how the novel was from the beginning associated with women writers and readers [see pp. 17–18]. The early woman-authored novel, for example the work of Aphra Behn, inherited from seventeenth-century French romance a set of idealised versions of male heroism, feminine beauty and absolute, passionate and potentially tragic love. The popularity of such fiction raised the anxiety that girls from the propertied classes might learn to expect and nurture such feelings, acquiring habits of sentimental self-indulgence at odds with the emotional self-control demanded of them by their actual social role as pure daughters and virtuous wives. The Gothic novel, with its idealised heroine, purely evil villain, unlikely plot and stimulation of feelings of horror and suspense, is itself a kind of romance, and became a particular focus for worries about the effects of feminine reading practices in the final decades of the eighteenth century.

In *Northanger Abbey* the possibility that the female reader might interpret reality through the categories of the Gothic novel is most obviously raised once Catherine arrives at Northanger Abbey itself, old religious houses, like castles, being a characteristic setting for abduction, incarceration and murder in the genre. Here she concludes, from various slender indications, that the late wife of her host, General Tilney, must have perished at his hands, or even remain alive, imprisoned somewhere in the building (II.vii–ix). Chapter II.ix ends with an apparently conclusive explosion of this interpretation by Henry Tilney, the General's son:

> ". . . Consult your own understanding, your own sense of the probable, your own observation of what is passing around you—Does our educa- tion prepare us for such atrocities? Do our laws connive at them? . . . Dearest Miss Morland, what ideas have you been admitting?"
>
> (II.ix.186)

Northanger Abbey, read thus, becomes the story of how a young woman's per- ception of the world is warped by the wrong sort of (romance) reading, how she makes terrible mistakes as a result, but is rescued from her errors by the forces of reason, embodied in a male figure of some kind of authority (Henry will after all become Catherine's husband).

Northanger Abbey is not the first novel to tell this kind of story. It is one of a series of novels that can be called 'anti-romances', whose ultimate ancestor is Miguel de Cervantes's *Don Quixote* (1605, 1615). It is useful to remember that the novel itself is a young form in the eighteenth century, and is still in a process of defining itself in opposition to the romance. Romance was a genre of low status from which the novel drew much and from which it was accordingly keen to distinguish itself. Most (especially early) eighteenth-century novels engage in something like this negative self-definition as *not* romances, their subject matter defined as the particularities of everyday reality, of 'common life', rather than the ideal and the extraordinary as in romance [see p. 17]. Such generic self-consciousness is certainly very marked in *Northanger Abbey*. As well as the role in its plot of the Gothic in general and *The Mysteries of Udolpho* in particular, *Northanger Abbey* also contains the remarkable defence of the novel in I.v, in which contemporary writers of the domestic novel, Frances Burney and Maria Edgeworth, are praised, and Radcliffe is prominent by her absence:

> "And what are you reading, Miss—?" "Oh! it is only a novel!" replies the young lady; while she lays down her book with affected indifference, or momentary shame.—"It is only Cecilia, or Camilla, or Belinda;" or, in short, only some work in which the greatest powers of the mind are displayed, in which the most thorough knowledge of human nature, the happiest delineation of its varieties, the liveliest effusions of wit and humour are conveyed to the world in the best chosen language.
>
> (I.v.346–7)

There are, however, a number of problems with reading *Northanger Abbey* as an anti-romance in this way. First, except for II.vii–ix, Catherine's problems in interpreting the world around her do *not* originate with her reading Gothic novels. Second, her rejection of romance that follows from Henry's outburst at the end of II.ix is not the climax of the plot. Rather, it is merely a prelude to Catherine's summary and genuinely traumatic ejection from the Abbey when the General discovers that she is not the prospectively wealthy heiress he had been told she was, and thus not after all a suitable match for Henry, the younger son who will not inherit the Northanger estate. This crisis is linked in no way to any flaw in Catherine's perception of the world around her: it is in no sense brought on by her bad reading or any other kind of mistake on her part.

Northanger Abbey cannot be reduced to the anti-romance of II.vii–ix for another reason. We have seen the novels of Burney and Edgeworth praised in I.v: yet nearly all of the conventional narrative elements ironised in the first two chapters are as much a feature of their fictions of contemporary life as of Radcliffe's Gothic fantasies. As well as centring on very clever, very pretty young women, Burney's and Edgeworth's novels, just as much as Radcliffe's, must end with the heroine surviving tribulations (albeit of a more plausible kind) and marrying a wealthy young man [see pp. 17–18]. Mrs Allen is credited with knowing that 'if adventures will not befal a young lady in her own village, she must seek them abroad' (I.i.18), a principle that holds just as well if 'abroad' is the public life of London or Bath as if it is a crumbling castle in the Apennines (the setting of a large part of *The Mysteries of Udolpho*). Mrs Morland could have learnt of the 'general mischievousness' and 'machinations' of 'lords and baronets' (I.ii.19) from the novelists that Austen praises as well as from those she seems to condemn. This is not to say that Austen is asserting her novel to be as different from Burney's and Edgeworth's as it is from Radcliffe's: its setting, at least, clearly gives it much more in common with the former. It *is* to say that the irony of the first two chapters is at the expense of the type of novel that *Northanger Abbey* actually *is* as well the type that it is not, as many of the generic conventions alluded to ironically here are ones that this novel will in fact go on to deploy.

I commented that, in the defence of the novel, Radcliffe was prominent by her absence. Yet that defence does not explicitly contrast Burney and Edgeworth with Radcliffe: indeed, the defence takes its occasion from Catherine and Isabella reading novels together, a joint activity which is not criticised here as it is in I.vi (see above), and the novels they are reading are presumably the Gothic ones to which they are addicted. Rather, I.v ends by contrasting (female-authored) novels in general, *including* Gothic ones, with the *Spectator*, that repository of polite wisdom discussed in Part 1 [see pp. 9–10]. There are a few other references to periodical and essay writing of this authoritative (and mostly male-authored) kind in *Northanger Abbey*. Fun has already been poked at Richardson's rule 'that no young lady can be justified in falling in love before the gentleman's love is declared' (I.iii.29) in Samuel Johnson's periodical the *Rambler* [see pp. 18–19]. Later, Catherine's mother will attempt to reconcile her dejected daughter to her fate with a volume of Henry Mackenzie's the *Mirror*, one of many journals modelling themselves on Addison and Steele's (II.xv.225). The implication seems to be that this genre of moral generalisation is too distant from the emotionally complicated particularities of social experience to be of any help in guiding conduct, in contrast to the novel which makes such particularities its central concern.

It is significant that we find Henry's own authority as Catherine's tutor (in, for example, current theories of what constitutes picturesque landscape) associated by his sister with just this kind of writing, when he criticises Catherine's use of the vague 'nice':

> "He is for ever finding fault with me, for some incorrectness of language, and now he is taking the same liberty with you. The word 'nicest,' as you use it, did not suit him; and you had better change it as soon as you can, or you shall be overpowered with Johnson and Blair all the rest of the way."
>
> (I.xiv.103–4)

Addison, Richardson, Johnson, Blair: these essayists are presented here as a canon of masculine authorities with which this novel is in competition to the same extent, at least, as it is with the female-authored Gothic novel. And these writers give Henry his version of reality as surely as Radcliffe gives Catherine hers. When Henry dissolves Catherine's Gothic fantasy at the end of II.ix, he is not dispelling her faith in written texts by confronting her with simple reality. Rather, he is facing down one genre of writing, a feminine one, with another genre of writing, a masculine one. The fact that the Gothic (and perhaps the novel in general) provides the means whereby young women can think for themselves is perhaps the real threat that Henry is countering here. After all, as we have seen, Catherine's fantasy proves to be a way of imagining as evil a truth about the General that Henry never criticises: the absolute nature of his patriarchal power. The type of language that Henry uses does not originate with him: it is borrowed from the essays of Johnson, Blair and company, and gets its authority, its power over Catherine, from that masculine source. As a distinct type of language, available for speakers or writers to use but in general circulation in society, we can call this a *discourse*: Henry deploys the *discourse* of the Johnsonian essay. One could see this power, then, as a linguistic version of the patriarchal power of the General:

a way of controlling women, not physically by locking them up or removing them from a house, but by controlling their language, telling them what they may and may not say. The eighteenth-century anxiety, that we have already noted, about the effects of novel reading on young women appears, in this context, as an expression of a deeper anxiety about the element of autonomy from traditional, masculine, cultural authority inherent in women's authorship itself.

Having begun with the ironic language of an omniscient third-person narrator, *Northanger Abbey* rapidly turns to its other main narrative mode, dramatic dialogue between the characters. And within that dialogue, we find more irony; this time from Henry Tilney:

> ... Then forming his features into a set smile, and affectedly softening his voice, he added, with a simpering air, "Have you been long in Bath, madam?"
>
> "About a week, sir," replied Catherine, trying not to laugh.
>
> "Really!" with affected astonishment.
>
> "Why should you be surprized, sir?"
>
> "Why, indeed!" said he, in his natural tone—"but some emotion must appear to be raised by your reply, and surprize is more easily assumed, and not less reasonable than any other.—Now let us go on. Were you never here before, madam?"
>
> (I.iii.26)

The difference set up here between Henry's 'natural' tone (what he later refers to as being 'rational') and the 'affected' conventions of formal conversation is similar to the gap in the first two chapters between Catherine's 'character' and the heroine of the conventional novel. As in the previous chapters, conventional terms are being used by the speaker in order to expose their conventionality, to expose the gap between convention and truth. The bulk of the novel, in fact, is much more concerned with the functioning of social convention, with the genres of speech and other types of discourse, than with the specifically literary genres discussed so far.

We have already seen, in Part 1, the considerable political importance invested in the rules of 'politeness' or 'civility' by eighteenth-century British society as a means whereby members of the propertied classes could recognise each other and share social spaces in which the important distinctions between the landed and the moneyed, between gentry and merchants, could be at least temporarily suspended [see pp. 8–10]. The social interaction made possible in this way must produce a pleasure which is shared by the parties to a conversation (what Henry at I.x.74 calls 'mutual agreeableness'), a reciprocity of speech and behaviour which confirms in *both* parties their common status as members of this privileged social group, polite society.

Henry may ridicule the conventionality of formal conversation on his first appearance in the novel; however, the necessity remains of conforming to some such conventions, as a condition of participation in polite society. Henry's 'natural' speech, after all, remains *polite*: that is, 'politeness' has been 'naturalised' as a form of discourse that characters simply take for granted as the standard against which various other languages (assembly-room formality in this case, but also women's gossip or indeed the Gothic novel) can be judged as aberrations. To put this point another way, 'politeness' only *appears* 'natural' to these characters *because* it is understood as the opposite of other discourses, including the 'affected' speech mocked by Henry. In Catherine Morland Austen deploys a type of heroine most familiar to her readers from the novels of Frances Burney, namely the ingenue from the country who struggles to gain a foothold in a metropolitan society whose rules, in their difference from mere politeness, she does not yet understand. In the passage from I.iii quoted above, for example, Catherine turns away from Henry as he signs off his ironic riff, 'not knowing whether she may venture to laugh': even in response to his mockery of social convention, Catherine is embarrassed by her ignorance of it. And as late as II.xiii, as the novel moves towards its climax, Catherine is still unsure about how long it is appropriate to stay as a guest in a country house: 'perhaps it might seem an intrusion if she staid much longer' (II.xiii.206).

As in Burney, the heroine's acquaintances tend to be characterised in terms of their own conformity to or deviance from polite standards, and thus of their capacity to help the heroine acquire them. Most obviously, Mrs Allen, for all her status as the wife of a landowner, simply does not have the intelligence to participate in pleasure-producing conversation of the kind required. John Thorpe himself represents the corresponding masculine type of gentry vulgarity, concerned exclusively as he is with horses and gambling: he

> seemed fearful of being too handsome unless he wore the dress of a groom, and too much like a gentleman unless he were easy where he ought to be civil, and impudent where he might be allowed to be easy.
>
> (I.vii.44)

Civility, rather than the mere possession of land, ought to mark the difference between a gentleman and his groom. John Thorpe lacks civility: later in the novel he pays Catherine a compliment which, she complains, 'gives me no pleasure' (I.xiii.95).

Henry Tilney, in contrast, is the guide that Catherine needs in the new social world she finds herself in, and his very ability to instruct her is a large part of his appropriateness as her eventual husband: he is a 'lover mentor', a type again familiar from Burney [see **pp. 17–18**]. In I.iii, alongside the discourses of convention and 'naturalness', he introduces a third discourse: that of the young lady's private journal:

> "I shall make but a poor figure in your journal to-morrow."
>
> "My journal!"
>
> "Yes, I know exactly what you will say: Friday, went to the Lower Rooms; wore my sprigged muslin robe with blue trimmings—plain black shoes—appeared to much advantage; but was strangely harassed by a queer, half-witted man, who would make me dance with him, and distressed me by his nonsense."
>
> "Indeed I shall say no such thing."
>
> "Shall I tell you what you ought to say?"
>
> "If you please."

"I danced with a very agreeable young man, introduced by Mr King; had a great deal of conversation with him . . ."

(I.iii.26)

Thus is Henry established from the start as one who is at ease with the various types of language of the society in which he moves, the discourse not only of public sociability but of private biographical narrative; not only masculine discourse (public gallantry) but feminine discourse (private thoughts, dress, etc.). In this instance, Henry goes so far as to speak in Catherine's voice, to put words in her mouth in something like the way in which an author puts words in the mouth of a character. This lends Henry an authority to judge the discourse of others, and indeed to correct or direct it ('Shall I tell you what you ought to say?'). His refutation of the discourse of the Gothic novel in II.ix is only the climactic instance of this function of his in *Northanger Abbey*.

The association of the feminine voice with privacy reappears in Catherine's dealings with her two friends, Isabella Thorpe and Eleanor Tilney. We have already observed the way in which Catherine's friendship with Isabella is mediated by the novels that they read, but given the way in which this text draws back, as we have also seen, from a condemnation of the Gothic *as such*, this mediation on its own should not necessarily be read as a signifier of the friendship's shallowness. Its real flaw lies in its failure to enact the reciprocal pleasure-giving essential to 'polite' intercourse; and in I.xiii this failure occurs, significantly, through Isabella's referring explicitly, in front of Catherine's brother James, to Catherine's fondness for *both* Tilneys, brother and sister:

Catherine thought this reproach equally strange and unkind. Was it the part of a friend thus to expose her feelings to the notice of others? Isabella appeared to her ungenerous and selfish, regardless of every other thing but her own gratification.

(I.xiii.94)

The reciprocity on which politeness depends breaks down here through the exposure of private 'feelings' in public discourse: politeness appears here as that which governs, among other things, what counts as private or personal, as appropriate for discussion between female friends but not in front of others. To put this another way, the codes of polite conversation define and thus summon into being a space of feminine privacy which appears here as the space of 'feelings'.

Similarly, the contrastingly sincere and selfless female friendship between Catherine and Eleanor finds its expression in language as conventional as that ironised by Henry: their first conversation (in I.viii) follows just those 'first rudiments' (55) that he mocks in I.iii, and their better acquaintance is described thus:

Miss Tilney met her with great civility, [and] returned her advances with equal good will . . . and though in all probability not an observation was made, nor an expression used by either which had not been made and used some thousands of times before, under that roof, in every Bath season, yet the merit of their being spoken with simplicity and truth, and without personal conceit, might be something uncommon.—

(I.x.70)

This striking passage can be read as disturbing the connection made by Henry's irony in I.iii between the conventional, repeatable quality of formal conversation and its lack of 'naturalness'. The same words that are used by everybody else are repeated one more time by Catherine and Eleanor, but are a perfectly adequate medium for 'truth', for the reciprocity of 'civility', in which sincere friendship consists.

Northanger Abbey at first appears to be a satire on convention, whether in the novel or in speech, and a plea for its opposite, the 'natural'. In fact it reveals 'the common feelings of common life' to be just as much the product of conventions. It opposes the romance plot with a narrative of education [see pp. 101–4], in which the heroine learns to distinguish the 'truth' of everyday reality, the truth as constructed by the realistic novel, from the fantasy of Gothic fiction. Yet the plot of *Northanger Abbey* remains true to very similar narrative conventions; and what Catherine learns in this plot is that, so far as General Tilney's *character* is concerned, her Gothic reading was as good a guide as any: 'Catherine, at any rate, heard enough to feel, that in suspecting General Tilney of either murdering or shutting up his wife, she had scarcely sinned against his character, or magnified his cruelty' (II.xv.230).

Read in this way, *Northanger Abbey* appears as much an adaptation, naturalisation and vindication of the Gothic novel as it is a critique.

On *Northanger Abbey* in Part 3: on irony, see D.W. Harding and Clara Tuite [pp. 92–3, 98]; on gender politics, see Claudia Johnson [pp. 130–1, 133]; on nationality and language, see Miranda Burgess and Janet Sorensen [pp. 143–5].

Sense and Sensibility

Sense and Sensibility was first drafted in 1797–8, and revised for publication between 1809 and 1811. It was published by Thomas Egerton on commission: that is, with the author taking the profits after the publisher had taken a fixed sum, but also carrying any loss if the book did not sell. In fact the first edition sold out, and received an immediate, warm and extended review in the *Critical Review* of November 1811, as well as an equally positive if shorter notice in the *British Critic* in May the following year: the *Critical Review* was a liberal journal and the *British Critic* a conservative one, so this represented recognition from both sides of the political spectrum [see pp. 32–3] (for all contemporary critical reviews see Southam 1968a). Egerton brought out a profitable second edition in 1813. *Sense and Sensibility* thus marks Austen's first emergence as a successful published author, although the novel was of course published anonymously.

The story is basically as follows. Mrs Henry Dashwood and her daughters Elinor, Marianne and Margaret are left with little money when Henry Dashwood dies, as his estate passes to his son by a previous marriage, John Dashwood. Elinor falls in love with John's dull brother-in-law Edward Ferrars; Marianne falls in love with dashing stranger John Willoughby. Elinor discovers that Edward is trapped in an engagement with another, but keeps her grief secret; Marianne is noisily heartbroken when she finds Willoughby is to marry a rich heiress. Colonel Brandon, a family friend, reveals to Elinor Willoughby's history of seducing girls. All is resolved when Marianne, having nearly died after her abandonment by Willoughby, accepts Brandon as a husband instead; Edward's fiancée runs off with his brother, and he is at last free to marry Elinor.

In Part 1 we discussed the role of 'feeling', in its constitutive opposition to 'reason', in eighteenth-century thinking about ethics and society; the emergence of an ideal of the home as the site of such feeling; and the relation of these discourses of feeling and domesticity to the discourse of political economy and its account of economic self-interest [see pp. 19–21]. *Northanger Abbey* whisks its heroine away from home to have her feelings and perceptions tested by a wider, public world of strangers. *Sense and Sensibility*, on the other hand, is firmly located in the domestic circle and the extended family of which it forms a part. However, the opening chapters represent familial affection under siege in the Dashwood family. John Dashwood, Elinor and Marianne's half-brother, has inherited their father's estate by entail [see pp. 58–9], leaving his stepmother and her daughters in greatly reduced financial circumstances. Henry, Elinor and Marianne's father, and his wife had been bequeathed Norland Park by his uncle on account of their 'constant attention' to him, 'which proceeded not merely from interest, but from goodness of heart' (I.i.5). But John does not have 'the strong feelings of the rest of the family' (I.i.7):

> He was not an ill-disposed young man, unless to be rather cold-hearted, and rather selfish, is to be ill-disposed; but he was, in general, well-respected; for he conducted himself with propriety in the discharge of his ordinary duties.
>
> (I.i.7)

From the extraordinary duty laid on him by his father, to look after the financial well-being of Mrs Dashwood and the girls, John, encouraged by his wife Fanny, retreats. In the figure of John Dashwood, propriety or politeness functions not as a type of social solidarity, but rather as a way of masking economic self-interest.

In this context one should be wary of identifying 'feeling' with one part of the Dashwood household (Marianne and her mother) rather than the other (Elinor); for in opposition to John's selfishness, what the women have in common is at least as important as their differences. The difference between them centres on the relation of the familial intimacy cherished by all three to wider social bonds. For Marianne, such emotional openness provides the model for relationships in general: there is a continuity between the types of behaviour possible in the family and those appropriate in society at large. For Elinor, on the other hand, there is an absolute gap between the two. In II.iii, objecting to plans to go to London with the rich but vulgar Mrs Jennings, Elinor makes a ruthless distinction between her friend's private emotional capacities for sympathy (here as elsewhere figured as the 'heart') and her ability to function as a patroness in polite society: '[T]hough I think very well of Mrs Jennings' heart, she is not a woman whose society can afford us pleasure, or whose protection will give us consequence' (II.iii.149). It would thus be wrong to see Elinor as denying the importance of spontaneous feeling in intimate relationships; but she denies its governing role in other kinds of relationships, those conducted in public and open to public view. There, Elinor is committed to acting and speaking within the codes of politeness (or 'civility' or 'propriety') even when this involves a suppression of spontaneous emotional response. She explains this 'plan of general civility' (Edward Ferrars's term) to Marianne thus:

> "My doctrine has never aimed at the subjection of the understanding. All I have ever attempted to influence has been the behaviour. . . . I am guilty, I confess, of having often wished you to treat our acquaintance in general with greater attention; but when have I advised you to adopt their sentiments or conform to their judgment in serious matters?"
>
> (I.xvii.92)

Later, stunned that Edward's engagement has become public knowledge, Elinor struggles 'to collect her thoughts', but her thoughts are not what she speaks; she instead makes 'such observations as the subject might naturally be supposed to produce' (III.i.243–4).

Marianne, on the other hand, sees private sentiment and public behaviour as continuous with one another: the latter, like the former, has meaning in relation to its origins in the inner life of the individual, rather than in the effect it will have on those around her. '[I]t was impossible for her to say what she did not feel, however trivial the occasion, and upon Elinor therefore the whole task of telling lies when politeness required it, always fell' (I.xxi.118). When Elinor suggests that her enthusiasm for Willoughby is based on no more than a few shared tastes and opinions, Marianne counters: "I have been too much at my ease, too happy, too frank. I have erred against every common-place notion of decorum; I have been open and sincere where I ought to have been reserved, spiritless, dull, and deceitful . . ." (I.x.49–50).

These are not uniquely Marianne's terms: Elinor is later 'distressed' by the accusation of 'reserve' at II.v.162, and 'openness' and 'sincerity' are virtues ascribed to Brandon (albeit by Mrs Dashwood, at III.ix.314), for example. But Marianne has been 'frank' and 'sincere' and 'open' in the presence of people other than Elinor and her mother and Willoughby and Edward. In these contexts, Marianne's 'sincerity' becomes for Elinor 'indulgence of feeling' (I.xvi.83), a type of selfishness, ignoring as it does the consequences of one's speech for the feelings of others.

If it is indeed easy to miss how much the two girls have in common, it is largely because so much of the novel is narrated from their point of view, and the differences between the sisters are important to *them*. Thus a series of set-piece dialogues early in the novel, involving either the sisters or one of them and their mother (in I.iii, iv, viii, x and xiii), allow them to characterise themselves in opposition to each other, or (in the case of Mrs Dashwood and Marianne) in alignment with each other, but always in relation to each other. This is important for two reasons. First, such self-definition through opposition clearly functions not to divide the family but as its glue. Such conversation within the family allows its members to maintain themselves at a level of discourse otherwise unavailable in the lower strata of society in which they now find themselves on Sir John Middleton's estate in Devon. On one of the few occasions when we see them through the consciousness of an outsider, the difference between the sisters signalled by the novel's title is not observed:

> Because they neither flattered herself nor her children, she could not believe them good-natured; and because they were fond of reading, she fancied them satirical: perhaps without exactly knowing what it was to be satirical; but *that* did not signify. It was censure in common use, and easily given.
>
> (II.xiv.231–2)

Lady Middleton here makes no distinction between the sisters, and while this could be read as a sign of her general obtuseness, she identifies common characteristics binding them that the novel elsewhere confirms as setting them jointly apart from the other women in the neighbourhood: a commitment to moral judgement (they are 'satirical'), and a corresponding resistance to the gradation of civility according to the wealth or rank of one's interlocutor (they do not flatter her merely because she is the local lady of the manor). Significantly, Lady Middleton links this satirical role to their reading: the problem of 'taste' in books that separates the sisters (see below) vanishes here in their sheer *literacy* compared to those around them. Lady Middleton, for her part, cannot even understand the basic literary-generic term that she deploys here ('satirical'): the stunted version of polite culture that has reached Barton Park in the form of 'elegance' has given her such terms to use in conversation as mere signifiers of politeness itself, as terms 'in common use' among her class, and stripped of any more specific content. And if the sisters are satirical, one might note, then this is something they share with the narrator, satirical here at Lady Middleton's expense.

The second reason why it is important to recognise the degree to which the sisters and their mother *share* a set of values is that the very intimacy facilitated by these conversations, by this friendly construction of identities in terms of their difference from each other *within* a set of common terms and assumptions, is to some extent a model of proper human relations against which the other relationships of the novel can be judged. This intimacy is thus set up in the early chapters, to be disrupted by various types of secrecy demanded of the sisters, but finally restored: the last lines of the novel primarily celebrate not their new-found conjugal happiness but their restored sisterly closeness, their 'strong family affection' (III.xiv.353).

The secrets that disrupt this confidence are brought into their lives by their involvement with men. Elinor and Marianne have secrets from each other because Edward Ferrars and Willoughby have secrets from everybody. The dark hinterland of Willoughby's life prevents him from explicitly declaring his love for Marianne, let alone asking her to marry him, and conscious that she has been behaving in ways only permissible given their engagement, Marianne hides this omission from both her sister and her mother. Only when Willoughby reveals his engagement to Miss Grey in II.vii does Marianne confess the full truth to Elinor. Elinor at that point is, however, unable to reciprocate, having been coerced at the end of volume I into a contradictory secrecy with Lucy Steele, and feels herself bound to keep Lucy's engagement to Edward Ferrars secret, even from Marianne. Only when Edward's engagement becomes public knowledge at the start of volume III is 'confidence between them . . . restored to its proper state' (III.ii.253).

The difference that *does* exist between the two sisters is one in which the novel is itself implicated, however. Events are narrated from a perspective which tends to coincide with Elinor's, not Marianne's. The narrator tells us things when Elinor finds them out, not when Marianne finds them out, and often uses the vocabulary that Elinor uses: the novel thus frequently represents Elinor's subjective response to what is happening rather than any omniscient account that the reader can take as authoritative. This use of characters' language to represent their subjectivity, even though they are not actually speaking those words, is called free indirect discourse, and is increasingly characteristic of Austen's prose as her career as a novelist progresses. It allows for the achievement of some complex effects:

> Had Edward been intentionally deceiving her? Had he feigned a regard for her which he did not feel? Was his engagement to Lucy, an engage-ment of the heart? No; whatever it might once have been, she could not believe it such at present. His affection was all her own. She could not be deceived in that. Her mother, sisters, Fanny, all had been conscious of his regard for her at Norland; it was not an illusion of her own vanity. He certainly loved her. What a softener of the heart was this persuasion! How much could it not tempt her to forgive!
>
> (II.i.133–4)

A passage like this modulates between *reporting* Elinor's thoughts, marking them with an explicit attribution to Elinor ('she could not believe . . .'), and representing them without any *formal* marker (in grammar or punctuation) of such attribution. On the basis of grammar or punctuation, the statement 'His affection was all her own' could be the narrator's authoritative judgement: the reader must decide from the context *and content* of the sentence that it repre-sents Elinor's judgement and not the narrator's. This statement constitutes free indirect discourse. The last two sentences, however, fall somewhere between this and reported thought. The exclamation marks suggest, on a first reading, that this is the narrator's ironic commentary on Elinor's thinking, making her faith in Edward's love appear an exercise in self-delusion. However, the story in fact bears out Elinor's interpretation of Edward's situation, as he will be able to confirm in III.xiii. With this knowledge, one can read these sentences instead as Elinor's own habitual and rigorous examination of her own thought processes. Aware that the very comfort it offers her may be the ground for her belief in Edward's love, Elinor's self-scrutiny generates a sceptical counter-voice to her initial judgement. Her characteristic reaching for the judgement of others to reassure her that her own thought is not the mere product of self-serving 'vanity' does not dispel this scepticism: both possible interpretations remain, contained within a far from unified consciousness.

Free indirect discourse allows this novel to represent a consciousness that, while deploying the same terms as appear in public discourse, remains in itself private. Such a technique is of course especially useful for representing Elinor's thought, restricted in its outward expression both by her promise of secrecy to Lucy and by her commitment to propriety in public. By taking this form, by filling pages with this private subjectivity, the novel valorises the private consciousness as a source of meaning (*this* is what we need to know to understand a character; *this* is what the individual really consists in) over public speech and public behaviour. By splitting the narration between free indirect discourse and direct speech, between private subjectivity and public behaviour, the form of the novel itself seems to accept and embody Elinor's fundamental distinction between the private and the public self. To put this another way: this novel sets itself the task of constructing in language a private subjectivity, separate from, but both recognising the claims of and a source of criticism of, the public world, and the name of that private subjectivity is Elinor Dashwood.

However, it is this private subject's self-scrutiny, its consciousness of its own consciousness, that raises the possibility of *controlling* that consciousness, of disciplining the mind to admit only certain thoughts and feelings. This capacity appears in the novel as Elinor's 'self command'. Further, such self-scrutiny also issues in or produces a scrutiny of others: not of that public who require no more than 'general civility', but of those intimates whose moral status has consequences for the happiness of other family and friends. Hence, at the end of the novel, what was originally Elinor's *self*-command is turned instead towards her sister and mother. The restoration of confidence between the sisters is a condition of Marianne's reformation (if that is what it is) in the last volume, but it is a confidence established on subtly different terms. Rather than defining herself in opposition to Elinor, Marianne must now think of her as an example to follow.

> "Do you compare your conduct to his?"
> "No. I compare it with what it ought to have been; I compare it with yours."
>
> (III.x.322)

But precisely because Marianne is now trying to be *like* Elinor, the old reciprocity of their discourse, in which each defined herself by her *difference* from the other, has gone. In its place is a discursive situation in which Elinor is in control. 'Elinor, impatient to soothe, though too honest to flatter, gave her instantly that praise and support which her frankness and her contrition so well deserved' (III.x.323).

Elinor's 'praise and support' seem here to be conditional on Marianne's frankness and contrition: they depend on Marianne returning Elinor's own vocabulary back to her unmodified and uninflected. When Marianne says that from now on, 'my feelings shall be governed' (III.x.323), this self-government appears to be constituted by internalising Elinor's terms and attitudes: it is ultimately Elinor who is the governor here. At the start of the next chapter, Elinor is given several long paragraphs (in a conversation that includes their mother) in which to tell Marianne what her experience means, and how a marriage to Willoughby would have worked out: in effect writing Marianne's story for her (III.xi.326–8). Elinor also regulates the direction, duration and depth of the self-abasement of the other two:

". . . I have nothing to regret—nothing but my own folly."

"Rather say your mother's imprudence, my child," said Mrs Dash-wood; "*she* must be answerable."

Marianne would not let her proceed;—and Elinor, satisfied that each felt their own error, wished to avoid any survey of the past that might weaken her sister's spirits; she therefore, pursuing the first subject, immediately continued,

"*One* observation may, I think, be fairly drawn from the whole of the story—that all Willoughby's difficulties have arisen from the first offence against virtue, in his behaviour to Eliza Williams. . . ."

(III.xi.327–8)

Notice the authority that Elinor's perspective now has here. There is no longer any question of her consciousness demanding its own self-scrutiny: rather it is in a position to survey the consciousness of her mother and sister, direct them in particular paths, and draw moral generalisations from their experience (for 'narrative authority' in Austen, see Wallace 1995).

It is then tempting to understand the moral authority enjoyed by Elinor at the end of the novel as continuous with that of her author, and to take the judgements that she passes on others as the 'message' of the novel. There are at least two possible arguments for resisting this temptation. One is based on the sheer discursive and generic self-consciousness that this novel shares with *Northanger Abbey*. Just as that novel is in dialogue with various genres of female-authored novel, so *Sense and Sensibility* engages with the novel of sensibility [see pp. 21–2]. One of the most marked features of the novel of sensibility is the prominent role within it of a particular set of texts or other works of art which produce a powerful emotional response in a particular group of characters and mark them as more sensitive to beauty than those around them. So, in *Sense and Sensibility*, the principal way in which Marianne and Willoughby recognise each other as the same kind of person, sharing a high evaluation of spontaneous emotional response and a disregard for social convention, is through their shared aesthetic judgement of music, art, landscape and books. Edward earns Marianne's disapproval for his ignorance of the doctrine of the picturesque (I.xviii.94–6); on the other hand, the poetry of Thomson, Cowper and Scott (I.xvii.91) functions as a sign of the common sensibility she shares with Willoughby. That they are thus marked as members of an elite group, whose 'greatness of soul' sets them apart from the materialistic majority of mankind around them, is alluded to by Edward when he jokes that, if she were to become rich, she would buy up every copy of her favourite authors 'to prevent their falling into unworthy hands' (I.xvii.91).

Elinor's voice and perspective are equally implicated in a genre of writing, however. We do not know if Elinor reads domestic novels or feminine conduct books, but in these final chapters she speaks in the voice of the author of such texts, expressing the sorts of judgements and claiming for herself the sort of authority that the domestic ideology had made available to women writers. The well-regulated inner space of Elinor's mind, demonstrated as such by her handling of Lucy Steele's secret, legitimates her passing judgement on others in something like the way in which its origin in a virtuous domestic sphere legitimates the dangerous venture into publicity undertaken by the woman author [see pp. 13–16]. And it is striking that subjectivity in this novel is a largely feminine space. We have access to the consciousness of Marianne, sometimes Mrs Dashwood and occasionally Mrs Jennings and Lady Middleton. But men, those bearers of secrets and previous attachments in this novel, reveal themselves only very rarely in anything other than direct speech. But if we identify Elinor's moral authority with the authority of the feminine domestic author, we should not then simply identify this generic construct with Austen herself and see Elinor as her mouthpiece. Rather, the voice of the domestic author, as embodied in Elinor, remains only one among many in the novel, and could be understood as put into play with and against those other voices as part of this novel's exploration of the generic resources available to the woman writer between 1797 and 1811.

The second reason for being sceptical of the moral authority of Elinor's subjectivity concerns the way in which its concern with propriety can be seen to be driven by precisely the sort of economic concerns from which the privacy of the mind (or the 'heart') is supposed to be a refuge. That is, it might be mistaken to see the contents of Elinor's consciousness, as represented in free indirect discourse, as simply the truth about Elinor. For if Elinor justifies the subordination of feeling to propriety in moral terms, in terms, that is, of equal respect for the feelings of others, one can nevertheless see a family economic self-interest at work behind this ethics. For such subordination is also subordination to the necessary wider social solidarities of her class. Confirmation of the family's membership of the propertied classes by means of conformity to these codes could be seen as especially important for the Dashwoods given just how little property they are left with at the start of the novel. Lord and Lady Middleton can take risks with such codes, the former with his adherence to an older gentry lifestyle where a man's ability to drink, ride and shoot is more important than his ability to converse; the latter in her arrogant unwillingness to enter into conversation. They can afford to take such risks because their status is spread around them in the form of their estate, and is not dependent on what happens in their drawing room. Removed from that estate to the anonymity of London, Lady Middleton ceases to be quite so complacent about Sir John's vulgar conviviality (II.v.162). In the case of the disinherited Dashwoods, propriety has to take the place of property on a permanent basis as a signifier of their status. In this context, Elinor's concern with propriety starts to look like a strategy for maintaining a toe-hold in the landed classes so that they can regain their propertied status through the right kind of marriage. If Elinor is indeed the novel's representative of 'sense', we should note that this word is frequently attached precisely to financial self-interest. Elinor, watching the Steele sisters at work, 'soon allowed them credit for some kind of sense, when she saw with what constant and judicious attentions they were making themselves agreeable to Lady Middleton' (I.xxi.116). And John Dashwood is astonished that 'a man of Colonel Brandon's sense' (III.v.277) should give away the living on his estate to Edward as a favour when he could have sold it for a tidy sum.

To see Elinor's adherence to the codes of politeness not as a moral end in itself but as instrumental in the achievement of a basically economic goal is to make her stance oddly continuous with that of her much-detested half-brother John. 'Propriety' indeed allows the propertied classes to imagine themselves as defined by a set of manners and values rather than by a brute economic fact, their ownership of the means of production and exchange; allows them, that is, to imagine their power to be legitimated by something other than the economic circumstances that have in fact produced it. One can then take the novel's fundamental opposition to be, not the struggle between the claims of publicity and privacy that I have been discussing, but between a world of conversation and discussion in which this debate takes place on the one hand, and, on the other, the world of economic relations from which it claims to escape.

On *Sense and Sensibility* in Part 3: on Elinor as an example of modern self-disciplining subjectivity, see Lauren Goodlad [**p. 104**]; on Marianne and sexuality, see Eve Sedgwick [**pp. 111–12**]; on the novel's relation to anti-Jacobin rhetoric, see Marilyn Butler and Peter Knox-Shaw [**pp. 118–20**]; on the gender politics of the novel, see Claudia Johnson [**p. 131**]; and on Brandon as imperial story-teller, see Maaja Stewart [**pp. 141–2**].

Pride and Prejudice

Austen completed a first version of *Pride and Prejudice*, entitled 'First Impressions', in 1796–7. Her father offered this manuscript to the publishing firm of Cadell and Davies but they declined even to look it over. Austen revised this text under its new title in 1811–12, and sold the manuscript to Thomas Egerton for £110. Jan Fergus argues that the novel remains substantially that which was written in the 1790s (Fergus 1991: 81–2), and this is also the period in which it is set. The militia regiment billeted on Meryton for the winter leaves for the huge camp at Brighton at the end of May (anticipated at the start of II.xvi): the Brighton camp was not operational until August 1793, and barracks were in place for all regiments from 1796, placing the action of *Pride and Prejudice* in 1793–4 or 1794–5. The *British Critic* (February 1813) and *Critical Review* (March 1813) repeated the warm praise that they had bestowed on *Sense and Sensibility*.

The story is basically as follows. The Bennets have five daughters, all of whom will have very little money when Mr Bennet dies, as his small estate will pass to his nearest male relative, a Mr Collins. Jane falls in love with a wealthy young man who has rented a nearby manor; his aristocratic friend Darcy, who has already snubbed Jane's sister Elizabeth at a ball, gets Bingley away to London to prevent the relationship developing, as he has been put off the Bennets by the vulgarity of the mother and the younger girls. But Darcy finds he has fallen in love with Elizabeth despite himself. When he proposes to her in the most arrogant terms, she rejects him. But Elizabeth has also been prejudiced against Darcy by George Wickham, who visits their town with the militia, and who has charmed her. The rejected Darcy is able to put Elizabeth right on Wickham's true (bad) character, which is confirmed when he elopes with the youngest Bennet girl, the feckless Lydia. His feelings for Elizabeth unchanged, Darcy finds the runaway couple, gets them married and finds Wickham an income. Discovering that Elizabeth has come to love him, he proposes and is accepted; Bingley at last is enjoying similar happiness with Jane.

The presence of a militia regiment in the small country town that is the setting for this novel does more than date the action. The militia were mobilised in the 1790s in direct response to the threat of invasion by revolutionary France: *Pride and Prejudice* thus evokes a very specific historical context. Among the six completed novels, only *Persuasion* also does this, with its story set explicitly in 1814 and built around the return of naval officers ashore after Napoleon's first defeat that year [see **pp. 36–7**]. The historical setting of *Pride and Prejudice* might not seem to make much difference to *its* story. Yet the romantic-comic plot itself, culminating in a marriage (between Elizabeth Bennet and Fitzwilliam Darcy) that bridges a much wider social gap than those of *Northanger Abbey* and *Sense and Sensibility*, can be read as answering ideological needs in British society produced by the revolutionary threat embodied in Jacobin France.

In Part 1 we saw how codes of politeness and propriety made possible a certain type of social solidarity among the propertied classes in eighteenth-century Britain, and discussed the rise of an ideal of affective marriage which also allowed for alliances between the moneyed and the landed. *Pride and Prejudice* is particularly and energetically concerned with the grounds of this sort of social settlement. The ability of polite society to accommodate the very different types of wealth enjoyed by the novel's characters is shown to be threatened from a number of directions. On the one hand, the Bennet family itself is divided between those members who have mastered these codes of propriety (Jane and Elizabeth) and those who have not (all the others). On the other, Darcy (to begin with) and the Bingley sisters make the mistake of associating propriety with gentry status, of *explaining* Mrs Bennet's vulgarity by reference to her middle-class origins (one of her brothers is a country attorney and another is a merchant). Hence the importance to the novel of this latter brother, Mr Gardiner, and his wife; not only because they take Elizabeth to Darcy's house, Pemberley, in volume III (as the novel ends by reminding us), but more importantly as living refutations of Darcy's snobbery. Propriety can indeed be observed by the urban middle class. Darcy has himself broken the rules, as he later realises, by being so unready to give social pleasure to others as the code of politeness demands.

The novel opens with the arrival in Meryton of Charles Bingley and his sisters, whose money comes from trade, not land: the late Mr Bingley was a merchant, but his children now live off the interest accruing on the capital that he amassed. Darcy, who accompanies them, is a different type altogether. Although he is not a lord, his mother was the daughter of a lord, and his income of £10,000 a year places him among the wealthiest commoners in the kingdom. Much about the Bingleys becomes clear when this difference is kept in mind. The Bingleys are a family putting distance between themselves and the origins of their wealth by acquiring the 'manners' of, and seeking marriages with, the landed elite. Austen's narrator notes that the Bingley sisters

> had a fortune of twenty thousand pounds, were in the habit of spending more than they ought, and of associating with people of rank; and were therefore in every respect entitled to think well of themselves, and meanly of others. They were of a respectable family in the north of England; a circumstance more deeply impressed on their memories than that their brother's fortune and their own had been acquired by trade.
>
> (I.iv.17)

Conspicuous consumption, one might note, is a large part of the elite life-style that the Bingley sisters have acquired. One should also note the tension implied here between the 'respectability' of the Bingley family and the origins of its wealth. The sisters' thinking 'meanly of others', visible in their consistent snobbery towards the Bennets, Philipses and Gardiners, is a condition of their thinking well of themselves, not because they themselves are of a much higher rank, but because they are not. The Gardiners are different from the Bingleys only in the much smaller scale of their wealth, and because they have, quite literally, put no distance between themselves and their business: Mr Gardiner lives 'by trade, and within view of his own warehouses' (II.ii.137). Keeping her social distance from the middling sort is a condition of Miss Bingley's ultimate acceptance into the landed elite by marriage to Darcy, or a man like him.

It is in Charles Bingley's relation to Darcy, however, that the family's particular situation has its most direct influence on the plot of this novel. For Darcy is in effect Bingley's mentor or patron: Bingley's 'natural modesty' (II.xii.193), his 'diffidence' (III.xvi.351: these are Darcy's words), his readiness to accept Darcy's judgement on all matters without displaying the deference that would openly admit his inferiority are not simply character traits but the result of his transitional social status. Darcy acts as Bingley's guide to the fine discrimination of social differences that mark a member of the elite: the difference, for example, between real and assumed humility (I.x.47); or between a fine girl to dance with at a country ball and the fine lady whom one needs to marry in order to consolidate one's new social position. This latter distinction is the one on which Darcy acts when he separates Bingley from Jane Bennet, who falls decisively into the former category.

The question of inherited rank and its capacity to absorb new wealth without threatening the established political order is particularly insistent because of the threat presented to that order by the French Revolution. Inheritance is indeed a central term in Burke's *Reflections on the Revolution in France* (1790) [see p. 32]. A constitution passed on from generation to generation, subtly altered but never abandoned, will always, Burke argues, command the loyalty of its subjects as one drawn up from scratch on the basis of abstract principles (like that of the new French Republic) never will. To express the relation between each generation and the state Burke had recourse to an image that has direct relevance to *Pride and Prejudice*. The constitution, he explains, is like an entailed estate: that is, it is inherited by each generation from the last, but hedged around with restrictions on what the new generation can do with it. The landowner of an entailed estate cannot sell off his land, or cut down all its trees for easy profit, and so on. Rather, such an estate is already in a sense the property of the *next* generation, in that it is *their* interests that govern what he does with it: the landowner is in this way himself the tenant (albeit for life) of his own descendants. Such is the continuity of the British state, says Burke: no one generation has the right to wreck an inheritance such a long time in the making.

As a romantic comedy, *Pride and Prejudice* is concerned directly with continu-ity, with the reproduction of a society and its values by a younger generation, despite the barriers placed in their way by established conventions and alliances. Jane marries Bingley, Elizabeth marries Darcy, despite the gap between their families in terms of wealth and status. In this way, like most romantic comedies, it legitimates the established order by showing it to be capable of absorbing the new. Within this generic structure, however, Austen figures the *threat* to social continuity in exactly the legal metaphor in which Burke figures its guarantee: in the entailment of an estate. *Pride and Prejudice* makes the actual entailment of a particular estate the mainspring of its plot: it is because his family will *not* inherit Mr Bennet's estate on his death that finding husbands wealthy enough to maintain his daughters financially is such an urgent imperative.

Entailment is such a useful metaphor for Burke because, while it takes absolute control of an estate out of the hands of its present possessor, it does not impose an unchanging set of arrangements down through the centuries from an immemorial past. In England in the eighteenth century, the standard way of transferring land was through a form of entailment called a 'strict settlement'. In a strict settlement, the young Mr Bennet would have agreed with the previous holder of the estate that on the latter's death he would become only a life-tenant, with limited powers to alter or dispose of that estate. Mr Bennet is likely to have agreed to this arrangement, when he came of age at 21 or at his marriage, in exchange for some form of income from the estate until the death of his uncle put him in possession. Such a settlement also defines who will inherit after Mr Bennet: Mr Bennet's eldest son, and in the absence of a son then the nearest *male* relative, Mr Collins, rather than Mr Bennet's daughters. This is what is meant by 'entailed in default of heirs male' (I.vii.29). However, women were not *automatically* excluded from inheriting property, as the presence of two very grand heiresses in this novel, Lady Catherine de Bourgh herself and her daughter, should remind us.

In contrast to Mr Bennet stands the man who will take his place in Elizabeth's life, Fitzwilliam Darcy, the master of Pemberley. Corresponding to his exalted origins, Darcy represents all the concern for family continuity, all the virtues of responsible and self-abnegating stewardship, which for Burke are central to English national life. At first, of course, the personal and family pride which accompanies this sense of heritage is subject to some satire in the words of the narrator and Elizabeth herself. This pride needs to be reformed, indeed, by Elizabeth's salutary rejection of his proposal of marriage; but the social discomfort that it produces is shown by the novel to be of less consequence than the great good that Darcy's power allows him to do. Elizabeth, in the end, is awed by Pemberley, and her story ends with her delighted submission to Darcy in marriage. It is *gratitude* that forms the foundation of Elizabeth Bennet's *love* for Fitzwilliam Darcy: caught in a reciprocal gaze with Darcy's portrait at Pemberley, impressed with the evidence of his social power that surrounds her, Elizabeth 'thought of his regard with a deeper sentiment of gratitude than it had ever raised before' (III.i.240). Elizabeth's desire for Darcy does not happen *despite* the difference in their social situation: it is *produced* by that difference, and can be read as a vindication of the hierarchy which constructs that difference in the first place. This novel thus ends, it seems, by affirming the claims of a hierarchical social order to our loyalty and respect.

One can understand *Pride and Prejudice* as deploying an already established narrative pattern which attempts to reconcile the moral autonomy of its heroine, equated with the new social power of the middle classes, with the established social power of the gentry and aristocracy. It achieves this through the fantasy, familiar above all from Samuel Richardson's *Pamela; or, Virtue Rewarded* [see pp. 11–12], that the *resistance* of a lower-class woman to aristocratic power might in fact be profoundly attractive to handsome aristocratic males. Such narratives are engaged in the propagation of norms of behaviour on which master and servant might meet, by imagining such norms as produced by a woman's moral reformation of a man. This narrative of reformation is clearly developing the version of inter-gender relations, in which the characteristic faults of each gender will be cancelled out by the virtues of the other, proposed by Joseph Addison and Richard Steele as part of their propagation of polite culture as a set of moral and social values [see pp. 8–10]. It is precisely a union of this type that Austen imagines for Elizabeth and Darcy: 'by her ease and liveliness, his mind might have been softened, his manners improved, and from his judgment, information, and knowledge of the world, she must have received benefit of greater importance' (III.viii.295). But we must remember that, in *Pride and Prejudice* as in *Pamela* or the *Spectator*, the compromise being worked out in terms of the sexes is an expression of that being sought between the social ranks. Elizabeth's rejection of Darcy forces him to reform his manners to something more congenial to those of a lower rank in general, as well as making him deserving of Elizabeth's love in particular.

However, *Pride and Prejudice* is not only about the forging of solidarity between different ranks of the propertied on the established eighteenth-century model: it also imagines a new alliance between parochial and metropolitan ruling elites. The gap in lifestyles between the inhabitants of Meryton and the Bingley group is not only produced by the disparity in income between them: it is also produced by their differing relationships to the capital. London, for Darcy and his friends, is home for perhaps half the year, and their initial claim to be arbiters of manners results from their familiarity with *London* manners, referred to as 'fashionable' or 'elegant'. For Meryton people, London is a distant and glamorous place, for all its geographical proximity to Hertfordshire. The one local who has briefly entered the court is Sir William Lucas, and he has never really recovered from the experience. We should not lose sight of the fact that the local landed and professional classes, the Bennets, Lucases and Philipses, were the people responsible for the day-to-day political and judicial administration of England, in their role as councillors and Justices of the Peace and so on. When they refer to 'the country', they invariably mean the *county*, the local area, and not England or Great Britain. Sir William was mayor of his town: yet his awe of Darcy marks the deference of the provincial top-cat to his national superior. The Bennets send to a local apothecary when they are ill; the Bingleys call out a London surgeon. The young ladies of Meryton are always in danger of losing their fashionable lovers to the metropolis. Darcy's eventual concession of his role as arbiter of propriety to Elizabeth marks the establishment of a standard which transcends this gap and is thus *national* in a sense that neither local nor metropolitan standards alone could claim to be.

It is thus that the eighteenth-century compromise between the ranks of old and new wealth produces a culture that can claim to stand for England as a whole. The common culture forged among the polite turns into what would soon come to be thought of as a 'national culture', with 'culture' understood in a new sense: not as that which could be acquired to set one *apart* from one's forebears (in the sense that Bingley and his sisters have become 'cultured', as their father was not), but as that set of practices, social and aesthetic, specific to a nation, and passed on from one generation to the next irrespective of the individual's aspirations. Culture in the latter sense becomes important in this period as that which guaranteed a continuity of national identity in a period when industrialisation, as well as the threat from France, was transforming the country beyond recognition. And as a *national* inheritance, culture is necessarily in the possession of all, and not only the landed elite.

In most European countries, concepts of 'national culture' are developed by middle-class, urban writers using the customs, songs and folklore of the peasantry, or native smallholders and subsistence farmers, as the core of what that culture *is*, as opposed to an aristocratic culture which is essentially transnational and usually takes its models from (pre-revolutionary) France. In England, this does not happen. In *Pride and Prejudice*, we see an equivalent national identity emerging, but from the other end of the social spectrum. In England, the 'middling sort' plunder the culture of their social *superiors* for signifiers of a national, cultural identity. In opposition to the French Republic's persecution and execution of its aristocracy in the Terror [see p. 29], the English propertied classes define their nationhood by appropriating their own elite as custodians of national culture. Volume I chapter viii includes a telling exchange between Darcy, Bingley and the latter's sister on exactly how Bingley should attempt to emulate his friend. The conversation will turn to whether Bingley could build a house to match Pemberley; but the cultural inheritance for which Darcy is responsible, and to which Bingley cannot aspire, is not the house itself but what it contains:

> "I am astonished," said Miss Bingley, "that my father should have left so small a collection of books.—What a delightful library you have at Pemberley, Mr Darcy!"
>
> "It ought to be good," he replied, "it has been the work of many generations."
>
> "And then you have added so much to it yourself, you are always buying books."
>
> "I cannot comprehend the neglect of a family library in such days as these."
>
> (I.viii.38)

Bingley will never be able to build a family library like Darcy's as he might build another Pemberley, and this is one of the first suggestions that there might be more to Darcy than the pride on display at the Meryton assembly. But what does he (and Austen) have in mind by 'such days as these'? Here he refers to the specific historical situation of the novel's action, without saying exactly what makes it special; but part of what makes it special must be the books that it produces, books which can take their place on the shelves next to the purchases of his father and grandfather. Darcy's comment brings the story's historical moment into the novel as a cultural situation, as the presence of a militia regiment in Meryton brings that moment as a military and political situation. In neither case are the specifics of that situation mentioned in the text (what war, exactly, is being fought; what books, exactly, are being published). But where the soldiers represent a disruptive force arriving from elsewhere and leaving again in accordance with orders from a national government, the books can take their place in a library as part of a historical continuity of cultural production and consumption. The appearance of the militiamen represents national historical events as the rupturing of traditional, local patterns of life; Darcy's library promises that, under the custodianship of men such as himself, even this moment of rupture can be assimilated, by means of culture, in the ongoing history of a continuous English nation.

I say that *men* like Darcy are now the custodians of national culture; but unlike their political power, this cultural role is one in which *women* can also participate. Hence Darcy's addition, in this same conversation, to the list of the normal conduct book accomplishments required of a woman, of 'something more substantial . . . the improvement of her mind by extensive reading' (I.viii.39). This is not only a demand that women need information to fulfil their civilising role in polite conversation; in the context of Darcy's previous comments, it also demands that any future partner in marriage will be capable of sharing his function as carrier of a national culture, the latter understood as essentially separate from the political life that will remain a male preserve. Books are thus to be understood as 'aesthetic' objects which transcend the political-historical circumstances of their production, and women's cultural authority will be based on its strict demarcation from political power. And this prospect, held out for Elizabeth Bennet by Darcy's comment, is realised in the person of her creator. Jane Austen's prestige as a novelist, as measured in the praise of periodical reviews or in her appreciation by the Prince of Wales, is conditional on the exclusion of overt reference to politics; but as we have seen, the separation of cultural activities from politics has been made for profoundly political reasons.

On *Pride and Prejudice* in Part 3: on the psychological development of Elizabeth and Darcy, see Franco Moretti, Clifford Siskin and Susan Fraiman [**pp. 102–3, 104–5**]; on Elizabeth's individualism and its political meanings, see Marilyn Butler, Mary Poovey and Judith Newton [**pp. 118–19, 126**]; on the novel's gender politics, see Claudia Johnson [**pp. 132, 133–4**]; and on nationality, see Franco Moretti again [**pp. 145–6**].

Mansfield Park

Mansfield Park was written in 1811–13, and published by Egerton in May 1814. It was not reviewed in any of the periodicals, and yet the first edition had sold out by November, presumably on the strength of being 'By the Author of *Sense and Sensibility* and *Pride and Prejudice*' alone (as the title page proclaimed her). On the other hand, Austen lost money on the second edition, published by John Murray in 1816, an illustration of the hazards of publishing on commission [see **pp. 13–15**].

The story is basically as follows. Fanny Price is the daughter of a marine and his wife who married for love from a better background; she is adopted by Sir Thomas Bertram, a landowner who married Mrs Price's more fortunate sister. Among Sir Thomas's children at Mansfield Park, the quiet and sickly Fanny grows close to Edmund, the younger son; but Edmund is attracted to the vivacious and worldly Mary Crawford. On various occasions, including an attempt to put on a play in Sir Thomas's house during his absence in the West Indies, Mary Crawford and her brother Henry reveal themselves as bad influences: Henry, for example, is flirting with Maria Bertram, who is engaged to another man. After Maria marries, Henry proposes to Fanny; to the astonishment of both Sir Thomas and Edmund, she rejects him. She is proved right to do so when Henry later runs off with Maria. Both Edmund and Sir Thomas realise the superior moral vision of the long-neglected Fanny, and Edmund, now a vicar, marries her.

Patronage, already featured in the relationship between Darcy and Bingley in *Pride and Prejudice*, is the main mechanism governing the action of *Mansfield Park*. It ends with its heroine, Fanny Price, married to the vicar and established in a parsonage which has been throughout the novel the occasional residence of her enemies, the Crawfords, but which 'soon grew as dear to her heart, and as thoroughly perfect in her eyes, as everything else, within the view and patronage of Mansfield Park, had long been' (III.xvii.439). Usually one thinks of patronage as exerted for the advancement of young men in their careers, whether in politics, the army or navy, the law or the church [see pp. 5–6]. The influence exerted, first by Sir Thomas Bertram, and then by Henry Crawford, in the promotion of Fanny's brother William in the navy takes exactly this form: the informal use of personal contacts and the calling in of favours, of what is often referred to as 'interest'. But one can understand patronage in wider terms, as the use of power by the landed classes to establish personal bonds with those a step or two below them in status. Patronage is not simply benevolent: it establishes a debt of gratitude on the part of the recipient through which further power can then be exercised by the giver (Henry thinks of it as 'the means of conferring a kindness where he wished to oblige': II.vi.219). But by *appearing* as benevolence, patronage legitimates the power that makes it possible. Patronage, whatever other form it takes, is never impersonal; it is the means whereby networks of family and friendship are established and confirmed. But it also has a wider political function of displaying aristocratic and gentry power as enmeshed in a set of reciprocal obligations and duties that correspond to personal, emotional ties (as landowners' obligations and duties to central government, for example, are not, once government is no longer directly in the hands of the monarch). As the eighteenth century tends to understand human nature as essentially a set of emotional or sentimental responses, this emotional element has the effect of naturalising the power that goes with land; that is, of making it appear to correspond to a timeless natural order, rather than a contingent social one.

Originally, perhaps, patronage as described here was continuous with the feudal landowner's duty of protection towards his tenants. Even here, Henry attempts to build on the moral credit that his patronage of William has won him with Fanny by describing his concern over the actions of his self-serving steward: 'The mischief such a man does on an estate, both as to the credit of his employer, and the welfare of the poor, is incredible' (III.xi.382). But by Austen's time, the modernisation of agriculture (its reorganisation on capitalist lines) had abolished such duties: tenants are far fewer on much larger farms, and agricultural labour consists increasingly of a rural working class who can expect nothing from their employer beyond a daily wage when and if their labour is required [see pp. 20–1]. In such a context, the obligations of the landowner towards that much smaller group of 'connections' with whom he might be prepared to share his dinner-table become all the more important as a legitimation of his status. He can imagine the personal, sentimental bonds established by patronage networks as a survival from feudal or pre-capitalist modes of social organisation; they can then function as a way of disguising the impersonal (capitalist) system of exploitation on which the landowner's wealth is now in fact based. To put this another way, patronage allows the landowning classes to portray their power as in the service of something other than mere self-interest, as the expression in fact of a set of ethical values, as distinct from the self-interest governing economic relations more generally. It allows them, that is, to imagine their *social* authority as a type of *moral* authority (compare this to the role of politeness in the identity of the propertied classes more generally, as discussed in the case of *Sense and Sensibility* [see pp. 55–6].

Sir Thomas Bertram's adoption of his niece Fanny Price can be seen as an example of patronage in action, defined in these broad terms. His wife has married into a higher rank than the minor gentry into which she was born; her sister has married below this rank, and her household, as represented in chapters III.vi–xv, is the only detailed representation in Austen's novels of a family outside the codes and standards of the 'polite'. But Fanny's move from Portsmouth to Mansfield Park does not abolish the vast social distance between them; rather, it reinforces it. The former possibility is indeed present as a danger from the moment the adoption is proposed, and Sir Thomas is insistent on the need

> to preserve in the minds of my *daughters* the consciousness of what they are ... [I] would, on no account, authorize in my girls the smallest degree of arrogance towards their relation; but still they cannot be equals. Their rank, fortune, rights, and expectations, will always be different.
>
> (I.i.12; italics in original)

Fanny's other aunt, Mrs Norris, receives a lot of the blame for the miseducation of Sir Thomas's daughters in the last chapter of the novel, and elsewhere for treating Fanny poorly (in not arranging a fire in her work-room, for example: III.i.288), but her words are often no more than an echo of Sir Thomas's own, made shrill in the voice of a member of the rural middle class (she married a clergyman) anxious to preserve a hierarchy which offers her a place in elite society, however lowly: 'people are never respected when they step out of their proper sphere' she warns Fanny at II.v.204. Fanny's presence in Sir Thomas's home allows the Bertrams to confirm their high rank by repeatedly differentiating it from hers. The sentimental tie between the families, expressed through Fanny's adoption, is the means whereby their difference, rather than their commonality, is confirmed.

Accordingly, Fanny is required in return to feel the appropriate 'gratitude' towards the Bertrams, as the price she pays for being thus favoured. Feel it she certainly does: the most hurtful charge against her when she refuses to take part in the play is that of ingratitude towards her cousins (I.xvi.139) and her rejection of

Henry Crawford's offer of marriage is complicated by the necessity of gratitude both to Sir Thomas (III.i.294–5, 297) and for Henry's own patronage of William (III.ii.303). And accordingly, Fanny internalises her differential status by understanding herself partly in terms of her lack of 'consequence' or 'importance' to others. These are terms which sometimes name that which Fanny does *not* have in relation to the Bertrams or indeed her own family, but sometimes name the social authority which landed families like the Bertrams *have* in their county or the nation at large. In the former case, in Fanny's voice, it carries the association of something like 'moral or social usefulness'; in the latter case it tends to mean primarily displayed power or wealth. Returned temporarily to Portsmouth by Sir Thomas to enforce a sense of her precarious advantages at Mansfield Park, Fanny wants to be 'of consequence' to her younger sister Susan by teaching her polite manners and domestic economy; it is precisely the indolence of her mother, on the other hand, that would have made her 'just as good a woman of consequence as Lady Bertram' (III.viii.362). The ironic use of 'good' in the latter statement reveals the extent to which these two categories (social power and moral usefulness) *ought* to be co-present in the person of Lady Bertram but are not.

Of course, Lady Bertram is not the only character in *Mansfield Park* to fail to fulfil any useful social role in their society. The younger generation of the landed classes, as embodied in the Bertram children (except Edmund), the Crawfords, Mr Rushworth and Mr Yates, are all dedicated entirely to what the novel often calls 'pleasure'. Sometimes this word is used, as it is elsewhere in Austen, to name the means whereby polite intercourse produces social solidarity among the propertied classes [pp. 44–5]; but more often, and especially when linked with Henry, it is connected to a 'gratification' (I.xiii.115) which is not reciprocal and thus in the service of wider social aims but is more or less purely selfish. Henry's observation in chapter v that 'an engaged woman is always more agreeable than a disengaged . . . she feels that she may exert all her powers of pleasing without suspicion' (I.v.43) is an early indication that 'pleasure' or the 'pleasant' has been cut loose from its function in support of social institutions (such as, here, marriage) and is what one achieves *despite* social institutions. Henry's use of Maria Bertram to indulge his vanity, an attitude that leads to the disaster of her adultery, is already encapsulated in this comment.

In marked contrast to this younger generation, Sir Thomas retains a sense of the high moral standards that are the justification for his social power. But of his children, only Edmund has internalised a similar sense: for his older brother and his sisters, restraint in the name of virtue is something imposed on them from outside by a father who monopolises power within the family (his wife objects to Fanny's going to Portsmouth, 'But he was master at Mansfield Park'; III.vi.343). Sir Thomas, says Mrs Grant, 'has a fine dignified manner, which suits the head of such a house, and keeps everybody in their place' (I.xvii.149); but this very dignity or 'reserve' has only 'repressed' the flow of spirits of his daughters rather than channelled it in morally responsible directions (I.ii.20). Within the family context, at least, the very alignment of social power with moral authority, rather than legitimating the former with affective ties of gratitude and loyalty, undermines the latter by making it appear as arbitrary restraint. Rather than wider social relations being imbued with the emotional content of family ties, family ties have been stripped of feeling by their assimilation to power relations generally. The ethical remains a matter of government (by a patriarchal father) rather than of *self*-government. Hence, on his departure for Antigua, we are told of his daughters that '[t]heir father was no object of love to them, he had never been the friend of their pleasures, and his absence was most welcome' (I.iii.31). But one should note that Fanny, too, cannot miss Sir Thomas on this occasion. Although intensely conscious (as her cousins are not) that she *ought* to, her sense of gratitude does not find expression in that 'love' which would transform a power relation to her patron into an authentic emotional tie. Fanny's sources of pleasure may be very different from her cousins', but she too experiences a gap between spontaneous feelings of loyalty and regard and the inherited authority that she believes has a theoretical claim to them.

Mansfield Park as a whole can be read as an exploration of the problems that thus emerge: the location of moral *authority* in a society where it can no longer be taken to reside simply in the ruling elite (as the younger members of that elite have abdicated this role); and the location of moral *agency* in a society where spontaneous emotional bonds, both within that elite and between it and others, can no longer be relied on to enforce compliance (due to Sir Thomas's reserve).

There are two sources of moral authority in this novel, Edmund and Fanny. Edmund's views are set up throughout in opposition to those of his undisciplined siblings and the louche Crawfords alike. Nor, as a younger son, does he owe his influence to a future role as head of an influential gentry family. But Edmund's authority is identified, through his ordination into the Church of England, with one of the other governing institutions of English society. The authority of the clergyman is indeed not only put into play through Edmund's moral judgements in the course of the story, but is the object of a series of discussions between him and Mary Crawford. Mary cannot recognise the authority that religion might have *over* the claims of pleasure and the fashionable London life that she is used to: she can only comprehend the church as one more social institution, and judge its servants according to their wealth (usually minimal) and agreeableness (likewise minimal, in Mary's experience). When Edmund argues in the chapel at Sotherton for the crucial role of the clergy in 'the guardianship of religion and morals', she counters:

> "One does not see much of this influence and importance in society . . .
> How can two sermons a week, even supposing them worth hearing,
> supposing the preacher to have the sense to prefer Blair's to his own, do
> all that you speak of?"
>
> (I.ix.87)

Mary is partly basing her opinion on her observation of the Mansfield vicar, her brother-in-law, a lazy glutton. And where Fanny naively affirms that 'a sensible man like Dr Grant, cannot be in the habit of teaching others their duty twice a week . . . without being the better for it himself', Mary sensibly hopes that Fanny does not become 'the wife of a man whose amiableness depends upon his own sermons' (I.xi.104–5). Like the emotional bonds that are supposed to hold together gentry society, the moral authority of churchmen is more a matter of theory than practice.

Indeed, *Mansfield Park* is structured around two failures of moral perception on Edmund's part: his inability to stay aloof from his friends' production of a play at the end of volume I, and his backing of Henry's proposal of marriage to Fanny at the beginning of volume III. Edmund criticises two aspects of the play scheme: the disruption to the family home without permission from Sir Thomas (for example, turning Sir Thomas's room into part of a theatre); and the abandonment of decorum in respectable young ladies like Maria and Mary in acting out scenes of sexual passion on the stage, especially acute in the case of the already-engaged Maria. In both cases, of course, the objections do not stem directly from religious considerations. The crisis works as a test of Edmund's ability to govern the behaviour of others, and it is a test that he fails. Already at I.xiii.120, and at I.xv.134 and 137, Edmund is simply silent where he ought to speak out. The best he can do is to contain the impropriety by trying to prevent anyone outside their immediate circle being involved, but he can only do this by implicating himself in the indecorum that remains, by taking on the part of Anhalt, the clergyman love-object of Mary Crawford's Amelia in the play. This involvement of Edmund in what he knows he ought simply to condemn is telling, for it aligns him much more closely with Mary's sceptical version of the best that can be hoped from a clergyman than his own: in preserving the privacy of the Mansfield theatricals, Edmund is much more the 'regulator' of 'refinement' than a model of correct 'conduct' (his terms at I.ix.87). Even in Edmund's own person, the character of the clergyman seems easily seduced by a fashionable society which it ought to be his function, in part at least, to criticise, and it is this seduction that Mary Crawford will continue to threaten in the following two volumes.

There is, however, another source of moral authority available to the reader throughout this episode by which to judge Edmund's failure and that is Fanny's own. The relationship between Fanny and Edmund begins within the same hierarchical framework, and the same return of gratitude for patronage, that determines her relation to the rest of the family, but in the particular form of tutor and tutee. Edmund assists 'the improvement of her mind':

> he recommended the books which charmed her leisure hours, he encouraged her taste, and corrected her judgment; he made reading useful by talking to her of what she read, and heightened its attractions by judicious praise. In return for such services she loved him better than any body in the world except William.
>
> (I.ii.22)

So later, when Edmund appreciates her meditations on the moral effects of the sublimity of nature, she can reply, '*You* taught me to think and feel on the subject, cousin' (I.xi.106). This relationship is in fact another example (compare it to Catherine's relation to Henry in *Northanger Abbey*) of a heroine's relation to a lover-mentor, a man whom she can love because he is better and more knowledgeable than she is, promising a marriage in which the man's legal power over the woman is compensated for by turning his other types of advantage to her benefit. This relationship is most strikingly acted out in I.vii, in a discussion between them of the woman who will get in the way of this promise, Mary Crawford. Chapter I.v includes a conversation involving the Crawfords, Edmund and Tom (of which more later) in which Fanny is discussed; I.vi a long dinner

conversation at which Fanny is present. Chapter I.vii begins with Edmund
discussing Mary's contribution to the dinner conversation.

> ". . . But was there nothing in her conversation that struck you Fanny, as
> not quite right?"
> "Oh! yes, she ought not to have spoken of her uncle as she did. I was
> quite astonished . . ."
> "I thought you would be struck. It was very wrong—very
> indecorous."
> "And ungrateful I think . . . Do not you think," said Fanny, after a
> little consideration, "that this impropriety is a reflection itself upon Mrs
> Crawford, as her niece has been entirely brought up by her? She cannot
> have given her the right notions of what was due to the Admiral."
> "That is a fair remark. Yes, we must suppose the faults of the niece to
> have been those of the aunt . . ."
>
> (I.vii.60–1)

Edmund hears his own views returned to him from Fanny's mouth: in that
initial question there is the suggestion that Edmund is testing Fanny's moral perception, the teacher checking the correct application of his ideas by the apt pupil.
In the light of Edmund's later infatuation with Mary, however, he could be seen
here as seeking to confirm his moral judgement of her which he would prefer to
do without, by turning to Fanny's judgement as more reliable; making this an
exchange driven by an uncertainty not about Fanny's moral perception, but about
his own. This would then mark the point at which Fanny begins to emerge as a
moral authority in her own right, the dominant ethical subjectivity of the novel,
and one legitimated not by the established social institutions of the gentry or
the church, but, like Elinor Dashwood in *Sense and Sensibility*, by the very
self-consciousness and self-criticism embodied in the language of the novel itself
[see pp. 53–4].

This conditional autonomy of Fanny's moral authority becomes clearer in the
crisis over the play, when Edmund, having decided to take the part of Anhalt to
spare Mary acting a love scene with a stranger, asks explicitly for Fanny's approbation: 'I am not comfortable without it' (I.xvi.144). She never gives it, although
she expresses gratitude at Mary's stopping the attempts to coerce *her* into acting
the previous night, and Edmund takes this as approbation enough. Fanny's shock
at Edmund's inconsistency does not find its way into direct speech, but remains
private, in the form of free indirect discourse.

> After all his objections—objections so just and so public! After all that
> she had heard him say, and seen him look, and known him to be feeling.
> Could it be possible? Edmund so inconsistent . . . Alas! it was all Miss
> Crawford's doing. She had seen her influence in every speech, and was
> miserable.
>
> (I.xvi.145)

Fanny can be seen in this episode to be taking Edmund's proper place as moral
judge of those around them; in chapter xviii this substitution is acted out when

Fanny must literally play Edmund's part in Mary's rehearsal of her own (Mary recognises that this is a particular case of a replacement that occurs elsewhere, observing, 'You *have* a look of *his* sometimes'; I.xviii.156).

The crisis over the play is resolved by the early return of Sir Thomas from his West Indian sojourn, and simple patriarchal authority rectifies the errors that Edmund's moral authority was unable to prevent. Edmund, having abandoned the principled position maintained by Fanny, is brought to account by his father's mere looks, 'speaking a language, a remonstrance, a reproof, which *he* felt at his heart' (II.i.172). But if Fanny's moral perception is vindicated by Sir Thomas in this instance, in the crisis over Henry Crawford's proposal of marriage she is completely alone: Edmund and his father both back Henry's offer as an exceptional and never-to-be-repeated chance for Fanny to secure by marriage the wealth that she needs to support the lifestyle to which she has come to aspire at Mansfield Park. In contrast to the earlier episode, here Fanny must not only maintain her moral integrity in the *absence* of supporting patriarchal power, but in *opposition* to that power.

I have until now been concentrating on questions of moral authority in this novel, on the position of those voices in the text that are able to distinguish right from wrong. But in this separation of Fanny's moral authority from the power of the patriarch to change matters, the question now arises of moral *agency*: that is, her ability to put her moral judgement into practice and assert it in the world around her. For Fanny's moral authority goes hand in hand with a general power-lessness that leaves her the spectator of events rather than one able to intervene in them. So, for example, Fanny 'looked on and listened, not unamused to observe the selfishness which, more or less disguised, seemed to govern them all' in rehearsals for the play (I.xvi.123), and later comments to Edmund, 'As a by-stander . . . perhaps I saw more than you did' (III.iv.324). This position of 'by-stander' is also particularly marked in two other episodes in the novel. In the 'Wilderness' at Sotherton the party visiting Mr Rushworth's home fragments and separates, engaging in that rapid but purposeless movement that is a mark of the Crawfords (as before them of Marianne and Willoughby) and a sign of their moral rootlessness. Fanny, however, is left behind, her physical weakness fixing her to one spot, a still point in the forest from which other characters depart, return, separate and depart again. The narrative point of view stays with Fanny throughout, but she is as unable to influence the movement of her friends as she is to explain or justify it to others.

The episode invites an allegorical reading. The initial unifying 'one impulse, one wish for air and liberty' (I.ix.84) which propels the young people out of the house of Sotherton, with its ancient manorial legal rights (I.viii.77) and reminders of 'scenes of the past', suggests the general casting off of feudal ties and roles and manners by this new generation; the plantation in which they then lose each other and find each other again suggests the moral chaos into which this liberation has thrown them. That the forest is called the 'Wilderness' is suggestive, but so is the fact that this scene of confusion is in fact man-made. Perhaps more obviously, the specific movements of the characters act out prophetically their relationships as they will develop in the novel as a whole: Edmund leaves Fanny to spend far too long with Mary, but eventually returns; Maria runs away from Rushworth with Henry. In this context, Fanny's physical immobility becomes a sign of her moral steadfastness; and that immobility is adopted by the narrator as the perspective from which the truth of the other characters' behaviour can be revealed.

It is the crisis produced by Henry and Maria's actual adultery that is my second example of Fanny's status as bystander. Throughout the novel's climax at chapters III.xii–xvi, Fanny is absent at Portsmouth, and hears of developments only through letters from Mary, Lady Bertram and Edmund. Her subjectivity here consists of critical responses to these letters and thoughts about their content, but again, at no point can her judgements issue in anything like action. Fanny's consciousness is the dominant subjectivity of the novel, but her presence in the novel is for long periods purely *as* subjectivity, purely as the novel's perspective on events. It is a subjectivity structured by the gap between her moral authority and the lack of social importance that would allow her to put that authority to social use.

One should also note, however, that the omniscient narrator does increasingly qualify the reliability of Fanny's judgements, especially towards the end of the novel, and does so specifically to remind us that Fanny has her own self-interest at work in her judgement of the Crawfords, namely her unspoken rivalry with Mary for Edmund. Fanny cites a combination of her low social status and her specific debts to the Bertrams as the bars to indicating her attraction to Edmund.

> It was her intention, as she felt it to be her duty, to try to overcome all that was excessive, all that bordered on selfishness in her affection for Edmund . . . To think of him as Miss Crawford might be justified in thinking, would in her be insanity . . . Why did such an idea occur to her even enough to be reprobated and forbidden? It ought not to have touched on the confines of her imagination.
>
> (II.ix.244)

Here we see where Fanny's moral agency might principally lie: in the effort of self-control, of self-discipline, that calls to mind the similar effort of, once again, Elinor Dashwood. Unable to produce effects in the lives of others, Fanny works to produce a certain kind of *self* instead. The narrator is clear here that this attempt is in itself excessive:

> She had all the heroism of principle, and was determined to do her duty; but having also many of the feelings of youth and nature, let it not be much wondered at if, after making all these good resolutions on the side of self-government, she seized the scrap of paper on which Edmund had begun writing to her, as a treasure beyond all her hopes . . .
>
> (II.ix.244)

Despite this lack of direct social power, Fanny is, however, offered two types of *indirect* agency by the novel. One is the simple and negative agency of resistance. Given her dependent status at Mansfield Park, her ability to resist the pressure to accept Henry put on her by the men to whom she owes most in the family, Sir Thomas and Edmund, should perhaps be read as her great heroic act in the novel. This is a purely passive heroism, of course, implying a purely passive virtue; but one should not forget that what Sir Thomas and Edmund are trying to do in the third volume is to shape Fanny's feelings, to alter her perception of the world, and thus take control of that subjectivity which is the only realm over which Fanny enjoys control. At least since Richardson's *Pamela* this has been a standard model of feminine virtue [see pp. 11–12, 59].

The other type of indirect agency offered Fanny by the novel is just that which *Pamela* enacts, but is present here only as an unrealised possibility: the moral conversion of Henry Crawford by her example alone, and conversion of him into a man whom she could after all marry without danger to her own moral integrity. Edmund, in arguing the case for accepting Henry, holds out just this prospect of her ultimate reformation of him: '[Y]ou will make him everything' (III.iv.325). Her very moral steadiness makes her an attractive marriage prospect to Henry: when Fanny urges him to return to his estate and put it to rights in the interests of his tenants, he will comment, 'When you give me your opinion, I always know what is right. Your judgment is my rule of right' (III.xi.383). But he takes in London on his way home, visits Maria, and in place of finally settling into the local responsibilities of a good landowner he continues his career as rootless pleasure-seeker by running away with another man's wife. The extent to which Fanny's influence has genuinely begun to reform Henry, as Pamela's influence genuinely reforms Mr B, is left uncertain by the end of the novel. When Fanny finally perceives a 'wonderful improvement' in his manners, the narrator warns us to be sceptical: 'Not considering in how different a circle she had just been seeing him, nor how much might be owing to contrast, she was quite persuaded of his being astonishingly more gentle, and regardful of others, than formerly' (III.xi.384).

The story of Fanny and Henry can thus be read as Austen's questioning and refusal of Richardson's solution to the problem of (specifically feminine) agency. But Austen also broadens this questioning by opening up the possibility of a similar narrative for Edmund and Mary, but with Edmund as the moral standard, and Mary as the one who could be morally improved through love: on first getting to know Edmund, she finds 'a charm, perhaps, in his sincerity, his steadiness, his integrity' (I.vii.62) such as Mr B eventually finds in Pamela. This inversion of Richardson's gendering of virtue and vice perhaps suggests that, with the authority of the church in decline, and the gentry increasingly dedicated only to their own pleasures, men's virtue inevitably takes on the passive form traditionally associated with women, in the absence of working institutions through which a more active virtue could express itself. It is a pessimistic conclusion that perhaps called for the more optimistic version of gentry rule presented in Austen's next novel, *Emma*.

On *Mansfield Park* in Part 3: on irony and modern selfhood, see Lionel Trilling [pp. 108–9]; on psychoanalytic approaches, see Barbara Rasmussen [p. 113]; on Burkean conservatism, see Alistair Duckworth [pp. 116–17]; on feminism, see Margaret Kirkham and Claudia Johnson [pp. 128, 131]; and on the role of slavery, see Edward Said and his critics [pp. 134–41].

Emma

For her next novel Austen decided to switch publishers, leaving Egerton for the much more prestigious house of John Murray (Murray published Byron and Scott, the two most famous and successful writers of the period). *Emma* was written in 1814–15 and published by Murray on commission at the end of that year. A large and expensively produced edition made a profit for Austen but did not sell well, despite widespread and fairly positive notices in the periodicals, and a long and enthusiastic (although anonymous) review by Scott himself in Murray's important *Quarterly Review* [see p. 33] of March 1816.

The story is basically as follows. Wealthy Emma Woodhouse interferes to prevent her much poorer friend Harriet Smith marrying a farmer, to the fury of the local landowner, Mr Knightley, who is close to Emma but can see her faults. Emma herself flirts with Frank Churchill, the son of a local man who has grown up with relatives elsewhere. Realising that things are not as good as they might be with Frank, she hints to Harriet that he might be attracted to her; but Harriet takes the hint to refer to Knightley himself. Moreover, Frank turns out to have been secretly engaged to Jane Fairfax, a girl in the village with whom Emma has never got on. Shocked by the possibility of Knightley ending up with Harriet, Emma is forced to realise that she herself loves Knightley. Knightley, having been forced to a similar realisation through the threat of Frank, proposes to Emma and is accepted; Harriet ends up with her farmer after all.

One of the things that sets *Emma* apart from Austen's previous novels is a much more serious concern with the social interconnectedness of a small country town. *Pride and Prejudice* comes closest, but, as we have seen, concerned itself much more with the emergence of nation-wide networks of family and interest for which small town life is present as a foil. The Surrey town of Highbury, on the other hand, is an object of interest in its own right in *Emma*, a communal presence whose 'general interest' (II.iii.163) in the characters they have to recognise and negotiate. *Pride and Prejudice* begins with the lines: 'It is a truth universally acknowledged, that a single man in possession of a good fortune, must be in want of a wife'. But this 'universal truth' quickly reveals itself as Mrs Bennet's: its universality is not confirmed by the authority of the narrator, but nor is it underwritten by any general wisdom accepted in the community of which Mrs Bennet is a part. It is Mrs Bennet's subjective perception of a general wisdom that may not otherwise exist. In *Emma* we find something much closer to a genuinely communal voice, a point of view at work in the narrative that cannot be reduced to the subjectivity of any one character. This point of view appears both as something perceived by Emma, an external perspective on events and characters that the reader encounters as and when Emma recognises it; and as an independent discourse appearing in the text alongside the discourse of the narrator and the characters.

A particularly complex case in point is the return from Bath of Mr Elton, the local vicar whose proposal of marriage Emma has rejected, at the beginning of II.iv.

> The charming Augusta Hawkins, in addition to all the usual advantages
> of perfect beauty and merit, was in possession of as many thousands as

would always be called ten; a point of some dignity, as well as some convenience: the story told well; he had not thrown himself away—he had gained a woman of 10,000*l*. or thereabouts; and he had gained her with delightful rapidity—the first hour of introduction had been so very soon followed by distinguishing notice; the history which he had to give Mrs Cole of the rise and progress of the affair was so glorious . . .

(II.iv.170–1)

At first, the adjective 'charming' appears to be in the narrator's voice, as authoritative as the novel's opening description of Emma as 'handsome, clever, and rich'. But the following clause includes an association of the 'usual' with the 'perfect' which is on the verge of self-contradiction: 'perfection' is not 'usual'. It sounds as if there are two voices, two discourses, being juxtaposed here, to produce this tension. The following clause, with its passive voice ('as would always be called ten'), allows us to identify one of these discourses with the communal voice of general wisdom, the discourse of a community gossiping excitedly about a new member: it is in such gossip that a moderate fortune will always be rounded up in this way. The tension of the second clause then resolves itself into one between this discourse, eager to attribute 'perfection' to Mr Elton's fiancée, and the narrator, who can see how 'usual', how routine, such attribution is in gossip about a new bride. At this point the initial 'charming' begins to look as if it may not be the narrator's judgement either: the reader must wait until later in the story to discover just how far from charming Augusta Elton *née* Hawkins actually is.

The following phrases introduce new puzzles (and the reader might be wondering at this point why this paragraph consists of a series of clauses and phrases separated by dashes and semi-colons instead of Austen's more usual well-rounded sentences). Some 'dignity' and 'convenience' *may* accrue to the community by Elton's marriage to a wealthy woman; the passive voice of 'the story told well' once again, by not identifying a speaker, invites us to attribute this comment to the impersonal voice of communal gossip. But 'he had not thrown himself away': while this could well be an approving (and slightly envious) comment passed in a shop or street, it might also reflect Elton's own self-satisfaction in a good marriage; and the adjective 'delightful' must be his (only he was there, in Bath, to be delighted by the speed of his progress with Augusta). The dignity and convenience now look more like Elton's than Highbury's, and the final sentence that I quote above suddenly identifies a specific situation in which Elton might be making this speech: his telling the whole story to Mrs Cole. At this point the reader can look back over what had seemed impersonal gossip in the preceding paragraph and realise that all this information in fact comes from a single source: Mr Elton himself. Rather than circulating impersonal or communal judgements on Augusta and Mr Elton, that voice has been merely repeating the version of events that Mr Elton has given to Mrs Cole.

Frank, like Augusta, is constructed as the object of this kind of discourse, as a member of this *discursive* community, long before he physically sets foot in Highbury, as a result of his father's proud reports of him to his neighbours. 'He was looked on as sufficiently belonging to the place to make his merit and prospects a kind of common concern' (I.ii.18). And Emma's response to Frank is mediated by the way in which she imagines other people see them: by her belief, for example, that they must be seen as a potential couple, once his father has married her former governess: 'He seemed by this connection between the families quite to belong to her. She could not but suppose it to be a match that every body who knew them must think of' (II.xiv.112–13). Later, she anticipates his return by 'fancying what the observations of all those might be, who were now seeing them together for the first time' (II.viii.198).

At the same time, Emma is capable of an ironic distance from this communal voice (the same ironic distance as we have seen enjoyed by her narrator), as when she tells Jane of their young vicar, 'When you have been here a little longer . . . you will understand that Mr Elton is the standard of perfection in Highbury, both in person and mind' (II.iii.164). 'Perfection' once again marks the uncritical judgement of the community at large. The fact that Emma and the narrator share this ironic distance from the discourse of the community does, however, make it very hard to distinguish them when Emma's own subjectivity is the object of the irony. In a passage like the following, for example, where Emma is placing herself in relation to Frank, it is hard to tell the narrator's ironic commentary on Emma's consciousness from Emma's own ironic self-consciousness:

> This was all very promising; and, but for such an unfortunate fancy for having his hair cut, there was nothing to denote him unworthy of the distinguished honour which her imagination had given him; the honour, if not of really being in love with her, of being at least very near it, and saved only by her own indifference—(for still her resolution held of never marrying)—the honour, in short, of being marked out for her by all their joint acquaintance.
>
> (II.vii.193)

'Promising' and 'unfortunate' are clearly Emma's own judgements, but it is hard to tell if Emma is *conscious* that her high self-regard turns her estimation of his feelings into a 'distinguished honour', or if the irony here is the narrator's, revealing a truth about Emma's response to Frank that Emma herself is not aware of. With the ambiguities of knowledge in this passage comes a shifting attribution of agency. Emma grants herself an agency she does not have: the power to make Frank either in love or not in love with her through her interest or indifference. The final comment places ultimate agency elsewhere: Emma is only thinking in these terms because of the way that other people see both of them. On its own, this seems to be the judgement of the narrator, a truth hidden from Emma, and the passage as a whole seems thus to shift from free indirect discourse representing Emma's consciousness, to the commentary of an omniscient narrator, via a series of judgements that could be attributed to either. However, we know from the comment at I.xiv.112–13 quoted above that Emma is conscious that other people think of her and Frank in this way: so this final comment also could be Emma's criticism of herself, an awareness that her thoughts and feelings about Frank have their origin somewhere other than in her own judgement or imagination. Emma's subjectivity, that is, consists not only of judgements, and of her awareness of the subjective nature of those judgements (that her self-esteem turns this one into a 'distinguished honour'), but may also include an awareness that the origins of her subjectivity lie somewhere other than in herself. Her consciousness may appear at first as autonomous from the society around it; it is in fact produced by that society.

This problem of the relation of Emma's consciousness to the background noise of the communal life of Highbury is one that corresponds to the central problem acted out in the plot of *Emma*: the role of women in the construction and maintenance of that community. Unlike any of Austen's other heroines, Emma is born into the sort of wealth and position that allow her a leading role in her neighbourhood right from the start. Elizabeth Bennet and Fanny Price enjoy the moral authority of the virtuous domestic woman, but they must marry wealthy men if that authority is to be offered a wider social function beyond the home. Such a wider function for feminine virtue is what is figured in the marriages that close *Pride and Prejudice* and *Mansfield Park*. But Emma Woodhouse has this function to begin with. Frank describes her as 'She who could do anything in Highbury!' (II.vi.186); it is she, and not her father, who organises the charitable distribution of the produce of their estate to the likes of the Bates household (II.iii.162). When she comments to Harriet that she has 'none of the usual inducements to marry . . . Fortune I do not want; employment I do not want; consequence I do not want' (I.x.82) she identifies a difference, not only between herself and other women, but in the plot of her novel, whose culminating marriage will have some other type of ideological work to do than that of its predecessors.

This is not to say that Emma enjoys anything like the social power reserved for men in a patriarchal society. Knightley is not only the owner of Highbury but its magistrate (I.xii.96); we glimpse him at work in running his estate or governing the parish, though usually only after, for example, 'Mr Woodhouse had been talked into what was necessary . . . and the papers swept away' (II.iii.160). 'Parish business' is something engaged in by Knightley, Mr Weston and the other men once the ladies have withdrawn from the dining table (it is what Frank is eager to escape from at II.viii.205–6). Emma has a significant degree of agency of various other kinds. One is the feminine influence of example, as Emma's power over Harriet Smith is not just that of a mentor, but of a model to imitate: Harriet's habits are of 'dependence and imitation' (I.x.84). Perhaps more important is her active charity towards the poor, rather more concretely sketched in here (in I.x: see especially 84) than Fanny's in the previous novel. But the plot of the novel subjects Emma to a process of education whereby she discovers the limitations of her judgement and learns the superiority of Knightley's: theirs is a lover-mentor relationship such as we have seen in several of the other novels, albeit that Emma has far more confidence in her own abilities to start with than either Catherine Morland or Fanny Price. Even at the beginning of the novel, indeed, she has 'a sort of habitual respect for his judgment in general' (I.viii.64); by the end, once they are engaged to be married, she has nothing to wish for 'but to grow more worthy of him, whose intentions and judgment had been ever so superior to her own' (III.xviii.445).

Emma has sufficient authority in at least one further area to bring her into conflict with Knightley right at the start of the novel. This is the conventionally feminine area of courtship and marriage, but the argument with Knightley is one about the policing of distinctions of rank, and whether Harriet Smith belongs with the prosperous tenant-farmer class in the shape of her suitor Robert Martin, or with the property-owning class to which Emma and Knightley themselves belong. Knightley is ready to acknowledge Emma's real effect in improving Harriet's manners (I.viii.57); but having talked the illegitimate Harriet out of accepting Martin's proposal of marriage, Emma finds she must defend this use of her social power against Knightley's objections. One should note that Harriet's case is not one of feminine virtue or inner 'character' demanding recognition from masculine power: Harriet is not Fanny Price or Elizabeth Bennet. In fact the opposite is the case: Harriet is characterised throughout, and not merely by Mr Knightley ('Her character depends upon those she is with'; I.viii.57), as a blank surface on which Emma can inscribe whatever habits of thought or behaviour she chooses. Martin is described by Knightley, in contrast, in terms of his established and proven worth as friend, brother, son, farmer and businessman, his social identity fixed by his place in the networks of dependence that constitute the masculine community. Knightley's criteria for assigning someone to a particular rank go well beyond blood: 'What are Harriet Smith's claims, either of birth, nature, or education, to any connection higher than Robert Martin?' (I.viii.59–60). But they do not include the prettiness and good temper that are all he is ready to acknowledge in Harriet, and this remains a question of rank: what is at stake for Knightley is ultimately not the suitability of two people for each other as individuals but the maintenance of a hierarchy of 'connection'.

As indeed it is also for Emma, but the only connection that matters for her in this context is Harriet's to herself. Having adopted her as a friend, Emma must now find her a husband of high enough status to legitimate that friendship:

> "What! think a farmer, (and with all his sense and all his merit Mr Martin is nothing more,) a good match for my intimate friend! ... a man whom I could never admit as an acquaintance of my own!"
>
> (I.viii.60)

The intimacy and acquaintanceship that Emma cites here can be understood as forming a set of social connections distinct from, but not independent of, the masculine networks described by Knightley. Martin discusses his proposal of marriage with Knightley as, Knightley hopes, 'one of his best friends', but this friendship transcends a division of rank and is thus clearly not what Emma would call 'acquaintanceship': Knightley's friendship with Martin is inevitably closer to that of patron and client than the intimacy of two young women. 'Friendship' in *Emma* often refers to relationships where one party is in a position of power, is able to do favours for the other, including (and this is standard eighteenth- and early nineteenth-century usage) those we would now call relatives. To claim intimacy with someone, on the other hand, is to claim an equal social status with them. Mrs Elton is seen as a 'friend' to Jane Fairfax (by Emma at II.xv.265; by Miss Bates at III.viii.357) when she tries to find Jane a governess's position, but thinks of herself as enjoying 'intimacy' with Knightley (III.vi.332). Emma welcomes Mrs Elton's arrival in Highbury, on the other hand, as an excuse for dropping her own intimacy with her husband (on this occasion, 'former intimacy might sink without remark'; II.iv.172) while at the same time she tries to prevent a re-establishment of intimacy between Harriet and the Martins (II.iv.174).

In all these cases, what is being established by these terms is membership of or exclusion from a local ruling elite. Emma's argument with Knightley in I.viii is not about the justification of the existence of this elite: the necessity of hierarchy is not called into question by either. Rather, their disagreement is, at a superficial level, about where the boundaries of that elite should be set, and what qualifies one for membership; and at a deeper level, about who has the authority to police those boundaries. Such policing is precisely what Emma is engaged in when she persuades Harriet to reject Robert Martin as beneath her. Marriage, as the area where private feeling and public status most visibly interact, is one within which Emma, as the town's highest-ranking woman, can exercise a rival authority to that of Knightley, its highest-ranking man. The regulation of sexual relations, a role assigned largely to women, is necessarily central to the regulation of social relations more generally. *Emma* begins by dramatising this clash of rival masculine and feminine authorities within the private life of a small town.

The arrival of Augusta Elton, however, complicates this pattern. Mrs Elton quickly appropriates to herself the social authority previously assumed by Emma, and directs it to the social elevation of Jane Fairfax. This is an exercise similar to Emma's project with Harriet, but at once more reckless and less ambitious. On the one hand, Mrs Elton's goal is no more than to find the propertyless Jane, destined by limited means to the social limbo of a post as governess, a position with one of her much-vaunted wealthy acquaintances. On the other hand, her plan of 'noticing' Jane in the meantime (inviting her to parties and so on) does no more than exacerbate the pain of her existing position, that of having been brought up to the tastes and comforts of a class to which she cannot, in the long term, belong.

> "My dear Miss Woodhouse, a vast deal may be done by those who dare to act. You and I need not be afraid. If *we* set the example, many will follow it as far as they can; though all have not our situations. *We* have carriages to fetch and convey her home . . ."
>
> (II.xv.263)

She even goes so far as to claim to be 'Lady Patroness' of a day at Knightley's house at Donwell Abbey, implicitly taking Emma's place as Knightley's female counterpart (a move that Knightley firmly resists, of course; III.vi.332–3).

What makes Mrs Elton's claims particularly galling to Emma is, once more, a matter of rank. Her first sight of Mrs Elton suggests that she possesses 'ease' rather than 'elegance' (II.xiv.251): that is, a self-confidence in her equal (or superior) status to those around her which is just too taken for granted, rather than the subtle signifiers in dress and behaviour of a genuinely expensive upbring-ing and education. From this point in the novel, indeed, 'elegance' is frequently used ironically, in Emma's free indirect discourse, to describe Mrs Elton's self-conscious attempt to deploy these signifiers, which only serves to mark, in Emma's mind, the fact that they do not come naturally, and are thus not really *hers*. Emma's first conversation with her confirms this impression. She already talks of 'Knightley' rather than '*Mr* Knightley' (Emma's mode of address despite knowing him all her life; II.xiv.259); she flatly contradicts Emma on Surrey alone being called 'the garden of England' (II.xiv.254); and generally assumes an intimacy that she has not yet earned. This makes her 'pert and familiar'

(II.xiv.253), an 'upstart', 'vulgar' and 'under-bred' (II.xiv.259). These terms, one should note, refer not only to bad manners but also to the economic situation that produces them. Mrs Elton is in fact from exactly the background, though not quite so wealthy, as the Bingleys in *Pride and Prejudice*: the first generation of her family to be brought up on a country estate, Maple Grove, *bought* by her father with money earned from elsewhere. Her snobbery, like the Bingley sisters', comes from the precariousness of her claim to gentility, not from its security:

> "... I have quite a horror of upstarts. Maple Grove has given me a thorough disgust to people of that sort ... Mr Suckling [her brother-in-law], who has been eleven years a resident at Maple Grove, and whose father had it before him—I believe, at least—I am almost sure that old Mr Suckling had completed the purchase before his death."
>
> (II.xviii.288–9)

The true English gentry would count their residence on an estate not in years, but in generations.

Emma's social authority in Highbury, then, is defined in opposition to two alternative authorities: Knightley's and Mrs Elton's. With the former she shares a social rank: with the latter she shares a gender. I suggested above that the position of feminine social authority in a community like Highbury is a central problem for this novel. One can now read Emma's marriage to Knightley as a way of resolving this problem: the plot subsumes her feminine authority within the authority of her social class as a whole, explaining it decisively as the product of her rank and not her gender. Emma's recognition that she must marry Knightley is a recognition of the necessity of consolidating the power of their class and maintaining its exclusion, not only of the Harriet Smiths, but also of the Mrs Eltons, from their community. Mrs Elton indeed appears, on this reading, as a scapegoat with whom Emma's own presumption of power *as a woman* can be identified and then rejected. On this view, and in contrast to Austen's two previous novels, *Emma* works to legitimate established gentry power *defined in opposition to* an autonomous feminine authority over the regulation of social relations, and not through the vindication of such autonomous authority.

One *can* read the novel in this way, but it includes elements that seem to run counter to such a reading. For one thing, the novel is marked by a gradual widening of Emma's social sphere, an inclusion of a few of the previously excluded, a making more porous of the boundaries between the elite and other propertied groups. This process begins with her visiting the Bateses, purely to take Harriet's mind off Mr Elton, in II.i. Miss Bates, a spinster, and her mother perch on the very bottom rung of polite society, maintained there by a small income and a lot of charity from, mostly, Mr Knightley. Emma is 'negligent' in visiting them due largely to her 'horror of being in danger of falling in with the second and third rate of Highbury, who were calling on them for ever' (II.i.145). But such visits become regular as the novel proceeds. Similarly, she finds herself obliged to accept an invitation to dinner at the Coles, a family 'of low origin, in trade, and only moderately genteel' (II.vii.194) but whose recently increased income prompts them to reach out for social recognition to their longer-established neighbours. Emma's initial opinion is that the Coles 'were very respectable in their way, but they ought to be taught that it was not for them to arrange the terms on which the superior families would visit them' (II.vii.194). Yet once Knightley and the Westons accept their invitation, Emma goes along, and finds such company a comforting refuge from her continuing self-accusation over Harriet: 'all that she might be supposed to have lost on the side of dignified seclusion, must be amply repaid in the splendour of popularity' (II.ix.215). Similarly, when the ball is first mooted by Frank, Emma (it seems) objects that there are not enough 'proper families' in Highbury to make it worthwhile (II.vi.186). Frank cannot believe this,

> and even when particulars were given and families described, he was still unwilling to admit that the inconvenience of such a mixture would be any thing, or that there would be the smallest difficulty in every body's returning into their proper place the next morning;

and Emma judges that 'his indifference to a confusion of rank, bordered too much on inelegance of mind' (II.vi.186). Frank's father, Mr Weston, here as elsewhere in the novel a one-man principle of social inclusion, is put in charge, and witnessing the number of people invited early to inspect the improved facilities at the Crown Inn, Emma similarly reflects that 'a little less of open-heartedness would have made him a higher character.—General benevolence, but not general friendship, made a man what he ought to be.—She could fancy such a man' (III.ii.300). This of course should make the reader think of Knightley, the embodiment of social hierarchy put to benevolent ends. And yet not only is the ball a great success, but Knightley himself plays his part in it, not only dancing, against his usual habit, but doing so with Harriet, precisely in order to maintain the inclusivity of the occasion, after she is snubbed by Mr Elton.

It is through this series of successful social events that the social barriers policed by Emma and Knightley are gradually expanded. It is striking that the one truly disastrous social gathering, the trip to Box Hill, is not disastrous because it includes the Coles or the Coxes or any of the other representatives of new wealth in Highbury. From the start, 'There was a languor, a want of spirits, a want of union, which could not be got over . . . there seemed a principle of separation . . . too strong for any fine prospects, or any cold collation, or any cheerful Mr Weston, to remove' (III.vii.344). It may be that their very removal from Highbury, the very abandonment of the scene of their usual social duties to one another, is to be understood as producing this vague malaise. But the positive awkwardness that follows is produced by Frank's high-spirited if rather desperate attempts to overcome this internal division. The first consists of a demand to know what all their silent companions are thinking, offending a principle of mental privacy on which polite intercourse is grounded. The second is a demand that each of them say one very clever thing, two moderately clever or three dull, and it is this which produces Emma's thoughtless jibe at the voluble Miss Bates.

In many ways this is the crisis of the novel, trivial as it may seem. It provides the second knock to Emma's confidence in her own judgement after the debacle with Harriet and Mr Elton, and Knightley's censure begins the process of her realising her love for him. But the social circumstances that make such a blunder possible include a set of circumstances unknown to Emma and Knightley at the time: namely Frank's engagement to Jane Fairfax. For Frank's edgy flirtation with

Emma on Box Hill, the parade of good spirits so at odds with the general mood of the group, is produced by his own secret unhappiness regarding his row with Jane the previous day. I have not discussed this secret affair at any length, but at this point it clearly functions as much more than a way of complicating Emma's otherwise placid emotional life for the sake of the plot. In a novel in which characters are constantly under the surveillance of their neighbours, in which subjectivity is (as we have seen in the case of Emma) produced by such surveillance, Frank and Jane's secret puts them outside that community despite their physical presence within it. There are forces at work in Frank's discourse at Box Hill which are not transparent to his hearers. But Emma does not consider that his high spirits might come from somewhere other than his attraction to her, and plays along with, is seduced into, Frank's discordant verbal world. The hurting of Miss Bates follows from this partial withdrawal by Emma from the rules of language that normally govern social relations in polite society.

Another element in *Emma* that does not accord with the social homogeneity of its closing marriage is the presence of Jane Fairfax herself. For if Emma is the embodiment of a certain sort of female social power, Jane represents a much more usual female powerlessness, and specifically the possibility of downward as well as upward social mobility. Just as Mrs Elton has acquired a certain wealth and status without having properly naturalised the polite manners that should accompany that status, so Jane is a 'really accomplished young woman' (Knightley's words; II.ii.156) who is nevertheless destined to work for a living as a governess. To work for a living, as a woman, involves dropping out of the polite classes altogether [see pp. 7–8]. Leisured women like Emma and Mrs Elton may play at labour, picking strawberries in Mr Knightley's garden, but in the midst of this scene comes Mrs Elton's description of 'a most desirable situation' for Jane with a friend of her family: a reminder of the reality of the labour to which she is to be consigned (III.vi.337). If there is a story in *Emma* in which true personal (feminine) value wins recognition from a powerful man despite its lack of wealth and status, that story is not Emma's or Harriet's: it is Jane Fairfax's. But that story, the narrative pattern that is repeated here from *Pamela* and Burney, and *Pride and Prejudice* and *Mansfield Park*, is repeated under cover, as the novel's shaping secret, itself subordinated to a main plot in which gentry power is consolidated by the marriage of Emma and Knightley.

On *Emma* in Part 3: on point of view and moral, see Wayne Booth [pp. 95–6]; on irony, see Marvin Mudrick, Graham Hough and Walton Litz [pp. 98–9]; on free indirect discourse, see Casey Finch and Peter Bowen [pp. 99–100]; on morality, society and the modern self, see Lionel Trilling [pp. 107–8]; on sexuality and the body, see Susan Korba and John Dussinger [pp. 112–13]; on social hierarchy, see Arnold Kettle and Beth Tobin [pp. 114–15, 119]; on class and gender, see Nancy Armstrong, Margaret Kirkham and Claudia Johnson [pp. 123–4, 129, 132–3].

Persuasion

Persuasion was begun in August 1815 and finished one year later. It was the last novel that Austen completed: her health was already failing during this period, and when she died in July 1817 the novel remained unpublished. Her sister Cassandra, to whom she left almost all her property, arranged for John Murray to bring it out with *Northanger Abbey*, each novel comprising two volumes of a four-volume set. This duly appeared at the end of that year.

The story is basically as follows. Years before the novel opens, Anne Elliot was engaged to a young naval officer, Frederick Wentworth, but had been persuaded to break it off because of his limited prospects. Anne is now 27; the war having now ended (it is 1814), Wentworth returns to shore, promoted and wealthy, and their paths again cross. Although at first he remains cold to the woman who rejected him, his feelings for her begin to return: for her part, Anne has never stopped loving Wentworth. In Bath, where Anne's spendthrift father has retreated in order to rent their country estate to Admiral Croft, Wentworth accidentally discovers Anne's constancy; he proposes and is accepted.

In its handling of point of view and use of free indirect discourse *Persuasion* is as brilliant as *Emma*; in its use of a heroine slighted by those closest to her as a critical perspective on English society, it returns to the narrative strategy of *Mansfield Park*. It is in many other respects a radical departure from those, as from Austen's other novels. Like them, it culminates in the heroine's marriage, but this is a marriage which was originally proposed eight years before the novel begins, by Captain Frederick Wentworth of the Royal Navy to the 19-year-old Anne Elliot of Kellynch Hall, Somerset. For the course of the novel, then, the heroine's marriage figures in the narrative not as the end towards which it works, but as an event which has not happened, a non-event in the past which continues to shape Anne's perspective on the world and her relationship to Captain Wentworth when he walks back into her life in I.vii. In the other novels, hero and heroine must overcome differences of rank, or their own and others' mis-understandings, before their marriage can take place. Here, hero and heroine must overcome the sheer determining force of their own shared past before marriage is, for a second time, a possibility. The conventional courtship plot has already happened, as it were, before the start of I.i: and it ended in failure, in the rejection of the hero by the heroine. The plot of this novel will be a counter-plot to put that failure right.

We have seen, in the cases of *Pride and Prejudice*, *Mansfield Park* and *Emma*, at least, that these marriages can have a very particular political meaning: the recognition and absorption of moral or social virtue, embodied in women excluded from power, by men of the ruling class, in the case of the first two; or, I have suggested, the consolidation of gentry power by marriage within that class in the more conservative *Emma*. In all five previous novels indeed, the heroine marries a son of the gentry, one destined for, or already enjoying, the responsibilities of landownership (Colonel Brandon, Darcy, Knightley) or of the Anglican priesthood (Henry Tilney, Edward Ferrars, Edmund Bertram). Such absorption of the heroine by the established ruling class promises continuity in English life: the heroine's social energies, however subversive, or her moral authority, however independent, can be accommodated and productively channelled within an establishment which will remain essentially continuous with the past. Alone among Austen's heroines, Anne Elliot marries a man who not only owes his wealth entirely to his own efforts (and those of the crews who, under his command, have captured the French ships which have won them financial reward) but shows no indication of using this wealth to buy his way into the rural gentry: the penultimate paragraph refers to the newlyweds' 'settled life' (II.xii.235) but says no more about the location of this settlement. Buying an estate is, as we have seen, the tactic that brings the new wealth of the urban merchant classes into the country and wins them, in a generation or two, recognition as social partners from their longer-established neighbours. But even Admiral and Mrs Croft do not seem to intend to purchase an estate, but instead seem content to rent Kellynch Hall from Anne's father. Austen's version of the naval identity seems resistant to the social mechanism that characteristically assimilates new wealth to old in Britain's long eighteenth century. One might read the sailors of *Persuasion* as the most subversive characters in Austen's fiction, as the only ones who feel no *need* for the social recognition of the gentry, the navy's very 'national importance' (the novel's final words), as demonstrated by its role in the defeat of Napoleon, guaranteeing them a respected place in British society by other means. Indeed, taking these two differences together (the radical alteration of the courtship plot and the absence of a gentry hero) suggests that Anne's marriage to Wentworth, rather than embodying a hope for continuity with the past, represents rather a cancelling out of the past, and the prospect of starting again from scratch.

Not only is the hero not a member of the landowning classes but the representatives of the gentry offered by the novel are a particularly unimpressive bunch. Sir Walter Elliot, Anne's father, consists of nothing but family pride and personal vanity, with no discernible love for any of his three daughters. His fixation with the baronetage, and the record of his family's historical continuity that it provides, is abstracted from any real sense of the landowner's duties towards tenants and other dependants that, in men like Darcy or Knightley, legitimates this inherited social position. Elizabeth Bennet and Emma Woodhouse are struck by the social power and historical continuity embodied in the very buildings of Pemberley and Donwell Abbey: their age and size are meaningful because of the values that they embody. Here, in contrast, Anne is struck by her father's (and elder sister's) delight in their rented suite in Bath:

> She might not wonder, but she must sigh that her father should feel no degradation in his change; should see nothing to regret in the duties and dignity of the resident land-holder; should find so much to be vain of in the littlenesses of a town; and she must sigh, and smile, and wonder too, as Elizabeth threw open the folding-doors, and walked with exultation from one drawing-room to the other, boasting of their space, at the possibility of that woman, who had been mistress of Kellynch Hall, finding extent to be proud of between two walls, perhaps thirty feet asunder.
>
> (II.iii.129)

It is Anne who visits 'almost every house in the parish' to say goodbye when they leave Kellynch, not the landlord himself or his eldest daughter. The country estate has become, for Sir Walter, a sign of status detached from any corresponding set of social responsibilities. The younger Mr Elliot, heir to the Kellynch estate, is initially estranged from Anne's family by his real contempt for the trappings of lineage. In Bath, however, this contempt is strategically masked for the purposes of ingratiating himself with the widowed Sir Walter in an attempt to prevent him from remarrying and thereby, potentially, producing a son who would then take his place as heir. In any case, Mr Elliot is revealed as cruelly selfish in II.ix and likely to be an even worse landlord than Sir Walter.

The other landowning family represented in the novel, the Musgroves of Uppercross, represent a more complex case. The father and mother, living in the 'Great House', 'substantial and unmodernised' (I.v.35), are themselves 'in the old English style . . . friendly and hospitable, not much educated, and not at all elegant' (I.v.38–9). The daughters Henrietta and Louisa, on the other hand, have been to school, acquired accomplishments [see pp. 2, 24–5], 'and were now, like thousands of other young ladies, living to be fashionable, happy, and merry'. Anne, we are told, 'would not have given up her own more elegant and cultivated mind for all their enjoyments' (I.v.39). Although the narrator warns us that this may be an emotional mechanism on the older Anne's part to protect her from envy, the Musgrove girls are clearly not all that they could be, but they are all that a modern gentry lifestyle and its marriage market requires them to be.

But the generational gap set up by I.v is undercut by the description early in I.vi of the daily life of the whole family, where activities are divided along gender lines, and within the genders unite old and young alike in a shared 'social commonwealth': 'The Mr Musgroves had their own game to guard, and to destroy; their own horses, dogs, and newspapers to engage them; and the females were fully occupied in all the other common subjects of house-keeping, neighbours, dress, dancing, and music' (I.vi.40–1). The position of the heir, Charles Musgrove, is an interesting case in point. Good-natured and respectable, Charles proposed first to Anne, who, still measuring men against the standard of Frederick Wentworth, turned him down; he then was accepted by her younger sister Mary. Mary has never forgiven Anne for being Charles's first choice: but Charles, in the absence of a better wife, has clearly remained stuck in the unimproved masculine gentry world of guns, dogs and horses, when something more could have been made of him, by Anne's agency.

> Anne could believe, with Lady Russell, that a more equal match might have greatly improved him; and that a woman of real understanding might have given more consequence to his character, and more useful-ness, rationality, and elegance to his habits and pursuits. As it was, he did nothing with much zeal, but sport; and his time was otherwise trifled away, without benefit from books, or anything else.
>
> (I.vi.41)

A familiar version of marriage is being evoked here: the Addisonian model discussed in Part 1 [see pp. 9–10], in which it is the role of propertied women in general, and of wives in particular, to inculcate politeness or elegance in their husbands, expanding their narrowly masculine and class-based focus on business, politics or hunting. Anne, in rejecting Charles Musgrove, has rejected this role as an agent of modernisation. The novel tends to suggest that she is right to do so. Her mother had found herself in just this sort of marriage with Sir Walter, and the narrator does not describe her place as a particularly happy one:

> She had humoured, and softened, or concealed his failings, and promoted his real respectability for seventeen years; and though not the very happiest being in the world herself, had found enough in her duties, her friends, and her children, to attach her to life, and make it no matter of indifference to her when she was called to quit them.
>
> (I.i.6)

That friends and children alone attach Lady Elliot to life, and alone make death something other than a matter of indifference to her, suggests a terrible emptiness in her relation to her husband. On the other hand, a more genuinely mutually improving marriage seems in prospect for the lively Louisa Musgrove and the melancholy Captain Benwick: 'he would gain cheerfulness, and she would learn to be an enthusiast for Scott and Lord Byron' (II.vi.157). But then Louisa and Benwick are the novel's representatives of the fickleness of youth. Anne even jokes to herself that Louisa's knock on the head in Lyme Regis in chapter xii has produced this change, as the passage continues,

> . . . of course they had fallen in love over poetry. The idea of Louisa Musgrove turned into a person of literary taste, of sentimental reflection, was amusing, but she had no doubt of its being so. The day at Lyme, the fall from the Cobb, might influence her [Louisa's] health, her nerves, her courage, her character to the end of her life, as thoroughly as it appeared to have influenced her fate.
>
> (II.vi.157)

A contrast between Anne and Benwick, both grieving lost loves, has already been set up in I.xi, where Anne contrasts her feminine constancy to Wentworth's memory with Benwick's masculine redirection: 'He is . . . younger in feeling, if not in fact; younger as a man. He will rally again, and be happy with another' (I.xi.91). Both parties' ability to change makes the imagined Addisonian marriage between them a suitable one, for such a marriage depends upon the ability of each to change the other. Anne is not like this, and fortunately, as it turns out, neither is Wentworth. The plot of *Persuasion*, rather than depending on the principal characters' ability to change, depends upon them remaining exactly the same. Or to put this another way, rather than 'character' being constituted as that which can change in order to accommodate an essentially unchanging social reality (as in the other novels) [see pp. 101–3], here the central subjectivity of the novel remains true to itself, to its own memories and emotional commitments, as a source of stability in a society where landlords abandon their estates and heirs-at-law have only contempt for the rank they are to inherit. The general social continuity once guaranteed by gentry rule in the world around Anne is collapsing, at least on the Kellynch estate; the continuity of Anne's emotional life then appears as its internal equivalent and compensation, the survival at the level of personal sentiment of a fixity no longer apparent in the outside world. Anne and Wentworth do not need the promise of a country estate to render them 'settled' at the end of the novel, for their settlement is one of feeling, and not of property.

I noted above that Anne's feeling of emotional superiority over the Musgrove girls is accounted for by the narrator as a defence against envy. Significantly, all that Anne *does* admit to envying Henrietta and Louisa is their 'seemingly perfect good understanding and agreement together' which she does not enjoy with her own sisters: the 'confidence' that we have seen between Elinor and Marianne, and Elizabeth and Jane Bennet, that allows them to combine in mutual understanding against a world determined to impose its own meanings on them. Anne does not, and more importantly her younger self did not, have this resource: her only confidante at their age was Lady Russell, the one whose advice persuaded her to reject Captain Wentworth's offer of marriage in the first place. Lady Russell is not, however, the sympathetic sister, occupying a place in opposition to but also equal to that of her interlocutor. Rather, she is given the place in Anne's life of her late mother, with the authority that accrues to a parent. One should, however, note the context in which this happens: a description of her intervention to prevent Anne's engagement to Wentworth, narrated from Lady Russell's point of view: 'It must not be, if by any fair interference of friendship, any representations from one who had almost a mother's love, and mother's rights, it would be prevented' (I.iv.27). Lady Russell, that is, at least implicitly, *claims for herself* the place of Anne's mother. The use of free indirect discourse here leaves open the possibility that she does so explicitly, as part of her argument against the engagement when discussing it with Anne. Anne herself, we are told (again through free indirect discourse), 'had always loved and relied on' Lady Russell: this is enough to make her submit to her advice, but it falls short of a recognition of the maternal role Lady Russell grants herself. Similarly, we are told that Lady Russell is quickly reconciled to Anne's ultimate marriage to Wentworth, by 'attaching herself as a mother to the man who was securing the happiness of her other child' (II.xii.233). Again, this is Lady Russell's perspective on herself rather than Anne's.

If Anne is unwilling to accept Lady Russell's self-appointed maternal role, it is because she seems to desire to take the place of the mother herself. Although Lady Russell, we are told, loves all three sisters, 'it was only in Anne that she could fancy the mother to revive again' (I.i.7). Anne may be critical, as we have noticed above, of her father's lack of feeling for Kellynch Hall, his readiness to be pleased with any other residence that looks correspondingly expensive; yet on her first return to Kellynch after the Crofts have moved in, she is struck by how little emotion *she* feels for the place, except in its connection to memories of her mother:

> In such moments Anne had no power of saying to herself, "These rooms ought to belong only to us. Oh, how fallen in their destination! How unworthily occupied! An ancient family to be so driven away! Strangers filling their place!" No, except when she thought of her mother, and remembered where she had been used to sit and preside, she had no sigh of that description to heave.
>
> (II.i.117)

I have suggested that the continuity of Anne's feelings are set up by this novel in contrast to the discontinuities in the social world around her. Here, the place of the mother provides the only link between the two, the only site where the shifting of social relations has any purchase on Anne's emotions. The fall of ancient families and their replacement by newly wealthy strangers is a common locus for sentimental effusion in eighteenth-century writing, and a theme familiar to the novel from Maria Edgeworth's fiction set in Ireland such as *Castle Rackrent* (1800), and already, in 1818, from the novels of Walter Scott. At this point, near the end of her career, Austen, like Edgeworth, and unlike Scott, refuses to mourn. The Crofts, whose only claim to the estate is that they can afford to rent it, are nevertheless better landlords than the family who have lived there for generations. I noted above that Anne's 'settlement' at the end of the novel is one of feeling, and not of property. What is significant here is perhaps less the priority of feeling over property, as the fact that these two are opposed in the first place. We saw in Part 1 how Burke aligns sentiment with landownership and other inherited social institutions [see pp. 31–2]: in *Persuasion*, only the maternal link between mother and daughter seems to lend the inheritance of an estate any legitimacy on the basis of feeling or of the instinctive loyalties that according to Burke are the ground of social cohesion.

It should, however, be observed that the maternal role at stake here is not that of the sentimental educator of children, the affective centre of the home and inculcator of Christian values, that made the English mother so important to the rhetoric of anti-revolutionary writers of the 1790s [see pp. 34–5, 127–30]. Little is said about the late Lady Elliot's effect in this regard, and nothing at all about Anne's wanting children of her own to love and educate. The examples of maternal feeling we come across in the novel tend to be problematic. Mary cannot wait to leave her injured son to Anne's care in order to spend a social evening at the Great House. Anne proposes maternal feeling as a general fact of human nature: 'A sick child is always the mother's property, her own feelings generally make it so'; but Mary crossly inverts this: 'You, who have not a mother's feelings, are a great deal the properest person' (I.vii.53–4). Anne is left with the consolation that she is, indeed, 'of the first utility to the child' (I.vii.55); of more utility, that is, than its actual mother. Even more striking is the mockery visited by the narrator in the following chapter on the elder Mrs Musgrove, Charles's mother, for her sentimental mourning of a son who had died early in an unpromising naval career which included a spell under Wentworth's command: a mockery so unsparing that the narrator feels obliged to apologise for it. This merely has the effect of extending the satire, in a series of ironic generalisations, for another paragraph.

> Captain Wentworth should be allowed some credit for the self-command with which he attended to her large fat sighings over the destiny of a son, whom alive nobody had cared for.
>
> Personal size and mental sorrow have certainly no necessary proportions. A large bulky figure has as good a right to be in deep affliction, as the most graceful set of limbs in the world . . .
>
> (I.viii.63–4)

A curious disgust with the maternal body finds expression in this satire of the emotional self-indulgence with which it is equated. What matters to Anne is not this kind of sentimental connection between mother and son which finds expression only in death, but the social power that the place of the mother represents: the sheer social recognition that being a landed lady demands and that she is able to bestow on others. We hear nothing of the late Lady Elliot's education of her daughters: we *do* hear that she was the only one with the taste to appreciate Anne's piano-playing (I.vi.44). Hence the important memory Anne has of her mother is of one who 'presides', not one who feels. For Burke [see pp. 31–2] reverence is due to political constitutions on a parallel with the reverence due to fathers and grandfathers: here Austen identifies affective social continuity with a particular version of the mother. Hence, it is striking that when Lady Russell advises Anne to think seriously about Mr Elliot as a possible husband, she no longer lays claim to the place of the mother; rather, the one powerful incentive she can offer Anne to accept the heir of Kellynch Hall is the prospect of Anne's thereby taking the place of her mother herself.

> "... to look forward and see you occupying your dear mother's place, succeeding to all her rights, and all her popularity, as well as to all her virtues, would be the highest possible gratification to me ..."
> ... For a few moments her imagination and her heart were bewitched. The idea of becoming what her mother had been; of having the precious name of 'Lady Elliot' revived in herself; of being restored to Kellynch, calling it her home again, her home for ever, was a charm which she could not immediately resist.
>
> (II.v.150)

But she does not trust Elliot, and she is right not to, and the novel ends with this alternative, matriarchal version of social continuity being rejected together with its patriarchal counterpart.

Along with the novel's rejection of the Addisonian model of marriage comes a shift in the role of conversation. We have seen an ideal of conversation deployed in the other novels as the pleasurable medium of social cohesion in the propertied classes: conversation as the means whereby the interlocutors confirm each other in their common membership of an elite social group. In *Persuasion*, two important conversations have meaning in relation not to the identity of the speakers but to that of a third party who overhears them. The first of these is Louisa's conversation with Wentworth in I.x, overheard by Anne. This interrupts Anne's consoling recollection of poetry on the autumnal countryside around them with a consciousness of a real passion between the other two. Commenting on Admiral Croft's inability to drive a carriage, Louisa comments:

> "... If I loved a man, as she loves the Admiral, I would be always with him, nothing should ever separate us, and I would rather be overturned by him, than driven safely by anybody else."
> It was spoken with enthusiasm.
> "Had you?" cried he, catching the same tone; "I honour you!" And there was silence between them for a little while.

Anne could not immediately fall into quotation again. The sweet
scenes of autumn were for a while put by . . .

(I.x.78–9)

The episode appears to contrast the private, inward '*pleasure*' (I.x.78; italics in
the original) Anne derives from the inner recitation of verse to the social pleasure
derived by Louisa and Wentworth from their mutual recognition; the originality
and spontaneity ('enthusiasm') of that exchange with the clichéd nature of the
poetry ('some few of the thousand poetical descriptions extant of autumn',
I.x.78); and the erotic suggestiveness of Louisa's hypothesis, with its evocation
of a pleasurable danger in being 'driven' and 'overturned', with Anne's desire
'not to be in the way of any body' (I.x.78). And yet this scene of enthusiastic
mutual recognition is itself a cliché borrowed from the fiction of sentimentalism;
for the reader of Austen's other novels, it is additionally reminiscent of the
similar exchanges between Marianne Dashwood and Willoughby in *Sense and
Sensibility*. If its effect is to stop the poetic musings in Anne's mind, it as effectively silences the other two as well. And the plot of the novel will confirm that
the bond between Louisa and Wentworth that might seem to be established here
is indeed a superficial and short-lived one. What Anne overhears is a mistake: her
interpretation of it, the melancholy produced in her by it, is also a mistake.

The second crucial such conversation, in II.xi, between Anne and Captain
Harville, overheard this time by Wentworth, is the climax of the novel. This takes
the form of a long debate about the respective capacities for emotional fidelity
of men and women. It begins with Harville's reference to Benwick's rediscovery of
love with Louisa after the death of his fiancée, Harville's sister Fanny.

"Poor Fanny! she would not have forgotten him so soon!"
"No," replied Anne, in a low feeling voice. "That I can easily
believe."
"It was not in her nature. She doated on him."
"It would not be in the nature of any woman who truly loved."
Captain Harville smiled, as much as to say, "Do you claim that for
your sex?" and she answered the question, smiling also, "Yes. We certainly do not forget you, so soon as you forget us. It is, perhaps, our fate
rather than our merit. We cannot help ourselves. We live at home, quiet,
confined, and our feelings prey upon us. You are forced on exertion. You
have always a profession, pursuits, business of some sort or other, to
take you back into the world immediately, and continual occupation
and change soon weaken impressions."

(II.xi.218)

This discussion tends to the general, with no explicit reference to individuals
present in the room, in contrast to the earlier one between Wentworth and Louisa
('If *I* loved a man . . .'; '*I* honour you'). Yet it has particular effect, allowing
Anne to communicate something to Wentworth which the laws of feminine modesty make it impossible to communicate in any more direct way [see pp. 8, 18, 35,
126–7]. Anne's evocation of feminine confinement, that is, is the means whereby
she escapes that confinement.

Half way through, Wentworth, writing at a nearby table, drops his pen, and Anne becomes aware that he must be overhearing their conversation. Rather than stopping, she carries on, consciously conveying to Wentworth a meaning unavailable to her ostensible listener.

> "... All the privilege I claim for my own sex (it is not a very enviable one, you need not covet it) is that of loving longest, when existence or when hope is gone."
> She could not immediately have uttered another sentence; her heart was too full, her breath too much oppressed.
>
> (II.xi.221)

Rather than alluding to the physical, as did Louisa's speech in I.x, Anne's speech here has physical effects, both on Wentworth and on herself. After Wentworth has dropped his pen, Anne's speech goes on to complain about male control of the writing of books and thus of descriptions of feminine behaviour: 'the pen has been in their hands' (II.xi.220). Wentworth picks up his pen again to respond directly, with a proposal of marriage, to Anne's indirect assurance of her continuing love for him. The effect of Anne's speech, that is, has been to interrupt and redirect the course of masculine writing, to have an effect on a masculine world of letters, without her picking up the pen herself.

In both these episodes, we find polite conversation put to something other than its usual social purpose: rather than creating solidarity between the speakers, its meaning lies in the response of a third party, ostensibly outside the context of the exchange. I have quoted from only two examples of such conversations, but this triangular structure is much more frequently repeated in the way in which characters *look* at each other. At I.xi.87 Anne worries about the way in which she and Wentworth, together once more, would look to Lady Russell. In the following chapter, in her first, wordless, encounter with Mr Elliot at Lyme, she sees Wentworth seeing the stranger noticing her, and understands the glance that he then turns on her, 'which seemed to say, "That man is struck with you,—and even I, at this moment, see something like Anne Elliot again" ' (I.xii.97). At Bath, Anne's elder sister will not, at first, acknowledge an earlier acquaintance with Wentworth: 'it grieved Anne to observe that Elizabeth would not know him. She saw that he saw Elizabeth, that Elizabeth saw him, that there was complete internal recognition on each side' (II.vii.166) but there is no outward expression of this recognition; and in the same chapter she sees the same gaze at Wentworth, and the same refusal of acknowledgement, from Lady Russell (II.vii.168). Climactically, and disastrously, she sees Wentworth seeing her together with Mr Elliot, now introduced to her, at the concert in II.viii, from which he concludes the rumours concerning their engagement to be true.

The effect of this triangulation of speech and gaze is to suggest a world of emotional and erotic action occurring not within but on the boundaries of polite sociability. There is nothing reassuring about the overheard conversation, the glimpsed gaze between two other people: their meaning for the listener or the observer is not already decided by the rules of politeness, but is left open, remaining undecided until further direct speech with the parties involved. One might compare these observed glances to the multitude of mirrors which Admiral

Croft is disturbed to find equipping Kellynch Hall. Sir Walter is addicted to the gaze, but all he sees is his own gaze, confirming his own high opinion of himself without any possibility of disturbance. This might provide us with an image of elite society in general as portrayed in this novel as a class trapped in its own self-image, trapped by the very success of polite convention in reflecting back from every surface the expected confirmation of its superiority. There are other forms of recognition between subjects at work here, however, whose meaning depends on the conventions of politeness, but which ultimately escape those conventions. Not only, then, does Anne's marriage to Wentworth give her a different sort of destiny to that of Austen's other heroines: the means by which she arrives at that destiny are similarly different to Lizzy's, Fanny's and Emma's negotiation of the codes of politeness.

On *Persuasion* in Part 3: on emotions and the mind, see Adela Pinch and Alan Richardson [**pp. 130–4**]; on narration, see D.A. Miller [**p. 110**]; on individualism, see Julia Brown [**p. 115**]; on feminism, see Margaret Kirkham [**p. 128**]; on the imperial context, see Suvendrini Perera and Clara Tuite [**pp. 136–7, 141–2**].

3

Criticism

Introduction

It is impossible to introduce every significant critical work on Austen in the space of a single chapter, and that is not what this part of the book attempts to do. Nor does it try to be a history of the critical reception of Austen from her own time to ours: see the introductions to Southam (1968a, 1987) for this. Rather, this part is structured around a series of issues which have been the focus of critical debate. It pays particular attention to those issues most hotly debated in the last fifteen years or so. The central three sections outline criticism informed by three of the most easily identifiable strains of contemporary critical thinking: the relation of writing to power informed variously by Karl Marx and Michel Foucault; feminism; and postcolonial theory. But the first section, on aspects of the style and narrative structure of the novels, cannot avoid critics who have their own theoretical commitments, and in particular those whose approach to Austen is informed by queer studies.

Style, plot and morality

The origins of academic criticism of Austen

The reputation of Austen's fiction may have suffered initially from the revolution in the scope of the novel initiated by Scott [see pp. 37–8]; but later in the nineteenth century it rapidly accumulated a particularly dedicated readership and Austen became once more a popular novelist. Indeed, by the end of the century Austen was 'popular' in a way that she was not in her lifetime. The process of fragmentation in the literary marketplace that we saw beginning then [see pp. 32–3] had continued, with book production divided along lines of the class, gender and generation of the various readerships in the way that we today take for granted. The spread of literacy in the working class, and the development of wood-pulp paper and powered presses allowing books to be mass produced and within the price range of the lower middle classes, had abolished the idea that to be a reader was necessarily to belong to an elite. In the twentieth century, for critics and commentators to call Austen 'popular' no longer simply means, as it did in her own time, that she had a lot of readers; rather, it means that she had a certain type of reader, one unwilling to rise to the challenges of more decidedly 'literary' novels, perhaps one looking for comfort rather than difficulty, familiarity rather than strangeness, in their experience of fiction.

Commenting in 1905 on the rise in Austen's popularity over the previous fifty years, Henry James, a novelist whose own practice is deeply indebted to Austen's, suggests that the tide of appreciation has risen above 'the high-water mark . . . of her intrinsic merit and interest', but then

> we are dealing here in some degree with the tides so freely driven up, beyond their mere logical reach, by the stiff breeze of the commercial, in other words of the special bookselling spirit. . . . For these distinctively mechanical and overdone reactions, of course, the critical spirit, even in its most relaxed mood, is not responsible. Responsible, rather, is the body of publishers, editors, illustrators, producers of the pleasant twaddle of magazines; who have found their 'dear', our dear, everybody's dear, Jane so infinitely to their material purpose, so amenable to pretty reproduction in every variety of what is called tasteful, and in what seemingly proves to be saleable, form.
>
> (Southam 1987: 230)

For James, the critic must rescue a true estimation of Austen from the 'mechanical' and 'material' pressures of an industrialised book trade: must save Austen, in a way, from the majority of her readers. In the following decades, what James calls 'the critical spirit' in the UK and North America was increasingly institutionalised in (mostly recently established) departments of English Literature in the universities. One of the things this newish academic discipline had to do was establish a canon, that is, a body of especially valuable work about which students need to be taught. And, clearly, Austen's popularity could not be entirely explained in James's commercial terms. Her fans included ardent upper-class devotees, aesthetes who turned Austen into a cult and called themselves 'Janeites': see the various discussions of this phenomenon in Lynch (2000). Academic critics who wished to include Austen in the canon were, like Henry James, anxious about this pre-existing popularity: for why teach something that lots of people enjoy anyway?

The classic expression of this anxiety is the essay by D.W. Harding, 'Regulated Hatred: An Aspect of the Work of Jane Austen'. This essay first appeared in 1940 in *Scrutiny*, an influential journal of literary and cultural criticism published out of Cambridge University by F.R. and Q.D. Leavis (of whom more below). Harding sets himself the task of reclaiming Austen from precisely the people who are her most enthusiastic admirers, because, he argues, they like her for the wrong reasons. What is more, these are wrong reasons already anticipated by Austen: 'her books are, as she meant them to be, read and enjoyed by precisely the sort of people whom she disliked; she is a literary classic of the society which attitudes like hers, held widely enough, would undermine' (Harding 1963: 167).

The key to Harding's argument is Austen's portrayal of the general society in which her characters move: the 'common life' that we have already discussed in relation to *Northanger Abbey* [see pp. 41, 47–8]. Most readers of Austen, says

Harding, regard this society as a lost ideal of polite social interaction, and Austen as 'expressing the gentler virtues of a civilised social order' (Harding 1963: 166). Twentieth-century fans thus find in Austen an escape from the contemporary nightmare of class conflict and industrialised warfare.

But, according to Harding, Austen also allows more observant readers to find in her novels an account of her society as its own sort of nightmare. He identifies a number of points where such a reading seems to be invited. In *Northanger Abbey*, Henry Tilney expostulates with Catherine Morland at the absurdity of projecting her Gothic fantasies onto a contemporary England which is Christian, modern, made public by newspapers and roads, and 'where every man is surrounded by a neighbourhood of voluntary spies' (II.ix.186) [see p. 42]. In *Persuasion*, Anne's elder sister tries to console herself for having failed to make a catch of their cousin Mr Elliot: his being widowed might not have been an objection, 'but he had, as by the accustomary intervention of kind friends they had been informed, spoken most disrespectfully of them all' (I.i.10). And in *Emma*, Miss Bates 'stood in the very worst predicament in the world for having much of the public favour; and she had no intellectual superiority to make atonement to herself, or frighten those who might hate her into outward respect' (I.ii.22). The polite intercourse that occupies much of the novels is revealed at such moments as a façade; neighbours are in fact spies, friends take pleasure in causing pain, and intelligence in a single woman of slender means (such as Austen herself as well as Miss Bates, Harding observes) can only be used as a private consolation or a means of intimidating others from treating one with contempt.

> This eruption of fear and hatred into the relationships of everyday social life is something that the urbane admirer of Jane Austen finds distasteful; it is not the satire of one who writes securely of her civilised acquaintances. And it has the effect, for the attentive reader, of changing the flavour of the more ordinary satire amongst which it is embedded.
>
> (Harding 1963: 169)

That is, Austen's apparent commitment to genteel civility is ironic: she is really attacking what she seems on the surface to confirm. The majority of Austen's readers find this distasteful because the 'spies' referred to by Henry Tilney, the 'kind friends' ironised in *Persuasion*, the 'public' that fears and loathes poor Miss Bates, represent not only the generality of society in these novels, or in Austen's time, but the generality of Austen's contemporary readers too, 'precisely the sort of people whom she disliked'.

Now, the first two parts of this book have tried to place Austen's work in the specific historical (political and cultural) context of the early nineteenth century, and Harding seems here to be erasing the difference between that context and his own, by imagining most of Austen's original readers to be interchangeable with most of those in 1940. Yet he may have a point, in so far as the reassurance that Austen offers modern middle- and upper-class readers depends on precisely this collapsing of historical difference. Such readers could only identify with the 'gentility' represented in her fiction if they were able to remove it from the historical context in which it performed a specific political function [see pp. 7–8]. By imagining this set of manners, apparently secure in its privilege, as continuous with their own, the modern propertied classes imagine their own values as timeless, and a secure escape from the violence and vulgarity of twentieth-century democratic Britain or America. This is to use Austen for conservative political ends, and while not identical to the conservatism of Austen's own time, it follows the pattern of Burke's construction of a present England defined by its attachment to a past from which it has gradually developed [see pp. 31–2]. One might also note the politics of Harding's own argument, however. Implicitly, Austen's true meaning, as encoded in her irony, can only be appreciated by the critical few. These few are those who are, like Austen, alienated enough from their social world to perceive its underlying cruelty. This alienation may of course (though not in Harding's case) result in teaching posts in English Literature departments: a position like Harding's serves to legitimate academic criticism as that which can discover the meaning of the text distinct from the pleasure it offers non-specialised readers.

Out of the establishment and expansion of English Literature as an academic discipline came new modes of teaching and criticising texts. One of the most successful of these, from the 1940s on, was referred to as the New Criticism, associated with American critics such as Cleanth Brooks (*The Well Wrought Urn*, 1947) and W.K. Wimsatt (*The Verbal Icon*, 1954). For such critics, the literary text is an aesthetic object that combines variety with a particular type of wholeness: it is judged by the complexity that it manages to unify within itself by various technical means such as paradox, irony and different kinds of patterning. It can thus be understood without reference to its author's intentions, the society in which she wrote, or the reader's response. As a work of art, the literary text is also an end in itself: it is not there to teach us a moral or make us better people, but only to give us a specifically *aesthetic* pleasure, an experience of completion denied us in the real world outside. Because it attends only to the organisation of the text in itself, New Criticism is a type of *formalist* criticism.

Even before the New Critics, something like their formalist approach appears in Mary Lascelles's 1939 book *Jane Austen and her Art*. A large part of Lascelles's book concerns Austen's biography, her roots in eighteenth-century literature, and her development as an artist from the early unpublished works onwards. When she turns to the novels themselves, however, these are praised in terms of their formal capacity to unify and harmonise the various elements of the text. For example, her characters' speech is diverse enough to strongly mark different characters, yet similar enough to be recognisable as versions of a single idiom. This technique Lascelles calls 'shallow modelling' or 'low relief', expressions borrowed from the plastic arts (Lascelles 1995: 94). Similarly, nothing is included in the novels which is not necessary for the story, and this gives them their particular 'integrity' (147); overall, stylistic effects are achieved by '[d]elicate precision, resulting from control of the tools chosen' (115). A later example of a New Critical approach to Austen is Reuben Brower's 1951 essay 'Light and Bright and Sparkling: Irony and Fiction in *Pride and Prejudice*' (Watt 1963: 62–75). Brower's delight is in the formal perfection of this novel: the 'complexity' (65) and 'shape' (69) of its dialogues in particular. Brower admits that, as well as forming a complex but unified whole, *Pride and Prejudice* also makes reference to the world outside art. But even this representation of reality figures in his argument as one more element included with others in an aesthetic unity. The novel's 'triumph' is 'to balance a purely ironic vision with credible presentation of a man and woman undergoing serious "change of sentiment" ' (75). These discussions of the novel in terms of its 'shape' perhaps finds their ultimate expression in Dorothy van Ghent's *The English Novel: Form and Function*, where the formal perfection of *Pride and Prejudice* is represented by a symmetrical diagram of its plot (Van Ghent 1953: 105).

Morality

However, purely formalist or New Critical accounts of Austen are fairly rare. Most critics in the 1940s, 1950s and 1960s connect the formal or aesthetic qualities of her novels with a moral code that they embody. We have already seen this in D.W. Harding. Austen's irony, the capacity of her prose to say one thing and mean another, is the formal technique which allows her to write in the language of genteel society while simultaneously exposing its moral rottenness. Similarly, for F.R. Leavis in *The Great Tradition* (1948), Austen's greatness lies in her development of an aesthetic form that perfectly embodies her moral interests.

> [H]er interest in 'composition' is not something to be put against her interest in life; nor does she offer an 'aesthetic' value that is separable from her moral significance. The principle of organization, and the principle of development, in her work is an intense moral interest of her own in *life* that is in the first place a preoccupation with certain problems that life compels on her as personal ones. . . .
> As a matter of fact, when we examine the formal perfection of *Emma*, we find that it can be appreciated only in terms of the moral preoccupations that characterize the novelist's peculiar interest in life.
> (Leavis 1948: 16)

This places Austen at the head of a line of novelists who together exemplify 'what is great in English fiction': George Eliot, Henry James and Joseph Conrad. But Austen herself receives little further attention in Leavis's book.

For an account of *Emma*'s union of formal perfection and moral significance we must turn instead to Wayne Booth's ground-breaking *The Rhetoric of Fiction* (1961). Booth is able to give a convincing account of exactly *how* this novel so successfully unifies its moral and formal concerns by taking 'form' to mean, in the first place, its handling of narrative point of view. Booth identifies three distinct perspectives on events that the reader is offered and which the text intertwines: Emma's own, Knightley's authoritative commentary, and that of a reliable third-person narrator. That so much of the novel is narrated from Emma's point of view is important, says Booth, because too many of her actions are in and of themselves those of a spoilt and selfish child, and this would alienate the reader from her as a character right from the start: only if we see those actions as *she* sees them can we be brought to care what happens to her. In fact, this technique allows us to know more about Emma than she does about herself, as her moral errors are only possible because her perspective on herself is limited and uncritical. The reader also has access to the critical perspectives of Knightley and the narrator, and can thus combine the sympathy brought about by intimacy with a recognition of Emma's faults of which she is, at first, incapable. What Emma must learn to do, on Booth's reading, is to see herself as the reader can.

It is worth spelling out Booth's critical strategy here. A *moral* problem in Emma's character (pride, which comes down to a lack of self-awareness) produces, or turns into, an *aesthetic* problem for the novel (how to balance sympathy for Emma with recognition of her faults); and this problem can then be solved by a particular narrative technique, the combination of these various points of view. Thus the success of the episode of Emma's insult to Miss Bates on Box Hill and Knightley's subsequent rebuke at III.vii.351–2 [see p. 79], Booth argues, depends on the reader sharing the novel's (and Knightley's) belief in politeness even in the face of someone as boring as Miss Bates: 'If I refuse to blame Emma, I may discover a kind of intellectual enjoyment in the episode ... But I can never enjoy the episode in its full intensity or grasp its formal coherence' (Booth 1961: 263).

Booth's incisive analysis of Austen's handling of point of view starts to explain how her brilliant prose style works in the context of the stories that she tells. What is missing in this account of *Emma* is any sense of a pressing historical or political context in which Emma's education takes place. The reader's distance from Emma is not a historical or political distance, but purely a moral one, and thus a distance that her education, as acted out in the novel, can eventually collapse. Booth admits that values other than these timeless moral ones, 'like money, blood, and "consequence," are real enough in *Emma*, but only as they contribute to or are mastered by good taste, good judgment, and good morality' (Booth 1961: 262). Historically specific values, related to the specific social settlement of Austen's time, are subordinated to moral and aesthetic values that are shared (the implication is) by Austen's society and our own.

Booth's reading of *Emma* links the moral purpose of the novel with two of its formal features: the nature of the prose in which it is written (for example, its handling of point of view); and the nature of the story that it tells (its narrative structure). This section will now proceed by examining what critics have said about each of these in turn. Of course, all the critics mentioned discuss both prose style and narrative structure, but some have more interesting things to say about one than about the other.

Irony, point of view and free indirect discourse

Austen's handling of point of view is often discussed as a form of irony. The representation of a character's perspective on events is ironic if it is not the same as the perspective the reader is being invited to take on those events. Irony in its broadest sense means simply 'saying something other than what is meant', and in this case the novel is telling us about events in one way and requiring the reader to notice that this is not the correct way of seeing them. One of the first to consistently address this aspect of Austen was Marvin Mudrick in *Jane Austen: Irony as Defense and Discovery* (1952). For Mudrick, as his subtitle would suggest, Austen's irony has two dimensions. On the one hand it is a symptom of its author's psychology, a means of defence against feeling, including feeling for those characters whose flaws her prose dissects. This may not be a failing:

> close observation without sympathy, common sense without tenderness, densely imagined representation without passion may not limit the comic novelist at all, may indeed be the ideal instruments for penetrating the polished surface of the bourgeois world to its unyielding material base.
>
> (Mudrick 1952: 36)

Irony suspends the reader's implicit belief in what the novel seems to say, and can thus also serve as a way of demystifying the reader's conventional beliefs and revealing them to be just that, conventions, comfortable but mistaken beliefs designed to hide a less pleasant reality underneath. Hence, Austen's irony in *Emma* is built around the 'deceptiveness of surface' (201) exemplified by the socially accomplished Frank Churchill. Emma Woodhouse, like her author, 'cannot commit humanly . . . her ego will admit nothing but itself' (200) and is thus a creature of the surface. Hence, 'the widening sum of delights in *Emma* is, first of all, our widening recognition of the decisive pertinence with which every word, every action, and every response of Emma's establish her nature, confirm her self-deception, and prepare for her downfall' (202–3). The irony consists in the difference between how Emma sees the world around her and the world readers recognise as her true one. At least readers can recognise this on a second reading, once they have discovered the truth of Frank and Jane's engagement and of Emma's feelings for Mr Knightley. That is, *Emma* is structured by a *narrative* irony, a gap between appearances and truth only eventually revealed by the plot. However, the story eventually rewards both Emma and Frank for their commitment to the surface: they are lucky 'because in their social milieu charm conquers, even as it makes every cruel and thoughtless mistake' (206). 'Charm', for Mudrick, is the means whereby a lack of feeling, ironic distance, makes itself attractive even to good people like George Knightley and Jane Fairfax, and indeed the reader (for an account of the role of the reader in relation to irony, point of view and plot structure, using Reader-Response theory, see Odmark 1981).

Austen's ironic handling of point of view finds its most sophisticated form in the type of narration known as free indirect discourse (also known as free indirect style or free indirect speech). We have already seen this at work in *Sense and Sensibility* and *Emma* in Part 2 [see pp. 52–3, 72–5]. Let us approach the issue of free indirect discourse via a detour through literary history. In his highly influential discussion of the origins of the genre, Ian Watt in *The Rise of the Novel* (1957) argues that the English eighteenth-century novel was set apart from previous prose fiction by its commitment to a certain type of realism [see pp. 17–18]. This commitment was the product of various developments in English culture and society. On the one hand, the philosopher John Locke (1632–1704) had explained the origins of knowledge in our experience of the world around us in *An Essay Concerning Human Understanding* (1690). This argued that our ideas of the world can be said to be true, not because they conform to abstract rules established by mental reasoning alone, but because they correspond to the external world as we perceive it. Knowledge is based on, and confirmed by, our experience of an objective world outside ourselves: this doctrine is called 'empiricism'. At the same time, the increase in the size and wealth of what Watt calls the 'middle class' produced new groups of readers outside the ruling elites. These groups tended to be sceptical about hierarchies of inherited power and inherited social identity. They espoused instead an individualism that was both economic (wealth was something you deserved because you worked for it) and spiritual (the more puritan or fundamentalist versions of English Protestantism asserted that the individual's private relationship with God was more important than that mediated through the church). According to Watt, it is this latter interest in the individual, in subjective experience, that finds expression in the first-person narratives of Richardson and Defoe [see pp. 11, 17]. In *Moll Flanders* (1722) or *Pamela* (1740–1), the leading protagonists describe their lives as they are experienced by themselves, a description inevitably limited by their subjective point of view. But the novels of Henry Fielding (1707–53), such as *Joseph Andrews* (1742) and *Tom Jones* (1749), instead place their emphasis on the objective reality of the world around the protagonists. Their stories are told by a 'third-person' narrator, that is a narrator who is not himself a character in the story, so that all protagonists are referred to in the third person and not the first. Such a narrator can describe everything that happens (that is, he is *omniscient*), and also assumes the authority to pass definitive judgement on the characters and actions he describes. (For the ways in which these novels undermine or call into question the narrator's authority, see Wallace 1995; for Austen's relation to Fielding, see Parker 1998.)

Austen appears in Watt's book as the crucial figure who combines and balances these subjective and objective tendencies in previous English fiction. She shares Richardson's interest in the subjective point of view of the individual on his or her experience, but she combines this with a third-person narrator who is able to provide other perspectives on events (Watt 1957: 308–10). It is in order to tie subjective and third-person perspectives more closely together that Austen develops free indirect discourse. Watt does not in fact identify this style by name in *The Rise of the Novel*: the most useful early discussion of it comes in Norman Page's book, *The Language of Jane Austen* (1972: 122–37). Page is to some extent a formalist critic in the New Critical vein [see p. 94] as he understands this aspect of Austen's style as primarily a source of aesthetic effects such as 'immediacy' or 'concentration' (130), that are in themselves a source of pleasure for the reader. More recently, Clara Tuite has suggested that we understand free indirect discourse in relation to Austen's play with genre. The combination of the limited perspective of a character with a narrative voice capable of revealing those limitations continues at the level of prose style the work of parody done by her early fictions: of the Gothic in *Northanger Abbey*, of the sentimental novel in *Sense and Sensibility* (Tuite 2002: 63, 69). That is, Austen's style must be understood in relation to earlier genres as Watt suggests, but that style criticises and demystifies those genres, rather than simply synthesising them as in Watt's account.

However, as Watt also sees social and political positions at stake in the handling of perspective in eighteenth-century fiction, one might also ask how such issues are played out in Austen's free indirect discourse. Gary Kelly considers this and suggests that by the 1790s, first-person narrative could seem to embody not merely a domesticated individualism such as Richardson's but instead the politically dangerous alienation from society felt by sympathisers with the French revolutionaries [see p. 31]. Austen's use of free indirect discourse to enclose the subjective within a framework of third-person authority can then appear as 'a formal homology for a hierarchical yet open social structure' (Kelly 1997: 161). That is, it expresses at the level of prose style the social settlement between inherited power and new money that characterised Britain in the long eighteenth century [see pp. 8–10] and reaffirms it as an ideal in the post-revolutionary decades. Graham Hough similarly points out that the authority of the third-person narrative voice is produced by its adoption of a particular vocabulary and syntax, specifically that of the moral writing of Samuel Johnson (Hough 1978: 55) [see p. 19]. The various characters in *Emma* (Hough's example) are judged by how closely their diction corresponds to the voice of their narrator, Knightley being closest of all. The moral hierarchy thus produced is comprehensive: everyone can be located at some point within it and rewarded accordingly by the plot. According to A. Walton Litz, this function of 'Knightley as standard' is what prevents the irony of *Emma* becoming the cynical celebration of manipulative surface that Marvin Mudrick sees it as (Litz 1965: 148). It is only thus that the 'local ironies and verbal qualifications' of Emma's misrecognition of her world can be 'directed and organised' towards the novel's moral purposes (147–8).

> [B]y allowing us to share Emma's inner life without being limited by it, Jane Austen has avoided the dichotomy between the sympathetic imagination and critical judgment which runs through the earlier novels. The very form of *Emma* makes such a dichotomy irrelevant.
>
> (149)

This produces a coherence between language, plot and character unique to Austen. But this is not, as Hough points out, the cohesion of the society in which she actually lived, but one produced by resources specific to the novel as a form. In a very useful discussion of Austen's irony, Julia Prewitt Brown argues against Hough and Litz, suggesting that there is no single narrative authority by which the various perspectives of the novel can be judged. Unlike Mudrick, however, she sees this as part of Austen's developing democracy of vision rather than as a symptom of a pathological fear of commitment (Brown 1979: 25–36).

One further account of free indirect discourse should be mentioned here. In their important essay ' "The Tittle-Tattle of Highbury": Gossip and the Free Indirect Style in *Emma*' (1990), Casey Finch and Peter Bowen develop Ian Watt's analysis of Austen's combination of objective and subjective perspectives, but do so in a context informed by the theories of Michel Foucault (1926–84) in, for example, *The Order of Things* (1970) and *Discipline and Punish* (1977). For Foucault, the autonomy of the private conscience from social coercion promised by the Enlightenment, the right to come to one's own conclusions on the basis of objective evidence and the use of one's own reason, is as much a myth as the claims of the church or the monarchy to have a privileged access to truth. For the assumptions from which the private conscience works are as much a product of shared cultural forms as the authority of bishops or kings. The autonomous modern self has simply internalised this authority: rather than the Inquisition or the secret police putting the subject under surveillance, the subject puts himself or herself under surveillance. Authority, rather than being embodied in particular agents of an ecclesiastical or state hierarchy, is dispersed within everyone. As such we tend to mistake it for a simple condition of selfhood, a fact of human nature, and not the effect of a particular type of political power.

For Finch and Bowen, free indirect discourse is the language of this sort of self-surveillance. The apparently private self is made public in this language, but in order for this to be possible that private self must be constructed in a public language to begin with (Finch and Bowen 1990: 5). This shared language allows the narrator to speak with the voice of everyone and no one. The authority of the narrator can then be taken for granted as a fact of human nature. And this 'naturalizing' of narrative authority as free indirect discourse is what it has in common with the gossip of a community like Highbury in *Emma*. 'Both function as forms par excellence of surveillance, and both serve ultimately to locate the subject . . . within a seemingly benign but ultimately coercive narrative or social matrix' (3–4). In this context, Emma's recognition that she really loves Mr Knightley is a recognition of an external social necessity; presumably the necessity of heterosexual union to perpetuate the ruling class, although Finch and Bowen do not specify this. But Emma does not perceive it as such. It seems to her as a revelation about her truest, deepest, if until now unconscious, self, for she has internalised, 'naturalised', this social necessity so completely.

> Free indirect style has here literally created the space of the unconscious as the natural source of Emma's inner desires, which, naturally enough, now discover themselves perfectly aligned with the overriding social imperative the novel has been at pains to establish from the start: "Mr Knightley must marry no one but herself!"
>
> (12)

In a response to Finch and Bowen, Frances Ferguson argues that the marriage plot (to which we will turn in a moment) is in fact in tension with their Foucauldian conception of discourse. We noted above that Finch and Bowen do not seem to explain why Emma (specifically) must marry Mr Knightley (specifically). Ferguson suggests they cannot answer this question, as if social authority is imagined as circulating throughout the community, the characters who articulate it appear interchangeable with each other (Ferguson 2000: 4, 14).

Narrative form: education and the marriage plot

In discussing the relation of prose style to moral message we have inevitably ended up discussing another aspect of form in Austen's novels: her handling of plot, of narrative structure. Narrative structure appears in the paragraphs above on the one hand as itself a medium for irony [see p. 97], and on the other as a means of rewarding the morally good characters with happy endings [see pp. 98–9]. These two allusions to the role of plot can be taken as representative of two ways of understanding the function of plot in Austen: in its relation to the subjective point of view and identity of the protagonists, or alternatively as romance, a plot structured by obstacles to the worldly fulfilment of the virtuous hero and heroine. Broadly speaking, this corresponds to two ways in which critics have discussed Austen's stories: as narratives of individual education or development, and as 'marriage plots'. We will now look at these in turn.

In addressing the narrative of education or subjective development, we should begin by noting that it is possible to see the subjective identity of the novel's protagonists as disconnected from narrative as such. For Howard S. Babb, for example, it is *dialogue* that 'reveals her characters in depth and shows them engaged in the most fundamental activities of personality' (Babb 1962: 5–6). This is to imagine Austen as essentially dramatic in her presentation of character, as it is in the theatre that we (usually) depend upon dialogue to tell us what we know about the protagonists. Because of the negative representation of amateur drama in *Mansfield Park* I.xiii–II.ii [see pp. 68–9], Austen is often imagined as being anti-theatrical. But two recent books have both identified Austen's personal enjoyment of the theatre and established her profound debt to the plays of her time in the construction of her novels (Gay 2002; Byrne 2002). Indeed, these books suggest that Austen can be seen as analysing social life as itself a sort of theatre, in which 'character' is a certain sort of performance offered to the appraising gaze of others. This is not Babb's assumption: dialogue is 'where characters define themselves', and thus where we find the truth about them independently of the particular 'biases' of the heroine's consciousness which colour the third-person narration (Babb 1962: 28).

But generally critics see 'character' as something inward, distinct from any public performance, and as something that changes and develops in the course of the novel as protagonists learn from their experiences. This conception of character can be seen as a product of the Enlightenment [see pp. 6–7] and specifically the theories of John Locke, for whom, as we have noted, all knowledge is the product of experience [see pp. 97–8]. It is in the context of Enlightenment theories of education, particularly those of Locke, that D.D. Devlin places Austen's fiction in *Jane Austen and Education* (1975). Indeed, it is through the theme of education that the novel as a genre most obviously adopts and adapts Enlightenment ideas. The novel of a hero's education is, like the Enlightenment, a Europe-wide phenomenon, and is usually referred to by the German word *Bildungsroman* (which means simply 'novel of education'). Typically, a *Bildungsroman* traces the development of a young person from youth to maturity through a series of encounters with the world in which he or she acquires an adult identity and learns how to be happy. For Franco Moretti in his book *The Way of the World*, this type of novel is the premier 'symbolic form' of modernity (1987: 5), of a society no longer bound fast by inherited tradition, but facing an unpredictable future in which new rules will have to be learnt, new codes developed: hence the *Bildungsroman*'s focus on youth and the unpredictable acquisition of experience. It is an optimistic genre: change is always possible that will allow for human fulfilment.

However, if the plot of the *Bildungsroman* opens up the prospect of unbounded possibilities for change, in its classical form it also works hard to contain those possibilities and reassert the values of the old order. One of Moretti's two examples of the classical *Bildungsroman* is *Pride and Prejudice* (the other is *Wilhelm Meister*, 1795–6, by the German poet and novelist Johann Wolfgang von Goethe). Elizabeth Bennet's capacity to judge Darcy and his friends comes from a distinctly Enlightenment scepticism: her 'prejudice' against Darcy is really 'distrust', and she 'does not err due to a lack – but due to an *excess of criticism*' (58). Speaking of both Elizabeth and Goethe's Wilhelm, the gross errors of these heroes are

> all resulting from their desire to be, 'without any reason', in alterity with the world. From their refusal – weak but stubborn echo of Enlightenment criticism – to trust in it *a priori*, and from their belief that being part of the world should not imply the individual's total assimilation to the whole.
>
> (61)

That is, Elizabeth defines herself in opposition to the world around her, defines herself by her ability to separate herself from it and thus to subject it to rational criticism. But this excess must eventually be curbed, and she must find her place in the world. The world defined by the *Bildungsroman*, says Moretti, is 'everyday life', understood as representing 'an unchallenged stability of social relationships' in contrast to the military and political convulsions endured by Europe in this period (54). For Moretti as for Kelly [see pp. 198–9], but this time at the level of plot rather than narrative discourse, social stability and individual reason are established as complementary rather than in competition.

> if the hero wishes to enjoy absolute freedom in a specific domain of his existence, in other sectors of social activity there must prevail instead complete *conformity*. Everyday life, we have seen, demands the *stability* of social relationships. . . . The omnivorous narcissism of private man has its counterpoint in the timidity that dominates him as soon as he ventures into the larger world.
>
> (Moretti 1987: 55–6)

Note that we have already seen the assumption of the private individual's 'alterity' with the world – the idea that the individual exists prior to the social world with which he or she must then negotiate in the way Moretti describes – identified as a specifically modern conception of personal identity by critics drawing their ideas from Michel Foucault [see p. 99]. A similar argument is developed by Clifford Siskin in a book that appeared shortly after Moretti's, *The Historicity of Romantic Discourse* (1988). For Siskin, the case of the *Bildungsroman* is one example of the emergence of 'narratives of development' more generally (autobiographical texts, fictional and non-fictional, in prose or verse, constituting his other examples). What matters about the 'development' that drives such plots is precisely that it is *internal*: the protagonist becomes happy not primarily by changing their outward circumstances but by changing their 'self' through a process of thinking about that 'self' (since it is the self that is doing the thinking, to think self-reflexively like this is already to embark on a process of change). Our modern category of 'character' is defined in terms of this self-consciousness of change. Psychological 'development' is invented in fiction in the late eighteenth and early nineteenth centuries as a way of coping with social and political upheaval, promising that the revolution can be internal and leave the inherited institutions of society still standing. Siskin's approach thus

> recognises development to be not a truth grounded in human psychology, but a formal strategy for naturalizing social and literary change: it functions to make change appear to make sense. . . . [Austen thus appears as] an author whose texts helped to redefine character as naturally 'round', that is, capable of the ongoing transcendence of developmental change. The self made continuously deeper by interpretative revision became the psychologised subject.
>
> (Siskin 1988: 126)

A contrast between Austen's plot and the traditional 'romance' plot might be helpful at this point. Siskin cites Henry Fielding's novel *Joseph Andrews* (1742), which concludes when a young servant, having defended his moral integrity against various temptations and undergone great tribulations as a result, is discovered, by a series of improbable coincidences, to be the heir to a country estate (having been kidnapped by gypsies when a baby); a discovery which allows him to marry his sweetheart.

> Elizabeth Bennet, on the other hand, knows who her parents are and, following Darcy's lead, decides they are inadequate. How, then, can the social gap be bridged and the marriage occur? In lieu of gypsies and luck, Austen posits what by the early part of the nineteenth century is understood as 'real' behaviour; she psychologises her characters' differences and posits a probable solution: development. They come to love each other as origins are reexamined and newly understood not as absolutely restrictive, but preparatory.
>
> (Siskin 1988: 139)

Darcy's pride and Elizabeth's prejudice are 'psychologised' by being recast as qualities of their individual minds that can be overcome by self-analysis, rather than aspects of their political identities as members of different classes.

This is 'real' behaviour and a 'probable' story primarily in contrast to the 'unreality' of romance plots like that of *Joseph Andrews*, rather than because the 'psychology' posited is that of actually existing people in the real world. However, several critics have recently noted that Austen is working within the context of new theories of perception and the mind, the origins of the discipline that we now call psychology, which might relate to her innovative portrayal of this 'deep' or 'developmental' self. Adela Pinch, in *Strange Fits of Passion* (1996), locates Austen's treatment of emotions as the objects of knowledge at the end of the eighteenth-century sentimentalist tradition of David Hume and Adam Smith [see pp. 20–1]. In *Persuasion*, Pinch finds their commitment to the 'social virtues' of feeling combined with a new scepticism about being able to know what one's own feelings *are*. In particular, this novel 'seems to break down the distinction between persuasions from without and internal states and desires' (1996: 154), calling into question the 'naturalness' of inner feeling and thus the 'alterity' of self from world that Moretti suggests is the precondition of the *Bildungsroman*. Alan Richardson also takes *Persuasion* as his example in *British Romanticism and the Science of Mind* (2001). But rather than looking back to the eighteenth century, he sees Austen as drawing on up-to-the-minute versions of the mind given in an emerging neuroscience. He notes that, when Louisa Musgrove bangs her head in her fall in Lyme Regis (I.xii.102–3), it permanently changes her character, suggesting that Austen is working with the material, physiological account of personality that was beginning to circulate in her time. Both Pinch and Richardson follow Susan Morgan's *In the Meantime* (1980) in arguing (against D.D. Devlin) that Austen does not follow John Locke's model of human perception and learning, with its clear distinction between an outer material world and an inner immaterial consciousness. It is indeed striking that it is through contemporary, post-Lockean theories of the mind, and not through questions of literary genre, that recent critics, again following Morgan, have most persistently linked Austen to Romanticism as a literary movement [see pp. 26–9]. Margaret Doody's (2001) essay on memory in Austen and the German Romantic poet J.C.F. Schiller, and Nicholas Dames's related article on 'Austen's Nostalgics' (2001), are another two cases in point.

On the other hand, Lauren Goodlad's essay on 'Self-Disciplinary Self-Making' in *Sense and Sensibility* sees 'realist psychology' and 'romantic character' as two quite distinct discourses within which the self can be described. We ended our discussion of irony and free indirect discourse by looking at Finch and Bowen's use of Michel Foucault's ideas; we can end our discussion of Austen and the *Bildungsroman* in a similar way with Goodlad's incisive analysis. Elinor's story in *Sense and Sensibility* exemplifies the self-liberation, the autonomy from an oppressive political reality, offered by the modern 'self-regulation' or 'self-discipline' that Foucault describes. But for Goodlad, as for the German Romantics but not for Foucault, this self-invention through self-scrutiny is still 'a potentially emancipatory act of political resistance' (Goodlad 2000: 62). This depends, says Goodlad, on a tension between 'psychology' and 'character', as Elinor must be both the object of her own observation, and the observer who grows as a result. Admittedly this tension collapses towards the end of the novel, and Elinor turns from a realistic character to a mere representative of 'selfless domesticity' (73). Generally, though, Goodlad is interested in the ways in which the interiorisation of social discipline that Foucault describes offers empowerment to the self rather than mere conformity to social ideals, so that 'power's rule over consciousness depends at least partly upon a self that has consciousness of power' (78).

The other set of terms in which critics often discuss Austen's narrative is its ending in marriage. If the novel of education is a specifically Enlightenment form, the marriage plot uses a much older set of generic conventions: the conventions of comedy, and specifically romantic comedy. This is a genre developed first of all on the stage, in English most notably by Shakespeare, and to which the eighteenth-century novel has a profound structural debt. The comic plot can be understood in purely aesthetic terms, as a source of pleasure for the reader who knows roughly how it is going to end up (in the marriage of the hero and heroine), and who is put in a state of pleasurable suspense by the obstacles that delay this ending.

To think of Austen's novels in these terms is thus to bring questions of *gender* to the centre of our attention. For where the *Bildungsroman* plot explores the subject's development as a character and is, in principle, available to a protagonist of either gender, the choice of a marriage partner is a fraught one for young women as it is not for young men [**see p. 24**]. The *Bildungsroman* plot allows the character to assert an identity distinct from that imposed by society; the marriage plot insists on the heroine's eventual submission to the overwhelming social imperative for women to marry. Susan Fraiman, in her chapter on *Pride and Prejudice* in *Unbecoming Women* (1993), argues that the female *Bildungsroman* cannot offer us a single story about its heroine, the story of her education. Rather, alongside the 'tale of Elizabeth's enlightenment as to Darcy's true character and her own true feelings' there is another, 'overlapping tale of her "humiliation" ' (Fraiman 1993: 10). So there are two Elizabeth Bennets: 'a character introduced as reliable, whose clarity of vision is obviously the author's own, is re-presented – in the context of her marriageability – as prejudiced' (82). For Stuart Tave, similarly, there is a discontinuity in Austen's novels between their stories of female education and their happy endings. Where the male *Bildungsroman* hero reaches happiness by learning, what Austen's heroines learn is precisely to accept a seemingly inevitable unhappiness. Then an unpredictable plot twist allows them a happy ending anyway. For the heroines, this

> happy ending is not guaranteed by their actions. What seems to be more important than the sudden and fortunate event, however, because it precedes the ending again and again, in whatever manner the end is produced, is that the heroine be prepared to accept unhappiness.
>
> (Tave 1973: 17–18)

This disjunction between two types of ending, between the end of a learning process and finding happiness in marriage, can be understood as produced by the gap between Austen's feminist agenda [**see pp. 24–5, 126–34**] and the demands of the genre in which she is writing (Shaffer 1992: 52–3). In drawing attention to this split, feminist critics [**see pp. 124–34**] have also drawn attention to the extent to which critics generally, on the contrary, tend to collapse the difference between these two elements in Austen's plot. Wayne Booth, for example [**see pp. 95–6**], sees *Emma*'s marriage as the result of, and reward for, her increased self-knowledge: 'The good for Emma includes both her necessary reform and the resulting marriage. Marriage to an intelligent, amiable, good and attentive man is the best thing that can happen to this heroine' (Booth 1961: 260). This is one instance of what Claudia Johnson has called the 'Girl Being Taught a Lesson' model of narrative analysis of Austen's fiction (Copeland and McMaster 1997: 222). Much later, prompted by feminist criticism, Booth returned to this issue and acknowledged that in fact the marriage plot looks more like a conventional ending demanded by Austen's genre, one which much else in the novel contradicts or undermines. Still, that conventional ending carries its own moral message (happiness for a woman is 'protective instruction and care from the right kind of man') which may drown out 'the moral instruction implicit in everything the author does in other respects' (Booth 1988: 429, 431).

Morality again

In this section we have discussed critics who address problems in Austen's prose style and narrative structure. Many of them, like Booth, have linked these formal aspects of Austen's novels to a moral message that they express. At this point, one should note that by calling the values that are at stake in these novels 'moral' or 'ethical', they tend to assume that these values remain as valid for late twentieth-century readers as they were for Austen's contemporaries. It may be, however, that the values expressed are specific to Austen's society, and moreover to a particular section of that society. Now, there are some commentators on Austen for whom the idea that her values are specific to a historical period different from ours, and the idea that they are universally valid, are not inconsistent. The most notable of these is Alastair MacIntyre in his book *After Virtue* (1981). This study is a critique of that element of the Enlightenment project that tries to discover a universally valid set of moral rules, through the individual's exercise of their own rationality alone, independently of the values that they have inherited from their society. For MacIntyre, this attempt is mistaken from the start: potentially, every individual will use their own reason to come up with their own set of rules, and a society with no shared moral rules will descend into the sort of moral anarchy from which, he argues, we now suffer. Rather, your moral rights and duties are always those that are embedded in particular social practices and a particular idea of 'the good life for man', specific to your own society. Anything else is not really a morality at all. Morality is about fulfilling the duties that you have as a result of the social position in which you find yourself. Developing those personal qualities of character ('virtues') that allow you to do this well will make you happy, and being happy (in this quite specific way) is the end goal of life. However, for this to work, your society needs to be something like the small city-state of classical Greece. Austen, for MacIntyre, assumes a similarly anti-Enlightenment position, although the country neighbourhood has to fill in for the Greek city-state, and a particular idea of marriage has to take the place of a wider vision of 'the good life for man' (MacIntyre 1981: 238–9). Austen's values may be specific to her society, but precisely for that reason they *are* moral values in a way that values that claim to be universally valid cannot be.

MacIntyre's version of ethics is one he traces back to the classical Greek philosopher Aristotle (384–322 BC). He is not the only philosopher to identify Austen as an Aristotelian: Gilbert Ryle did so too, in explicit opposition not to Enlightenment rationalism but to a Christian, and specifically Calvinist, version of ethics (for MacIntyre, Aristotle and Christianity are perfectly compatible). In his essay 'Jane Austen and the Moralists' (Southam 1968b: 106–22) Ryle notes that Austen's 'ethical vocabulary and idioms are quite strongly laced with aesthetic terms' (117), perhaps the reason for that strong connection made by the critics we have looked at between her artistic strategies and her moral message. On the other hand, she is very chary of using explicitly religious vocabulary, preferring (for example) the term 'mind' to the term 'soul' (120; for Austen as an illustration of Aristotelian ethics, see David Gallop's 1999 essay). David Lodge argues that Austen in fact distinguishes sharply between the language of social virtue or good 'manners', and a more properly moral or 'spiritual' vocabulary. This latter vocabulary allows for the individual to go against the group in the name of 'conscience', 'duty' or 'principle' (Lodge 1966: 99). 'Spiritual' these terms may be according to Lodge: it remains true that there is hardly any discussion of religious issues as such in Austen's fiction. More rigorously, Oliver MacDonagh has argued that in fact Austen is deeply engaged with contemporary religious controversy, at least in *Mansfield Park*, but that this is encoded in the text as subtly as her political position (MacDonagh 1991: chapter 1), and there has been at least one full-length study of the 'religious dimension' in Austen's work (Koppel 1988).

Austen is an important writer for MacIntyre because she is the last writer who is able to describe communities where morality can be lived out as the development of 'virtue', but she can only imagine such communities as 'enclaves' (the country neighbourhood, the good marriage) within a modern and already individualistic society (MacIntyre 1981: 238). Aileen Douglas points out, in a critique of MacIntyre's reading of Austen, that the enclosure of morality within the enclave of the home is in fact 'the creation of contemporary ideology', as we noted in Part 1 [see p. 24]. Austen's households are thus a specifically modern moral unit and not 'a shrunken surrogate for the Greek city-state' (Douglas 1999: 151). Austen is moreover intensely aware, as MacIntyre is not, that the domestic ideal she deploys is one she has inherited from other fictions and not from real life (Douglas 1999: 158). MacIntyre is not the only commentator on Austen to ignore the difference between the society Austen represents in her novels and the one she actually lived in. For Q.D. Leavis, for example, the moral vocabulary that Austen inherits from Johnson (see discussion of Graham Hough above, p. 99]) reflected a society that really was unified and coherent as ours is not (Leavis 2000: 124).

A position such as MacIntyre's, arguing for the universal validity of the version of ethics offered by Austen, is unusual among literary critics. More often, the values found in Austen's novels are understood as those of a specific section of society at a specific point in its history, different from those of other groups and in competition with them. They are understood, that is, as *political* values, the expression of a particular political ideology. In the next section, we will discuss critics who have placed Austen in her historical and social context in just this way. But before we move on, it is worth mentioning a few critics who explicitly question the linking of the formal features and moral message of these novels that has been a recurring feature of the critics we have examined so far.

The first of these is Lionel Trilling. In some ways, Trilling's account of Austen is the opposite of MacIntyre's. Where MacIntyre sees her as the last exponent of a pre-modern, pre-individualist idea of virtue, Trilling sees her as the first novelist to grapple with a distinctively modern version of the individual self. In his 1957 essay 'Emma and the Legend of Jane Austen' he identifies the importance of *Emma* precisely in the intensity of Emma Woodhouse's relationship with her self, of her 'moral life' (Trilling 1967: 47). And this moral life, in an apparent paradox, depends on what is otherwise her chief vice, her self-regard: 'Women in fiction only rarely have the peculiar reality of the moral life that self-love bestows' (48). It is this inner moral self-scrutiny which makes her a character with whom modern readers can identify:

> Jane Austen, conservative and even conventional as she was, perceived the nature of the deep psychological change which accompanied the establishment of democratic society – she was aware of the increase of

the psychological burden of the individual, she understood the new necessity of conscious self-definition and self-criticism, the need to make private judgements of reality. And there is no reality about which the modern person is more uncertain and more anxious than the reality of himself.

(Trilling 1967: 54)

Of course, even if this is a recognisably modern version of the self, modern readers may not find Austen's description of it very appealing to read about: her modernity alone cannot account for the popular 'legend' of Jane Austen that Trilling (like James and Harding before him) begins by discussing. Austen's attraction is that she places this modern self in an England which is otherwise a rural idyll, an ideal society in which Emma can come to self-knowledge and control her personal life without this conflicting with the community in which she lives. To suggest the possibility of such a society 'is indeed to make an extraordinary promise and to hold out a rare hope' (61). MacIntyre too posited a specific type of society as a condition for the 'good life', but for MacIntyre this existed in the pre-modern past, specifically in classical Greece. Trilling generously suggests that we 'should not be shocked and repelled' if some, like MacIntyre, 'think there really was a time when such promises and hopes were realized'. But in doing so they turn Austen from a novelist into 'a figure of legend and myth' (Trilling 1967: 61).

In an earlier (1955) essay on *Mansfield Park*, Trilling discusses the darker side of modern selfhood, 'the terrible strain it imposes upon us . . . the exhausting effort which the concept of personality requires us to make' (Watt 1963: 139). The greatness of *Mansfield Park*, he argues, lies precisely in its refusal to dress up the 'uncertainty and difficulty' (135) of modern selfhood in the aesthetic pleasures offered by Emma's Surrey utopia. Austen's irony, so all-pervasive in *Emma*, can appear from the perspective of *Mansfield Park* as 'but the engaging manner by which she masks society's crude coercive power', a power which in *Mansfield Park* is visible 'in all its literal truth, before irony has beglamoured us about it and induced us to be comfortable with it' (126). A Marxist critic [see pp. 120–4] might argue that what Trilling is identifying here is the ideological function of style, its ability to reconcile the reader to uncomfortable social realities by incorporating them in the aesthetic pleasure offered by, for example, beautiful language. Indeed, for Trilling, it is not just that *Mansfield Park* reveals such realities. To some extent this novel is about the attraction and danger of style, its tendency not to express morality, but to replace it. The embodiments of this danger in the novel are Henry and Mary Crawford, charming, graceful, yet morally corrupt.

The idea of morality as achieved style, as grace of ease, is not likely ever to be relinquished . . . at a certain point in its development, morality seeks to express its independence of the grinding necessity by which it is engendered, and to claim for itself the autonomy and gratuitousness of art. Yet the idea is one that may easily deteriorate or be perverted. Style . . . can also hide the truth . . .

(Watt 1963: 135)

Two points need to be made here. For Trilling, Austen's irony is not, as it is for Marvin Mudrick [see pp. 96–7], a mode of moral detachment from the world she describes, but a way of comprehending it, of incorporating its 'contradictions, paradoxes, and anomalies' in a 'generosity of spirit' (Watt 1963: 124). In its questioning of style, *Mansfield Park* remains ironic in this sense, but one of the problems that it must comprehend is that of the moral status of irony. It is thus characterised by 'an irony directed against irony itself' (135). The other point, which Trilling does not make, is that by reasserting the *difference* between morality and aesthetics, Trilling identifies a problem in most of the criticism of Austen being written at the time of his essay and indeed for some time thereafter: namely, its readiness to identify a unity between Austen's formal strategies, including her style, and her moral message. Collapsing morality into style as her critics do is precisely the danger that *Mansfield Park* warns against.

Queer Austen, the body, and psychoanalytic criticism

A more recent critic of Austen, D.A. Miller, has gone further than this, and identified the value of Austen's style precisely in its complete autonomy from moral considerations and from any social or critical function. Watt and Hough [see pp. 98–9] see Austen's third-person narrative voice as appropriating the authority of, respectively, Henry Fielding's omniscient narrators and Samuel Johnson; Kelly [see pp. 98–9] sees this voice as embodying a defence of the established social order against the critiques of individual reason expressed in the first person. But it is possible to see the authority of Austen's narrative voice as deriving precisely from its *disconnection* with any already existing sources of literary, moral or social authority. This is the possibility explored by Miller in his recent book *Jane Austen, or the Secret of Style* (2003). In retrospect, we can see that *both* moral critics, like Harding or Booth, *and* formalist critics tend to assume that, because an Austen novel is a work of timeless beauty, this makes the whole work an expression of timeless truths, quite autonomous from the particular political or historical conditions in which the author was working. Miller returns to the question of style and insists on those aesthetic qualities that indeed separate her prose from other types of discourse. But he does so, not in order to avoid questions of politics, but to raise style as itself a political problem; in order to understand Austen's style, not as the expression of a coherent moral position, but in its fundamental disjunction from *any* moral position. Far from Austen's narrative voice being identifiably Johnsonian or Fieldingesque, it owes its authority to having no personal characteristics at all. It is self-contained, complete in itself. In this it resembles the heroines of the novels at the start of their stories: the Elizabeth Bennet happy in her ironic distance from her family, the Emma who never wants to marry. But it does not resemble the characters these girls become, the girls who need marriage to a man to make them complete. And of course the heroine must come to feel this lack for there to be a story.

In this aspect of his argument Miller draws on his much earlier work, *Narrative and its Discontents* (1981). There, he distinguished between 'narratable' and 'nonnarratable' or 'closural' elements of a text. The former are those questions or open-ended situations that generate a story: Elizabeth Bennet's desire, the question of Darcy's true nature, in *Pride and Prejudice*, for example. The latter are those that close down the possibility of further narrative development: most notably, the perfectly happy marriage. Miller identifies the fundamental tension in Austen's work between its moral commitment to stasis, settlement and definitive truth (the nonnarratable), and the demands of narrative form itself for movement, change and doubt (the narratable). Her work thus tends 'to disown at an ideological level what it embraces at a constructional one' (Miller 1981: 54). *Persuasion* is a particularly interesting exploration of this problem, ending as it does with a marriage which could and should have happened before the novel even begins, and in which the narrative, rather than changing Wentworth (for example), 'merely awakens his sense of what he has always been' (Miller 1981: 102).

Narrative and its Discontents in some ways embodies a formalist approach to Austen. Unlike the earlier critical approaches to form in Austen that we have looked at, it is concerned to identify tensions and contradictions in Austen's work rather than coherence and completeness, but its concern remains with the interrelation of the various elements of the text itself rather than with their relation to social or historical contexts of production or reception. In this it is an example of American 'Deconstruction', the critical practice developed from the thinking of Jacques Derrida, mostly by Yale University professors such as Paul de Man and (crucially for the study of prose fiction) J. Hillis Miller. *Jane Austen, or the Secret of Style* develops this approach in a very particular direction. Clearly, Austen's narrative voice itself is here identified as what the earlier book called 'nonnarratable'. Miller comments of that brilliant first sentence of *Pride and Prejudice*, the assertion of the universal truth of a single man's want of a wife, that 'no one who writes with such possession can be in want of *anything*' (Miller 2003: 34). The narrator of an Austen novel is fundamentally alienated from the story she narrates, above all by the absence on her part of the heterosexual desire assumed as a universal norm by that story. The dazzling verbal style of that narrator is what marks her as apart from the society she narrates. And Miller links this to the deep commitment to style that traditionally marks a whole group alienated from heterosexual society: homosexual men. The aesthetic qualities of Austen's novels cannot be reduced to or explained in terms of their social or political meanings, but this is not because the aesthetic realm embodies universal truths that transcend any particular social or historical context. Rather, the distance between the aesthetic and the social is itself produced by a particular fact about Austen's, and our, societies. This is their assumption that heterosexuality is a moral norm from which all other forms of desire, and indeed the absence of desire, can be classed as deviant, and thus that heterosexual marriage is a necessary condition for personal fulfilment and a happy life. The self-sufficiency of style is what Austen's narrators, like gay men, have instead of participation in this narrative.

Miller's book takes as its starting point the popularity of Jane Austen among gay men, which this shared commitment to 'style' (understood in this very particular way) explains. It could be argued, in fact, that professional academic criticism as a whole begins in exactly the same place. Claudia Johnson suggests that the rage of Leavis, Harding and others against her upper-class fans, the Janeites, is a rage against just the sort of 'queer' reading of Austen that Miller supplies. The tendency among mid-twentieth-century critics, noted above, to translate her formal qualities into moral positions might be seen as an attempt to close down that separate sphere of 'style' from which the socially alienated can assert an alternative, non-moral, type of authority. 'The process of straightening Austen out, then, occurs in conjunction with the development of a view of narrative that presumes its province to be desire (hegemonic, heteronormative) rather than manners (which may be practiced self-consciously, skeptically, and strategically)' (Lynch 2000: 39).

Accordingly Clara Tuite has argued that the critical construction of a strictly heterosexual Austen has been a crucial step in her inclusion in a literary canon embodying British national identity: she is the 'foremother' of the British realist novel (Lynch 2000: 118). To recognise what she has in common with gay male novelists, as Tuite does in her essay 'Decadent Austen Entails' (Lynch 2000: 115–39), is thus to call into question the way in which the canon has appropriated Austen as a signifier of national culture (Tuite 2002: 16–19). We will return to the question of Austen and nationality later [see pp. 142–7, 153–6].

Eve Sedgwick takes as *her* starting point a more familiar expression of the tendency of critics to take heterosexuality as the natural order to which the heroine must learn to conform: the validation of the 'marriage plot' as the novel's primary moral mechanism by many, mostly male, critics [see pp. 104–5]. In 'Jane Austen and the Masturbating Girl' she picks out Tony Tanner's account of *Emma* as particularly 'vengeful' in its attitude to the heroine (Sedgwick 1991: 125; Tanner 1986: 176–207). We have discussed the Austen novel as a *Bildungsroman*, a novel of education embodying an Enlightenment ideal of self-criticism and personal growth [see pp. 101–3]. Such narratives imagine the truly human as already present in all subjects, requiring only education and experience to be released from the mistaken self-images, inherited from the past or imposed from without, which had repressed it. But we have also seen that many critics, drawing on the work of Michel Foucault among others, understand such Enlightenment narratives as themselves constructing an equally artificial model of the self, but one that will now internalise repression in the form of critical self-scrutiny [see pp. 104–5]. Sedgwick accuses male critics of discovering this process in Austen as a way of perpetuating just such repression: they find in Austen a normative heterosexuality because they are trying to perpetuate heterosexuality as a moral norm.

Sedgwick's bold move in 'Jane Austen and the Masturbating Girl' is to juxtapose three examples of feminine suffering and discipline. These are Marianne Dashwood at the height of her frustrated obsession with Willoughby in *Sense and Sensibility*; a late nineteenth-century account of female masturbation as a medical disorder and its gruesome treatment; and Tanner's discussion of *Emma*. Sedgwick suggests the female masturbator as described in eighteenth- and nineteenth-century medical writing (self-absorbed, flushed, distracted) as a model for Marianne's sexual identity in Austen's novel; and she suggests the surgical torture proposed as a cure in those textbooks as a model for the disciplining of feminine sexuality celebrated by Tanner. Sedgwick does not discuss the extent to which the painful cure is imposed on Marianne by Austen herself through her plot (Quinn 2000: 320). Nevertheless, her fundamental point is a useful one: that there are models of sexual and social identity available in Austen's texts other than the dominant heterosexual one. By choosing to notice only heterosexuality the critic may be continuing the ideological work of one aspect of the text, the marriage plot, at the expense of others. The comparison between masturbation and self-indulgent reading is one made by eighteenth-century critics of female novel reading, long before Sedgwick (Tuite 2002: 81–2). Thus when she finds in masturbation subversive metaphors 'for independence, self-possession, and a rapture that may owe relatively little to political or interpersonal abjection' (Sedgwick 1991: 111), she sets a precedent for Miller's celebration of the self-containment of art as a crucial tactic in a queer resistance to compulsory heterosexuality.

The 'queer' readings of Sedgwick and Miller question the role of heterosexual desire as the primary source of identity for Austen's characters, and alert us to the ways in which other, mostly male, critics assume that the purpose of the plot is to educate the heroine in this form of desire. Feminist critics on the other hand have long pointed out the importance of female–female relationships in Austen's life and work. Some see the female communities portrayed in the novels as empty, stifling and shaped entirely by the presence or absence of a man (Auerbach 1978). Others, however, see the Dashwood or Bennet households as reflecting Austen's own network of female friends and relations which provided the 'enabling context of her writing' (Kaplan 1992: 5), so that female–female relationships in the novels act out a set of values alternative to those asserted in the heterosexual ones [see pp. 50–1]. Eventually it may become difficult to keep apart these female–female relationships, whether competitive (Auerbach) or supportive (Kaplan), from the non-normative types of sexual identity identified by Sedgwick. Susan M. Korba, for example, has drawn on psychoanalytic explorations of 'erotic domination' to explore the perplexing relationship between Emma Woodhouse and Jane Fairfax. Power and sexual desire are markedly linked in the relations between men and women in Austen's work, and the power-play between Emma and Jane can be seen to carry a corresponding erotic charge (Korba 1997).

At this point it must be acknowledged that many readers cannot accept the idea that Austen has anything at all to do with sex. Sedgwick's essay in particular caused a storm of controversy in the context of the 'culture wars' then being fought in American education between radicals and traditionalists (for discussions of the reception of Sedgwick's paper see Johnson in Lynch 2000: 25–9; and Quinn 2000: 305–10). One should note that it is perfectly possible to find in Austen a complete lack of interest in physical experience, and to see this as a positive thing, in a way that relates to the dichotomy between education and marriage plots discussed above [see pp. 101–2]. Jane McDonnell points out that in eighteenth-century novels, 'a woman is identified with her sexuality' in that her only story is her progress towards marriage, and this is a story in which she herself does not change. Only by rejecting this definition of woman as no more than a potential mate does Austen make possible 'the Bildungsroman emphasis on subjectivity and mental history' (McDonnell 1984: 199). Similarly Susan Morgan explains 'Why There's No Sex in Jane Austen's Fiction' by answering another question: 'What did female sexuality mean in British fiction before Austen? It meant male sexual power': to express sexual desire for, let alone have a physical relationship with, a man was to give up what very little power a woman had over her own life (Morgan 1989: 40). Thus the 'story' that eighteenth-century heroines like Burney's [see pp. 17–18] have to endure is a series of threats from outside of a more or less sexual nature. But in Austen, 'plot is not a threat to character, life not an assault on self. . . . The notable absence of sexual definitions of character in Austen's novels is inextricable from their equally notable premise that experience is good' (Morgan 1989: 41). More radically, Ruth Perry has argued that sex can be regarded as no more than an appetite in this period. Citing the evidence of Charlotte Lucas's apparent indifference at having to breed with the obnoxious Mr Collins, she concludes that sex just does not have the role of defining one's innermost identity that it tends to have for us today (Pucci and Thompson 2003: 213–28).

On the other hand, this reading of the Austen novel as *Bildungsroman*, concerned above all with the development of 'character', tends to ignore other, physical aspects of the self that are acknowledged or otherwise make their presence felt in the course of the text. 'Character', as we have seen, tends to mean the self that the protagonist is conscious of: it is self-consciousness. Austen's characters tend not to think about their bodies, and yet physical experience plays an important role in these narratives. Several critics have been concerned to understand the role of physicality in Austen's novels. John Dussinger's *In the Pride of the Moment*, for example, concentrates on the encounters between selves through which the story progresses, but which may include many elements that do not contribute to that narrative progress. For example, Mr Knightley's rebuke to Emma over her rudeness to Miss Bates on Box Hill is a stage in Emma's coming to a greater knowledge of herself, but it also produces in her a 'thrill of being punished' which neither she nor the narrator ever interprets (Dussinger 1990: 59). Such responses cannot be assimilated to the story of Emma's education or even comprehended by the social identity she will assume at the end of the novel: 'While one part of the story satisfies the appetite for the resolution of conflict, another brings into doubt not only the possibility of fulfilment but even the freedom of the character engaged in the process of willing' (Dussinger 1990: 46).

The type of criticism most concerned with the way in which the body resists the meanings we impose upon it and the stories we tell ourselves about our identities is that informed by the psychoanalytic ideas of Sigmund Freud (1856–1939), Jacques Lacan (1901–81) and their followers. Several elements of Dussinger's book are good examples of this sort of criticism, although he uses the specialised vocabulary of psychoanalysis very sparingly. For a more thorough application of a particular psychoanalytic category see Francis L. Restuccia (1994) and Elizabeth Dalton (1995) on 'Melancholia' in *Emma* and *Persuasion* respectively, understood in the first instance as developed by leading French psychoanalyst and feminist Julia Kristeva, and in the second in more generally Freudian terms. For a comprehensive run-through of how psychoanalytic thought can be brought to bear on the problems of reading Austen, see Barbara Rasmussen's (1993) use of Lacanian theorist Shoshana Feldman's ideas to read *Mansfield Park*. Rasmussen's comment that, like the patient's narrative in psychoanalysis, 'the narrator's voice only divides the story further from itself', that is from any meaning we can imagine the story having prior to the narrator's telling it, is particularly intriguing. Psychoanalytic categories might provide another way of thinking through the disjunction between narrative voice and the story it narrates that D.A. Miller (2003) identifies in *Jane Austen, or the Secret of Style*. Rasmussen's account of *Mansfield Park* might also be usefully compared to Anna Mae

Duane's diagnosis of Fanny Price's 'hysteria' as the condition discussed by Freud (Duane 2001). Finally, it should be noted that it is possible to discuss the body in Austen without resorting to the joint concern of psychoanalysis, feminism and queer studies with issues of sexuality and sexual desire. John Wiltshire convincingly argues in *Jane Austen and the Body* that corporeality makes its presence felt in Austen most consistently in problems of health and illness. While I have suggested that these other critical approaches understand the body as resisting the social development undergone by the heroine, for Wiltshire, in the case of Fanny Price in *Mansfield Park* for example, 'it is impossible to separate . . . psychosocial development from her bodily and sexual condition' (Wiltshire 1992: 63–4). The feelings that Fanny cannot admit, envy, jealousy, rage, are kept out of consciousness and 're-experienced physiologically' as bodily symptoms (73) whose connection to the story must be inferred by the reader.

Austen and society

The next two sections will look at two, interrelated, ways of understanding Austen's work: in terms of its relation to the social hierarchy and historical developments of her own time, and in relation to questions of gender.

A problem

We began the last section by identifying an anxiety on the part of academic critics concerning the popularity, amounting to a cult, surrounding Austen. Those critics committed to the role of literary studies in building a democratic culture have often expressed a related anxiety about Austen's novels themselves, in their apparently uncritical acceptance of the decidedly undemocratic society of her time. Among the earliest of these is Arnold Kettle, in the first volume of *An Introduction to the English Novel* (1951). Kettle begins by praising *Emma* in terms, familiar from Leavis, Trilling and Booth, of the 'fineness of feeling' and intense 'moral concern' that it evokes in the reader (Kettle 1951: 92). However, Kettle then asks, 'exactly what relevance and helpfulness does *Emma* have for us today?' (94). This is a problem, because unlike Trilling in his essay on *Emma*, or Booth in *The Rhetoric of Fiction*, Kettle is ready to admit that 'the standards we are called upon to admire may be inseparably linked with a particular form of social organisation' (99). Trilling, in a later essay called 'Why We Read Jane Austen' (Trilling 1982: 204–25), and Booth, in *The Company We Keep*, later admit this historical specificity of Austen's values. But this is a particular problem for Kettle as 'the particular form of social organisation' involved is one that modern readers, as democrats, are bound to find unpalatable, in its rigid social hierarchy and ruthless economic exploitation: 'The values and standards of the Hartfield world are based on the assumption that it is right and proper for a minority of the community to live at the expense of the majority' (Kettle 1951: 99). Kettle concludes that Emma remains 'a warm and living work of art' which should be appreciated for its 'humanity', but it remains fundamentally limited in its social vision.

The limitation and the narrowness of the Hartfield world is the limitation of class society. . . . [T]he question at issue is not Jane Austen's
failure to suggest a *solution* to the problem of class divisions but her
apparent failure to notice the existence of the problem.

(Kettle 1951: 98–9)

We suggested in Part 1 that the language of 'class' is slightly anachronistic
in discussing Austen, as it does not become current in political discussion
until the 1820s [see pp. 5–6]. But Raymond Williams, developing Kettle's observation, finds a 'class viewpoint' already implicit in the writing of the great radical
journalist William Cobbett (1763–1835) in Austen's own time and indeed in
her own county (Williams 1973: 109). In a brilliant passage in *The Country and
the City* Williams describes Cobbett's journeys through Austen's Hampshire,
chronicling the miseries of the rural working class that Austen's fiction ignores.

What he [Cobbett] names, riding past on the road, are classes. Jane
Austen, from inside the houses, can never see that, for all the intricacy
of her social description. All her discrimination is, understandably,
internal and exclusive. She is concerned with the conduct of people who,
in the complications of improvement, are repeatedly trying to make
themselves into a class. But where only one class is seen, no classes are
seen.

(Williams 1973: 117)

It is precisely because Austen is still concerned with the eighteenth-century
problem of relations between different 'ranks' of the propertied that she cannot
understand the 'propertied' as a group, defined by their opposition to another
group, propertyless labour [see p. 5].

In *Jane Austen's Novels: Social Change and Literary Form* (1979), Julia Prewitt
Brown sets out to counter this complaint about Austen's 'limited' vision by identifying the transition from traditional to modern society happening *within* her
houses. She does this by showing how Austen chronicles the emergence, not of
class identity, but of the modern individual, alienated from *any* meaningful social
identity. *Persuasion*, for example, demonstrates 'the social and moral necessity
for a democratic individualism that nonetheless meant powerlessness and
alienation for the heroine' (Brown 1979: 5). As we mentioned above, Brown sees
Austen's irony as the stylistic means of democratically including a multitude of
voices without imposing a hierarchy of significance on those voices [see p. 99].
Persuasion, however, is also modern in this darker sense: the collapse of the
old hierarchical certainties has produced, not a democracy, but a society split
into 'disparate parts', leaving individuals like Anne Elliot 'disoriented, isolated'
(137, 138), and unable to fulfil themselves in a world which resists their claims for
recognition as human subjects. Brown does not describe herself as a Marxist
critic, but in this description of modernity as it figures in the novel she draws on
the theories of the Hungarian Marxist Georg Lukács and particularly his *The
Theory of the Novel*, first published in 1920 (Lukács 1971; Brown 1979: 129,
139). Lukács, one might note, was also a major influence on the declared but
similarly pragmatic Marxism of Raymond Williams.

Austen as Burkean conservative

Along with the Marxist-inflected studies of Williams and Brown, the 1970s saw the development of another way of relating Austen to her social context, not in terms of the broad categories of class or modernity, but by tracing in her writing specific political or cultural controversies of her time. This was the work undertaken by Alistair Duckworth in *The Improvement of the Estate* (1971) and Marilyn Butler in *Jane Austen and the War of Ideas* (1975). For Duckworth, the political and moral values expressed in Austen's writing closely follow those of Edmund Burke [see pp. 31–2]. Austen follows Burke, he argues, in taking the country estate as representative of the English nation as a whole, an inherited institution that has grown organically over the centuries and now embodies those centuries' accumulated wisdom. This country estate is more than the economic basis on which a gentry family survives: it is the source of their status, of their identity. And this specific dependence of the gentry on their land represents the wider dependence of the individual generally on the social forms and inherited relationships (national or familial as well as local) on which their identity depends.

> Isolated from a stable and inherited 'estate', an individual suffers more than loss of station; he is, more importantly, excluded from the 'grounds' of being and action. Without the customary reference points of a structured inheritance, he may feel at a loss how to act.
>
> (Duckworth 1971: 4)

In this emphasis on inherited social identity, Duckworth sees Austen as engaging in an argument against the economic individualism represented by the discipline of political economy [see pp. 19–21] and her novels as treating 'the dilemma of an individual in a society in which traditional values are giving way, or are felt to be giving way, to new economic and individualistic ones' (Duckworth 1971: 16). Burke's conservatism is formulated in response to a specific event, the French Revolution of 1789; Austen's conservatism, while making full use of Burke's categories, appears convincingly in Duckworth's account as a response to much longer-term changes in English society, and the deeper 'cultural instability' that they had produced (Duckworth 1971: 23).

This is not to argue either that Austen was against change, or that she saw no need for change in the landed society she portrays. Indeed, in a novel like *Mansfield Park*, Duckworth's starting point, the functioning of the country estate, has already been corrupted. Precisely that character most alienated from the life of the estate is the one who understands how it *ought* to be organised: Fanny Price (72). The 'moral autonomy' of the Austen heroine, that is her ability to criticise the society in which she lives, is not 'individualism' but a commitment to its opposite, an ideal of social interdependence. '[E]xcessive individualism' (23) is precisely what the Austen heroine criticises in others. Indeed, like Burke, Austen in Duckworth's view can also allow for the 'improvement' of estates (and by extension social institutions generally). New practices and ideas are acceptable, so long as their aim is the health of the whole, and they are introduced with respect for what has gone before. Here Duckworth is able to relate the novels to another, apparently non-political, controversy specific to Austen's period. No one in *Mansfield Park* actually mentions Burke, but they do discuss the merits of various contemporary practitioners of landscape-gardening, such as Humphrey Repton, who has transformed the estate of a friend of Rushworth according to his fashionable but controversial taste. Rushworth accordingly decides that his own estate, Sotherton, 'wants improvement ... beyond any thing' (I.vi.51). The 'improvements' of Repton and his imitators were designed to improve the way an estate looked, and could involve anything from cutting down trees and diverting streams to moving whole villages, all to improve the view from the big house and its approaches (the issue crops up again in Henry Crawford's sweeping plans for Edmund's parsonage at Thornton Lacey in II.vii.23–5). Many voices were raised against such irreparable damage to the products of long ages of growth, and Austen is drawing on their arguments. The eventual triumph of Fanny and her acceptance into the Bertram family represents the absorption by traditional society of the new, not for the sake of fashion but for the necessary maintenance-through-evolution of that inherited order.

Like Duckworth, Marilyn Butler sees Austen as a fundamentally conservative writer in *Jane Austen and the War of Ideas* (1975). In contrast to Duckworth, Butler considers that conservatism much more strictly in the context of the British reaction to the French Revolution that we looked at in Part 1, and begins an examination of the cultural politics of writing in this period that continues to be a fruitful source of Austen criticism to this day. Butler's book in fact places Austen's writing in *two* productive contexts. One is the revolution controversy (see Sales 1994 for a counter-argument to this). The other is the sentimental model of the human mind developed in the writing of David Hume and Adam Smith [see **p. 21**]. The latter Butler identifies as a dominant influence on the novel in the later eighteenth century, the 'age of sensibility'. Novels of sentiment or sensibility focus on the feelings of individual protagonists, on their subjective response to the world, rather than on their social commitments to others. Sometimes the protagonist of sentimental fictions such as Laurence Sterne's *Sentimental Journey* (1768) or Henry Mackenzie's *Man of Feeling* (1771) is shown responding with deep feeling to a victim of the present social order: the seduced and abandoned servant-girl, the old soldier, the evicted smallholder. But that feeling is almost always an end in itself: it is involuntary, and does not come from or produce a thought-through critique of society that might issue in political action to eradicate such misery. Indeed, for those English radicals who sympathise with the French revolutionaries, the sentimental model of the individual is strictly *useless*, as it leaves the individual powerless before his own emotions and the outside world that plays upon them (Butler 1975: 36).

Instead, radical novelists in Britain turn to reason, not emotion, as the source of their critique, and write stories in which the protagonist educates him- or herself into a position where they *can* enjoy some control over events. *A Simple Story* by Elizabeth Inchbald (1791), *Anna St. Ives* by Thomas Holcroft (1792) and *The Memoirs of Emma Courtney* (1796) by Mary Hays are examples of such novels. They can be seen as a radical appropriation of the novel of education or *Bildungsroman* discussed above [see **pp. 101–4**]. On the other hand, the arch-conservative Burke adopts the strategies of sentimental fiction in his *Reflections on the Revolution in France*, casting Queen Marie Antoinette of France as the sentimental heroine whose tears we are invited to share; and for Burke, the power-lessness of the individual to change anything is in general a good thing. On the basis of these texts, sentiment would seem to lend itself at least as easily to a conservative political position as to a radical one.

Yet in the heated political controversy of the 1790s, the reactionary, anti-Jacobin press [see pp. 32–5] identified the emotional self-indulgence of sensibility with political radicalism. For example, it was easy to equate any critique of the institution of marriage, however well reasoned, with an attempt to license sexual promiscuity, and thus explain it as the product of a culture of sensibility that recommended giving in to one's impulses rather than restraining them. Jean-Jacques Rousseau [see p. 35] was also a useful figure for the anti-Jacobin writers, as both a writer of sentimental fiction, a hero to the Jacobin party in Paris, and someone who had confessed to various sexual indiscretions in his autobiography, the *Confessions* (1781).

Butler argues that Austen shares in this identification of sensibility with political radicalism, and that her criticism of emotional self-indulgence and individualism in, for example, *Sense and Sensibility*'s Marianne Dashwood, encodes her conservative, anti-Jacobin politics. '[H]er manner as a novelist is broadly that of the conservative Christian moralist of the 1790s' in the argument 'between the advocates of a Christian conservatism on the one hand, with their pessimistic view of man's nature, and their belief in external authority; [and] on the other hand, progressives, sentimentalists, revolutionaries, with their optimism about man, and their preference for spontaneous personal impulse against rules imposed from without' (Butler 1975: 164–5). As Butler herself has shown, this rejection of sentiment was one shared by radicals and reactionaries in this period, however much the reactionaries might have pretended otherwise. Since anti-sentimentalism is not *in itself* reactionary, the task Butler sets herself is to show that Austen's anti-sentimentalism is marked in the novels themselves as being a reactionary stance, and not as a more general rejection of sentimentalism's 'absorption . . . in the conscious and unconscious mind, because implicitly it put the individual before the group' (8). The difference between Elinor and Marianne Dashwood then

> is one of ideology – Marianne optimistic, intuitive, un-self-critical, and Elinor far more sceptical, always ready to study the evidence, to reopen a question, to doubt her own prior judgements. . . . Elinor was never intended to be infallible, but to typify an active, struggling Christian in a difficult world.
>
> (Butler 1975: 192)

For Butler, 'the characteristic recourse of the conservative . . . is to remind us ultimately of the insignificance of individual insights and even individual concerns when measured against the scale of "the universe as one vast whole" ' (130; the last phrase is a quote from Maria Edgeworth).

As in Duckworth, this conservative version of Austen seems to hang on what the critic means by 'the individual' or 'individualism'. This becomes a particular problem in Butler's reading of *Pride and Prejudice*, the novel most difficult to fit into her conservative paradigm. Elizabeth Bennet's lively and rational criticism of

Darcy, defiance of Lady Catherine de Bourgh, and (by extension) her scepticism towards inherited authority in general, make *her* individual perspective seem a much more likely candidate for the label 'proto-Jacobin' than Marianne's. Butler indeed makes this case, and reads *Pride and Prejudice* as fundamentally about the reformation of this unruly subversive: Elizabeth learns in the course of the novel that her irreverence is potentially as socially irresponsible as her father's withdrawal from his family into his library, unless it can be used to renew and revitalise the old institutions of power represented by the Pemberley estate. The marriage of Elizabeth and Darcy thus represents just that negotiation of inheritance with innovation which Burke sees as essential to national continuity. The problem then faced by Butler is that Elizabeth's witty refusal to be awed by Darcy as a man is so attractive, so entertaining, that it is hard to feel that it is fundamentally wrong, as Butler herself acknowledges (Butler 1975: 216–7). Elizabeth, in the end, is awed by Pemberley, and does marry its owner. But if this novel *ends* by affirming the claims of a hierarchical society over the perspective, rationality and feeling of the individual, the experience of reading it is nevertheless an immersion in that perspective, that rationality and that feeling.

Austen, political economy and Marxist criticism

Recently, critics placing Austen in her historical context have turned from the specific debates about landscape improvement and sensibility to the broader shifts in social categories which these particular controversies acted out. The 'individualism' being debated here may be as much the economic individualism of capitalism as it is the emotional individualism of the cult of sensibility (though the two are related, as we saw in Part 1: [**see pp. 19–22**]). The historical context in which Austen needs to be placed is thus, in this view, not the aftermath of the French Revolution, but the rise of capitalism as an all-pervasive economic system. The new discipline of political economy, the 'science' which explained and justified capitalism, provides a very powerful set of terms with which to describe social and economic change, but these terms are not necessarily compatible with Burke's influential rhetoric of emotional attachment to inherited social power and national identity.

   Beth Fowkes Tobin, in 'The Moral and Political Economy of Austen's *Emma*' (1990), backs up Duckworth on this point, seeing this novel as defending a traditional ideal of the landowner as paternal guardian of his community (Knightley) against the irresponsibility of mere money cut loose from this inherited social role (Emma). Other critics point out that Adam Smith, the greatest of the political economists, was himself worried that capitalism would erode traditional social virtue, and that Austen may thus be adopting his model of society rather than rejecting it. Elsie Michie suggests that, in the marriages of Edward Bertram and Fanny Price, and Darcy and Elizabeth, Austen 'unites virtue and wealth without conflating the two' (Michie 2000: 17): capitalism and social responsibility pull in different directions but they can be reconciled. These novels are thus trying 'to acknowledge and work through commercial culture's ambivalent feelings about its own materialist drives' (21). In a similar way, Peter Knox-Shaw sees a problem in Butler's assumption that the cult of sensibility was necessarily connected to radical politics. As we saw above, pro-revolutionary novelists of the 1790s tend to be as critical of uncontrolled emotion as their conservative opponents, and Knox-Shaw finds striking similarities between *Sense and Sensibility* and *St. Leon* (1799), a novel by notorious radical philosopher (and Mary Wollstonecraft's husband) William Godwin. What Austen has in common with Burke in *Sense and Sensibility*, she could also be said to have in common with Adam Smith (Knox-Shaw 1998: 183–208).

David Kaufmann has gone further than this in an important essay on the same novel, reading Austen as a full-blown economic liberal, like Adam Smith expressing a 'civic jurisprudential' model of society (Kaufmann 1992: 396). What she shares with Smith is the conviction that virtue is exercised most effectively in private life rather than in public politics. The law that guaranteed economic individuals control of their property finds its equivalent within the home in the rules of 'propriety' that allow one 'the privacy of sentiment' (391). Elinor's propriety thus negotiates between 'the claims of an assertive individualism and the demands of the social totality' (397). And this propriety is not an inheritance of the landed elite from the fine manners of their chivalric ancestors, as Burke would have it, but a specifically modern code that addresses this specifically modern cultural situation: 'Elinor does not use the past as her authority: she, unlike Burke, does not appeal to precedent. ... [P]ropriety in *Sense and Sensibility* is not the atavistic outcropping of tradition but the expression of an experience of radical change' (399). It is precisely because Austen's fiction does this work of establishing the space of the emotional personality within capitalism that James Thompson places her at the conclusion of his full-length study, *Models of Value: Eighteenth-Century Political Economy and the Novel* (1996). So, in *Mansfield Park*, 'Austen creates an ironic voice capable of violating and then repairing the equation between love and money' (Thompson 1996: 186).

But other critics see Austen as much more critical of capitalism and the theories that legitimate it. Later, we will discuss Fraser Easton's 1998 essay 'The Political Economy of *Mansfield Park*' in the context of the role of slavery in that novel [see pp. 140–1]: enough to note here that he sees this novel, published in 1814, the year of Napoleon's first defeat, as distant from the revolution controversy of the 1790s, and consequently as registering 'the social cost of Smithian economics rather than Painite politics' (Easton 1998: 461). An article we have already looked at in the context of the *Bildungsroman*, Lauren Goodlad's on *Sense and Sensibility*, argues directly against Kaufmann (1992): in this novel, 'Austen turns civic jurisprudence *against* the commercial self-interest it was developed to legitimate' (Goodlad 2000: 63). Rather than offering a 'utopian promise' of reconciliation between individual and society (Kaufmann 1992: 397), *Sense and Sensibility* offers more evidence of 'liberalism's failures to transcend dominatory relations' (Goodlad 2000: 76) as Marianne, in the end, has to be bullied into the modern self-disciplining selfhood demanded by propriety (74).

If Lauren Goodlad is right, and Austen turns the language of political economy against the capitalism it was designed to serve, she therein anticipates a thinker from later in the nineteenth century, Karl Marx (1818–83). For Marx too starts from the assumption of political economy, that technological and economic change are the engines driving political and legal change in human history. But

Adam Smith, with his other, sentimentalist, hat on, sees human relationships as grounded in shared feelings that are *not* the product of their economic environment [see pp. 20–1]. Marx, on the contrary, sees capitalism as determining even the realm of feeling that we think of as personal, intimate, domestic. All human relationships are reduced by capitalism to the 'cash nexus', to types of economic exchange between individuals who have no other bond than calculated shared self-interest.

Marx's ideas are accordingly useful in thinking about the relation of Austen's fiction to her society. In *Jane Austen and the State* Mary Evans, for example, finds in Austen a criticism of bourgeois capitalism not a million miles from that of Marx. She acknowledges Austen's concern for the 'stability of human relationships and communities' but asks why Butler and Duckworth should regard such concern as a 'conservative' one (Evans 1987: 37). For criticism of 'conspicuous consumption' and 'the individualisation of feeling' (41) are as much a feature of a socialist thinker like Marx as they are of Burke. Austen accordingly asks her readers to 'recognise the needs that all share – for material provision, social recognition, commitment, and the means to support their children', rather than pursuing ever greater individual consumption of commodities (42). Evans in fact sees Austen as prefiguring in these demands the institutional agenda of Victorian social provision, the establishment of the principle that the state has a duty to defend the community against the limitless greed unleashed by a free market economy. This is the principle that underlies the modern welfare state. Evans's book is, among other things, an intervention in contemporary British politics, as it is this welfare state that the Conservative administrations of the 1980s were seen to be dismantling (81). Austen is often claimed as an ideological ally by late twentieth-century conservatives [see pp. 146–7, 153–6]. Evans's book is an attempt to claim her back for the social-democratic left.

James Thompson in *Between Self and World* (1988) develops Evans's position through a much more rigorous use of Marxist theory, specifically that of Lukács in *History and Class Consciousness* (1972). In particular, Thompson is interested in Austen's attempt to find a realm of freedom and autonomous subjectivity in a capitalist world where economic relations seem to determine all others, where human relations seem to be subordinated to material necessities. In other words, Austen's novels address 'the problematic status of the individual subject' that follows from the 'rationalization of the social world caused by commodity production' (Thompson 1988: 10). He draws attention to Austen's portrayal of the material world of her characters, one full of consumer goods, a theme we will return to in our discussion of film adaptations of the novels [see pp. 155–6]. But at the same time Austen's protagonists distinguish themselves from this world of mere commodities.

> This technique of . . . revealing a world of commodity while distancing it with moral ideas, at once announces and denies the presence of economic determinism. . . . In this way, then, Austen's characters do and do not live in the material world; they can and cannot rise above it, for Austen insists upon as much as she obscures the cold world of economic necessity.
>
> (Thompson 1988: 43)

In Marx's terms, this work of simultaneously revealing and obscuring the material basis of society is the work of 'ideology'. Ideology includes all cultural practices that represent the world in such a way that the perspective of the ruling group in society is reproduced as the only true perspective on the world. Austen insists that her heroines enjoy the capacity to reason autonomously and thus judge morally, but this self-definition is at the same time 'inevitably determined by the alienating effects of capital'. In claiming the first and acknowledging the second, Austen's novels act out 'the essential ideological contradiction' of capitalist society (13).

Here is Marx himself on ideology: '[I]t follows that every class which is struggling for mastery . . . must first conquer for itself political power in order to represent its interest in turn as the general interest' (*The German Ideology*; in Marx 1977: 169–70).

Marx's formulation here makes the prior grasping of political power a condition for a class to represent its own interests as general in this way. But one could read the slow ascendancy of the moneyed classes in Britain in the long eighteenth century as the opposite: 'polite' forms of writing, and the theories of the political economists, represent the commercial interests of the middle class as the interests of all those with property, and identify these with the interests of the nation as a whole, *before* the middle class gains any political power. In contradiction to Marx, the middle classes *first* take control of the way in which society is represented in texts, *then* make a claim to political power, a claim that only begins to yield fruit in the Reform Act of 1832 [see p. 5].

It is in this long historical perspective of class conflict between the middle classes and the aristocracy that Nancy Armstrong places Austen's work in *Desire and Domestic Fiction* (1987). Armstrong shares with Marxist critics a perception of wider class-political issues being acted out even in the most intimate recesses of family life and the private self, even in what makes a man or a woman sexually desirable. But by understanding political power as something achieved *through* textual representations, rather than seeing texts reflecting an already established political situation, Armstrong is much closer to Michel Foucault than to Marx. Her focus on sexual desire as the effect of political power relations draws particularly on Foucault's *History of Sexuality*, Volume I (1979).

For Armstrong, the novel itself was the genre of writing that allowed the modern individual, as described by Foucault, to come into being. It did this by constructing a space outside the state in which this individual could be imagined as enjoying an existence prior to any commitments to society as a whole, whose only commitments would be personal ones to friends and family. This space is the domestic space of the home. The modern domestic subject can then be imagined as freely choosing to give up elements of her liberty in exchange for protection from the state in a 'social contract'. The state is legitimate precisely to the extent that it can be imagined as freely entered into by originally autonomous beings in this way. The novel emerges to explain how that original autonomy could be possible:

> Shaped by this logic, the social contract characteristically offered a
> private solution for problems that were inherently political. . . .

As it gave rise to modern liberal discourse, the social contract produced a contradiction on which the rise of the novel depended.
The novel developed sophisticated strategies for transforming political
information into any one of several recognizable psychological
conditions.

(Armstrong 1987: 36)

In other words, the novel located the identity of the modern individual in the
private needs and desires that could be accommodated within the framework of
the state, but whose origins could be located outside the state in that pre-political
'natural' humanity. The plots of novels then appear as designed to show these
needs and desires being met without reference to the state, in private solutions,
above all marriage, that overcome what would otherwise be political problems
that would require the reform of the state.

Furthermore, in a society in which state politics remained an exclusively male
arena, this modern individual was first imagined as *female*. It was, Armstrong
argues, in conduct books for middle-class women [see pp. 7–8] that the
redefinition of subjective identity in terms of private 'qualities of mind' rather
than status was first tried out. The novel then takes this feminine identity
developed in the conduct book and uses it in the construction of both male and
female characters in terms of their inner lives and private relations rather than
(and in opposition to) their inherited rank and political power. By portraying the
individual as in the first instance separate from political power, and as defined
instead by something as 'natural' as sexual desire, the novel thus took an essentially middle-class situation and made it represent 'human nature' in general. The
novel thus won for the middle classes a certain kind of cultural, and ultimately
political, authority, purely by means of writing: 'By virtue of their apparent disregard for matters that were supposed to concern men, plots turning on the sexual
contract offered the means of passing off ideology as the product of purely human
concern' (Armstrong 1987: 42).

Armstrong takes *Emma* as her example of Austen's version of this sexual/
political contract that legitimates middle-class moral authority. For Armstrong,
Emma dramatises the relations between different types of language and social
class. It is precisely in Austen's establishment of a particular version of polite
English as a standard to which the (literate) nation in general should aspire
that she serves the interests of the middle classes [see pp. 44–5, pp. 144–5]. And,
crucially for Armstrong's case, that standard is not only about the vocabulary
and rules of propriety used in public, but about the internalisation of those rules
as constitutive of the individual's perspective on the world and ability to separate
that perspective from the world itself. The rules are constitutive, that is, of their
subjectivity, of their status as a 'self'. The reader, by accepting the general
authority of this type of language, by accepting it as the norm, will come to see the
world through its categories and ideals, and thus be produced as this particular
kind of individual. Ideology, here as elsewhere, does its work of producing con-
sent to a particular social order not by presenting an already formed individual
with a set of propositions ('landowners have a right to rule', say, or 'middle-class
women are more virtuous than poor women') for our judgement, but by producing a particular type of identity for the individual, a perspective from

which he or she will make these judgements, and from within which these specific propositions will seem self-evidently true.

Austen gives her readers the chance to practise making the right judgements by offering them apparently much less momentous questions concerning the rights and wrongs of social life in a small English village. To read people's speech or writing is then to be able to place them socially and morally, and to acquire power over them, or not, accordingly. Thus for Austen, as for Foucault, 'representation constitutes a form of agency in its own right. In this way, she raises the question of how language may provide an accurate indication of an individual's value' (Armstrong 1987: 142). In Austen's novel, we are not told what Emma says in reply to Knightley's eventual proposal, only that it was 'what she ought' (III.xiii.404) because Emma is now the standard by which both politeness and correct interpretation of others' language are to be measured. Note the difference here from Graham Hough or Walton Litz, for whom Knightley sets the standard of judgement in this novel [see pp. 98–9]. For Armstrong, it is Emma herself who sets the example of learning to read others correctly that we must follow (Armstrong 1987: 136).

Austen and feminism

It is perhaps slightly misleading to set apart feminist studies of Austen from a section titled 'Austen and society'. On the one hand, the vast majority of feminist critics are concerned precisely with Austen's relation to her society, but see that relation as shaped by the category of gender. On the other, many Marxist or Foucauldian critics necessarily place gender alongside categories of class at the centre of their own analyses: we have just seen this in the work of Nancy Armstrong, and Mary Evans's study is avowedly feminist as well as Marxist.

One influential work in feminist literary studies must be mentioned which does *not*, however, pay attention to the particular historical circumstances in which Austen was writing. This is *The Madwoman in the Attic* by Sandra M. Gilbert and Susan Gubar. For Gilbert and Gubar, the male dominance of, and masculine perspective expressed in, the literary tradition is a problem for Austen as for all women writers. Women writers, in whatever period they find themselves, are confronted with a culture which is *patriarchal*: that is, a culture which imagines power as naturally the possession of men, and power in general as modelled on the power of fathers over their families [see p. 22]. In that tradition, woman, where she figures at all, invariably figures as the object rather than the subject: she is what is looked at and talked about, rather than the voice doing the talking, the perspective from which one looks. Accordingly, female characters tend to be reduced to stereotypes, angels (representing a masculine ideal of passive, silent, helpless femininity) or monsters (the opposite of that ideal), playing a role in the story of a man. Gilbert and Gubar take fairytales as their prime example of inherited narratives embodying patriarchal values and teaching silence and passivity to each new generation of women readers. And they figure this imprisonment in a masculine tradition with an image taken from a fairytale, Snow-White's glass coffin:

[S]ome stories have been imagined for women, by male poets as well as male novelists. . . . [But] most of these stories tend to perpetuate extreme and debilitating images of women as angels or monsters. Thus the genres associated with such plot paradigms present just as many difficulties to the woman writer as those works of literature which focus primarily on men. If she identifies with a snow-white heroine, the glass coffin of romance 'feels' like a deathbed to the female novelist.

(Gilbert and Gubar 1979: 68)

For the woman who wants to write, the precedents set by the texts of this tradition are thus experienced as silencing, creating for women writers a 'profoundly debilitating' 'anxiety of authorship' (51). All female-authored texts thus embody this experience to some extent or other [see pp. 13–16].

Austen's novels thus appear in Gilbert and Gubar as an attempt to take this masculine literary inheritance and subvert it from within: to take its originally patriarchal plots and stereotypes and develop new meanings for them. 'Austen admits the limits and discomforts of the paternal roof, but learns to live beneath it. . . . Austen makes a virtue of her own confinement, as her heroines will do also' (121). That last-quoted sentence expresses an important tactic in Gilbert and Gubar's analysis: the heroine's position in the family home and her relation to its master and his wife in the novels can be read as representations of the position of the female novelist in her relation to a patriarchal culture. The heroine's physical confinement expresses her author's cultural confinement; the tyranny or inadequacy of the novels' father-figures is also the tyranny or inadequacy of the patriarchal literary tradition in relation to women's needs and perspectives. Similarly, Austen does indeed borrow plot elements or motifs from Shakespeare or Sterne, but it is to 'demystify' them, to 'illustrate how such fictions are the alien creations of writers who contribute to the enfeebling of women' (121). More strikingly, Gilbert and Gubar's approach reveals as vehicles for suppressed feminist rage precisely those female characters who are, in traditional terms, monstrous. The 'wicked stepmother' figures, like Lady Catherine de Bourgh in *Pride and Prejudice*, Mrs Churchill in *Emma* and, especially, Aunt Norris in *Mansfield Park*, figure as embodiments of their author's creative energy and anger. 'Quite openly dedicated to the pursuit of pleasure and activity, especially the joy of controlling other people's lives, Aunt Norris is a parodic surrogate for the author, a suitable double whose manipulations match those of Aunt Jane' (171).

This is precisely why such figures must be defeated and expelled from novels otherwise committed to feminine modesty and decorum. They are expelled, that is, as scapegoats for the female author's *im*modesty in writing a novel in the first place. Heroines like Elizabeth Bennet, Emma Woodhouse and Anne Elliot, on the other hand, figure the author's compromise with patriarchy and survival within it, as they learn to 'exploit the evasions and reservations of feminine gentility' (183). This splitting of the author's situation into two parts, one compliant with society and one resistant to it, might incidentally recall to mind D.W. Harding's perception of the tension between Austen's writing in the discourse of civility and her ironic undercutting of it [see pp. 92–4]. But Gilbert and Gubar's feminist perspective seems to offer an explanation of *why* Austen's texts should be divided against themselves in this way: it is the female author's way of negotiating with the patriarchal conditions under which she writes.

As we initially observed, most feminist critics define Austen's society, not simply as a patriarchy like any patriarchy, but as a very specific patriarchy undergoing specific types of historical change. For example, in Part 1 we discussed the possibility that the eighteenth century sees the emergence of a new ideal of femininity, the domestic woman, in response to particular economic and social shifts in European society at the time. Female authors inevitably find themselves negotiating with this ideal in the way that Gilbert and Gubar describe, but the compromise they make with patriarchy will be shaped by the specific nature of this ideal: both the type of authority, and the type of limitations, that it offers will be different from the authority and limitations offered by the aristocratic ideal of femininity, for example [see pp. 24–5]. Linda Hunt, in A Woman's Portion (1988), looks specifically at how women novelists negotiated between the expectations created by the domestic ideal and their artistic commitment to realism in the novel. Where for Gilbert and Gubar subversion of patriarchal fantasy from within was the only tactic that made women's writing possible, for Hunt realism is always available as a corrective from outside.

Many feminist critics of Austen take as their starting point the didactic literature (that is, literature that aims to teach) that set out to propagate the domestic ideal in the decades before Austen began to write. The 'conduct books' did this most obviously [see p. 8]. Mary Poovey, in The Proper Lady and the Woman Writer (1984), was among the first to look at the problems and opportunities that the ideology of 'propriety' offered women writers. The 'proper lady', above all, is one who does not express her own desire (Poovey 1984: 4). Qualifying Marilyn Butler's position on Pride and Prejudice [see pp. 118–19], Poovey argues that in this context Elizabeth Bennet's wit is defensive rather than subversive, a means of resisting the meanings that the men around her would otherwise impose on her (196). Still, the novel as a whole legitimates Elizabeth's desire for Darcy only by dissociating it from this wit and instead making it appear as the product of 'the mortification of pride' (201). Judith Lowder Newton also addresses the role of the conduct books in shaping the English female novel tradition. She makes a similar point to Poovey's about Pride and Prejudice. Elizabeth is at her most impressive once she turns her critical intelligence on herself, but once married to Darcy she is fated to 'dwindle by degrees into a wife' (Newton 1981: 80–1, 84). 'Modesty' in Ruth Bernard Yeazell's Fictions of Modesty (1991) occupies much the same role as 'propriety' does in Poovey, but Yeazell spends more time on the conduct book origins of this concept. As it appears there, 'modesty' is both a standard of outward behaviour (Yeazell 1991: 6) and the young woman's ignorance of her own sexual desires. To consciously conform to modest standards of behaviour is thus not to be modest at all, as it implies a knowledge of the desire that requires to be hidden. The double-bind in which this placed women is well illustrated by Mr Collins's proposal to Elizabeth in Pride and Prejudice (I.xix), where her refusal is interpreted as 'modest', that is, a conventional gesture rather than a heart-felt rejection (Yeazell 1991: 143–4). The valorisation of a woman's ignorance of herself seems designed expressly to leave decisions concerning her in the hands of men.

In this context what Jan Fergus calls the 'emotional didacticism' of Austen's first three novels, *Northanger Abbey* and *Sense and Sensibility* as well as *Pride and Prejudice*, can be seen in two ways (Fergus 1983). By this phrase Fergus means that Austen sets out to cultivate her reader's emotional responses to social situations as a type of moral training. The feelings being cultivated by reading these novels may be perfectly modest; but the type of self-knowledge necessary to this cultivation empowers the female reader in the way the conduct books warn against. Something like this gap may also produce Austen's irony, discussed earlier [see pp. 96–7]. For Rachel Brownstein (1994), Austen's irony is produced by her resistance to the types of fiction for women that have shaped the market for her own novels. It is a way of distancing herself from the didactic fiction of Richardson or Burney while still exploiting the conventions they developed. More recently, Clara Tuite has taken this argument a step further. She suggests that Austen's achievement was to take the tactics of the didactic novel and refine them to such an extent that they became a source of aesthetic pleasure in themselves, turning the domestic novel into 'a polished, finished, aesthetic artefact' by 'the transformation of pedagogical irony into something so stylized and formal and abstract that it does not even appear to resemble moralizing or "instruction" ' (Tuite 2002: 80–1). This might explain why critics, as we noted earlier, tend to read Austen's moral message as inhering in her formal brilliance, but it also explains why most modern readers manage to enjoy the novels while ignoring their moral message altogether.

So far in this section we have looked at what feminist critics have to say about Austen. Devoney Looser, in her introduction to *Jane Austen and the Discourses of Feminism*, usefully outlines the multiple ways in which Austen can be read through feminist ideas (Looser 1995). But there is also a strong case to be made for saying that Austen is herself a feminist, in that eighteenth-century tradition that culminates in the work of Mary Wollstonecraft [see p. 25]. Lloyd Brown was the first to place Austen in this context in 'Jane Austen and the Feminist Tradition' (Brown 1973–4). In an essay in Looser's 1995 collection, Gary Kelly describes just how complex and multi-faceted this tradition is, and how interwoven with the different models of society in general that were in circulation in the eighteenth century.

The first full-length study to take seriously the idea that Austen might be drawing on the ideas of Wollstonecraft at least as much as on Edmund Burke was Margaret Kirkham's *Jane Austen, Feminism and Fiction* (1983). I noted above that Marilyn Butler uses Austen's hostility to extravagant 'sensibility' as a mark of her closeness to anti-Jacobin propagandists, even after she herself has pointed out that the 'Jacobin' novelists of the 1790s were hostile to sensibility too, on other grounds [see pp. 117–19]. Kirkham makes the same point with regard to sexual morality more broadly: the tightening up of sexual mores was a response to the political crisis across the board, on both sides of the political argument. And despite Wollstonecraft's posthumous savaging at the hands of the reactionary press, recognisably feminist arguments could be found on both sides of the political argument too.

> Because Mary Wollstonecraft and Mary Hays were among that group
> [the 'Jacobin' writers], we tend to think of feminism as restricted to
> that group, but this is misleading; the feminist interest cut across other

political divisions to a considerable extent. If the moral and (by implication) political question which concerned Jane Austen most was the feminist one, her stance as a rational moralist does not carry the reactionary implications which it might otherwise appear to do.

(Kirkham 1983: xiii)

Owing to the way in which our history of the eighteenth century has been written, with the distinguished women usually mentioned, if at all, in connection with their association with better-known men and male-dominated movements, schools or other groupings, the continuity of feminist development, in all its manifestations, is easily overlooked. Our habit of thinking of Mary Wollstonecraft as a Jacobin, and Jane Austen as a Lady Novelist praised by Scott, makes it difficult for us to see connections between them; attention to the 'feminist tradition' of the eighteenth century, in its widest sense, shows that it is by no means bizarre to look for such connection.

(Kirkham 1983: 40–1)

Kirkham therefore places Austen in that line of feminist thinkers, from Mary Astell through Catherine Macaulay to Wollstonecraft, whose central aim was to have women recognised as the rational equals of men, and have them educated accordingly. Their Enlightenment feminism was, fundamentally, a resistance to the continuing definition of women in terms of the emotions rather than reason, a definition that the culture of sentiment had turned from the routine slander of earlier ages into a much more insidious limitation, by making irrationality and emotional self-indulgence an ideal which young women might internalise and attempt to act out as a way of making themselves more attractive to men. Anne Elliot's outburst in *Persuasion* ('Men have had every advantage of us in telling their own story. . . . The pen has been in their hands. I will not allow books to prove anything', II.xi.220) is, after all, at once a feminist rejection of gender hierarchy, and a restatement of the Enlightenment principle that the authority of established texts is not sufficient to guarantee their truth. By placing Austen in this context, Kirkham relates her to the deeper patterns of an ongoing struggle which the noisy party conflict of the 1790s brought into play but also obscured.

In the context of *Mansfield Park*, Kirkham makes the point that the conduct book version of femininity, which promised that self-effacement and ignorance would help reel in a husband, succeeded only in confusing the categories of morality and sexuality, so that qualities that were supposed to signal innocence and virtue in fact became highly sexually charged. In consequence, the reader is expected to be able to distinguish between Fanny's conduct book qualities of weakness and modesty which make her attractive to Henry Crawford, and the intelligence that makes her attractive to Edmund. That conduct book ideals tended to *infantilise* women is a running theme in Kirkham's analysis, and the praise of feminine physical weakness in a writer like Rousseau [see p. 35] is one of Wollstonecraft's targets in the *Vindication* when she writes that 'the first care of those mothers or fathers who really attend to the education of females should be, if not to strengthen the body, at least not to destroy the constitution by mistaken notions of beauty' (Wollstonecraft [1792] 1975: 127). Accordingly, Austen portrays Fanny's physical weakness at the start of the novel not as a quality essential to her, let alone a good thing, but the consequence of poor living conditions, and something that Edmund can train her out of. Mrs Croft, in *Persuasion*, represents a counter-ideal to the sentimental one, physically robust and energetic, and she is the one who hates to hear her brother 'talking so, like a fine gentleman, and as if women were all fine ladies, instead of rational creatures' (I.viii.65).

However, 'feminism' for Kirkham remains something worked out in the themes of these particular novels, in their overt subject matter. Kirkham has less to say about the extent to which Austen's *formal* innovations in the novel, such as her use of irony or free indirect discourse, offered specific generic resources to feminism. The tradition that matters is that of the 'female philosophers' Astell, Macaulay and Wollstonecraft, and the novel as a form is imagined as an empty vessel into which their ideas can be poured, and narrative as a means of expressing their ideas, without those ideas being in any way altered. This leaves Kirkham unsure of what to do with a different tradition, that of the female-authored novel, which very often and very obviously had ideas of its own. On the other hand she admits that 'it will not do to approach the female authors of this period and divide them into genuine feminists versus the rest, for at this period to become an author was, in itself, a feminist act' (Kirkham 1983: 33–5).

There is one other question raised by Kirkham's book. This is the role of rank and status in Austen's world. Kirkham gives a good account of Austen's feminist criticism of various institutions as they discriminate against women: the laws of inheritance in *Pride and Prejudice*, for example. But Austen is not obviously in the business of criticising the hierarchical structure of English society itself. Many of its office holders, fathers, landowners and clergymen alike, may fail to do their job properly, but the idea that authority should be the preserve of a particular class is never held up for questioning.

> As the novel unfolds, the education of hero and heroine, about themselves and one another as moral equals, is shown in a way which subverts the stereotype in which a heroine is educated by a Hero-Guardian. Emma, for all her faults, belongs with the Guardians of England as it ought to be – represented by Donwell Abbey, rather than Highbury – and Mr Knightley . . . is a hero who earns, or ought to earn, the respect of intelligent but far from perfect women.
>
> (Kirkham 1983: 139)

If Austen is an Enlightenment feminist, there are clearly limits to that enlightenment, to its capacity to rationally critique social institutions. Two pages before, Kirkham has argued that Emma, rather than exhibiting the self-indulgent feeling of the typical novel heroine, 'is truly sympathetic and sensitive to the wretchedness of the poor' (137). Are there still the wretched poor in 'England as it ought to be'? This is not a question that *Emma* is prepared to ask.

Claudia Johnson's *Jane Austen: Women, Politics and the Novel* (1988), like Kirkham's book, finds Austen's starting point in the reactionary politics of the 1790s, and understands Austen as a broadly feminist writer. But Johnson does so not by examining her debt to an Enlightenment feminist tradition culminating in Wollstonecraft. Instead, she locates Austen among the same contemporaries to whom Butler calls our attention, the women writers of anti-Jacobin reaction, Elizabeth Hamilton, Jane West and Hannah More; *not* because Austen simply shared their counter-revolutionary, anti-feminist agenda, as Butler would have it, but because Austen appropriates their typical plots and characterisation in order to subvert the anti-feminist assumptions that underlie them. Rather than placing herself outside the respectability of conservative women's fiction, Austen takes the conventions and myths of such writing as her raw materials, then uses them to establish a much more radical position on women's role in society than More or West could ever have countenanced.

Central to Johnson's argument is the discovery that the place of women was not just one of many issues that divided radicals from reactionaries in the aftermath of the French Revolution in Britain. Rather, it had a crucial and quite specific role to play in the rhetoric of the anti-Jacobins. As we have seen in Part 1, the domestic ideal developed by Richardson, and in the conduct books of Fordyce and Gregory, to describe a feminine realm outside politics was now appropriated for explicitly political purposes [see pp. 32–3]. Johnson observes,

> To be sure, women novelists had never been wanting for subjects before the Revolution in France. But after it, those largely domestic subjects, concerning which they had been acknowledged to have some wisdom, were brought to the forefront of national life and were infused with dignity as well as urgency.
>
> (Johnson 1988: 2)

In the reactionary novels of, for example, Hannah More [see pp. 34, 35–6], the threat of revolutionary subversion is thus translated into sexual terms: threats to the political status quo, from France as from radicals within, are figured as threats to paternal authority over the family:

> With the countryside full of Jacobin riffraff out to ruin English families by seducing women away from fond fathers and rightful husbands, female modesty – that is to say, the extent to which women do not feel, express, and pursue their own desires – is no less than a matter of national security.
>
> (Johnson 1988: 18)

In this context, Austen's clear-eyed examination of the domestic sphere can itself be seen to disengage it from the conservative political function that it had been able to perform as long as it remained an unquestioned ideal, even while she adopts the domestic sphere as the setting for her stories. The 'female modesty' that conservatives see as guaranteeing the integrity of family life is critiqued for its silencing of women's voices, even as Austen goes through the motions of the self-effacement that it demands of a woman author. This Johnson calls her 'procedure of using apparently conservative material in order to question rather than confirm it' (21). The rhetoric of anti-Jacobin reaction is not only cooled in Austen's novels, but examined and its assumptions criticised.

In *Sense and Sensibility*, for example, the fate of the Dashwood sisters and their mother reveals the gentry family to be an arena for competing economic self-interest rather than the scene of moral and emotional nurture. In *Mansfield Park*, the family closes in on itself, instead of being the origin of the 'extended affections' that bind the neighbourhood and the nation as Burke says they should. Fanny ends up marrying a cousin, Edmund, who had previously presumed (as had everyone else) that she was too close to him in blood for this to be a possibility. And they end up living close to the Park itself: 'the principals in *Mansfield Park* gather together in a tighter knot of consanguinity because the larger world outside has always proved more than they could manage' (Johnson 1988: 119). Johnson begins her reading of *Northanger Abbey* with a reminder that Radcliffe's Gothic novel (like the culture of sensibility in general) can cut both ways politically in its representation of tyrannical patriarchs driven by monstrous passions: it can represent a conservative demonstration of the need for the heroine to discipline the emotions, but also a nightmare version of the patriarchal oppression that structures her everyday life. Austen's novel then appears as an exploration of the connections between the political and the generic. General Tilney, for example, 'is not only a repressive father, but a self-confessed defender of national security' (35). The confusion between Eleanor and Catherine over that 'something very shocking indeed, that will soon come out in London' (I.xiv.107), which Eleanor assumes is an actual riot rather than a novel, is not just satirising Catherine's confusion of 'fiction' and 'reality' but suggesting that they have something in common, and confirming that 'political unrest and Gothic fiction are well served by a common vocabulary of "horror" because they are both unruly responses to repression' (Johnson 1988: 39). If Burke uses Gothic language to describe the political crimes of the Paris mob, Catherine Morland returns that language to the place that, in Burke's view, is the origin of all our virtuous political sentiments, the family home, and discovers oppression at its heart.

But Austen's deflation of conservative myths can also take the form of simple anticlimax. Fanny Price may be appalled by Maria's adultery in *Mansfield Park*, but the narrator treats it as an unexceptional piece of society gossip: it does not signal imminent defeat by the French. Similarly, in *Sense and Sensibility*, Austen refuses to let Marianne die once she is abandoned by Willoughby, the conventional fate of the abandoned heroine of a sentimental novel. This is the destiny fulfilled instead by Eliza, Colonel Brandon's first love, married and seduced like Maria Bertram, but then abandoned with a child. Brandon, discovering her in a debtors' prison, sounds relieved that she is going to see through her expected role: 'That she was, to all appearance, in the last stage of consumption, was—yes, in such a situation it was my greatest comfort. Life could do nothing for her, beyond giving time for a better preparation for death' (II.ix.196). But her daughter, in turn seduced and abandoned by Willoughby, does not die, and both men are rather surprised by her survival, as by Marianne's, as they reveal in their narrations in II.ix and III.viii respectively. A young woman in these circumstances is *expected* to die, and it is most convenient for the men around her if she does. The male narrators of these stories, that is, are working within the conventions of sentimental narrative which envisages only one fate for the abandoned heroine: they, rather than Marianne, are the ones seeing the world through the expectations created by this fictional genre. By including these male narrative voices, Austen reveals the narrative mechanics of patriarchal power that are at work *within* the sentimental novel; her own novel then frustrates them. In both of these cases, a 'modest', conservative heroine is witness to the desire of another woman being expressed in improper ways. In *Pride and Prejudice*, it is the other way round, and of all the novels this is accordingly the most clearly critical of the conduct books' demand that a woman should not express her own desires, but wait for a man to express them on her behalf. Reading Darcy's explanation of his interference in Bingley's relationship with Jane, Elizabeth realises that Jane's inability to express her feelings was one factor that allowed Darcy to behave as he did: 'She felt that Jane's feelings, though fervent, were little displayed, and that there was a constant complacency in her air and manner, not often united with great sensibility' (II.xiii.202).

I began this discussion of Johnson by noting that on her view, Austen's novels *both* appropriate *and* react against the conservative myths that they criticise. Appropriating them, even for the purposes of criticism, necessarily means repeating them. So that in *Mansfield Park*, for example, 'Austen accomplishes her critique of the gentry family by registering its impact on a heroine who, though a model of female virtue and filial gratitude, is betrayed by the same ethos she dutifully embraces' (96). Austen does this, Johnson suggests, because more direct social criticism would invite the sort of abuse and loss of authority incurred by Wollstonecraft and her allies:

> [B]ecause reactionary apologists arrogated all moral authority to themselves, effectual dissent on the subject of sexual difference and a host of topics constellated around it was difficult, not to say down-right dangerous. . . . To write novels of social criticism, authors had to develop strategies of subversion and indirection which would enable them to use the polemical tradition without being used completely by it.
>
> (Johnson 1988: 19)

Or in the words of another critic, who like Johnson sees Austen as a moderate feminist attacking the restrictions placed on women even as she worked within them: 'As a member of a clerical family, she was anxious to spare herself and her family any ugly notoriety, and so she adopted policies of thematic and rhetorical caution' (Sulloway 1989: 4).

Clearly Austen's novels both develop a conservative position and criticise it. But for Johnson, these two aspects of Austen's project are not just in tension. Rather, the former is always only a means to the achievement of the latter: the deployment of conservative assumptions about society is only a necessary condition of Austen's real goal, which is its criticism. The revelation of Fanny's betrayal by the gentry ethos must be ultimately more important than the dedication with which she embraces it in the first place. Marianne's subversive survival must be more important than the deadening discipline to which Elinor then subjects her. The temptation on Johnson's part is inevitably to treat such conservative counter-moves within the text as mere conventional gestures, demanded by the need to conform to the shape of the novel as Austen had inherited it; just as, having revealed the real oppression hitherto coded in the conventions of the Gothic novel in *Northanger Abbey*, Austen can only end up by ironically repeating the conventions, rather than reasserting the reality, because she does, after all, have a novel to finish somehow:

> Alluding to the 'tell-tale compression of the pages before them' which can only signal that 'we are all hastening together to perfect felicity' . . . Austen draws attention to the artificiality, rather than the *vraisemblance*, of her conclusion, and implies that the damage wrought by the likes of General Tilney is in fact not resolvable into the 'perfect felicity' of fiction, and that the convention of the happy ending conceals our all-too-legitimate cause for alarm.
>
> (Johnson 1988: 47–8)

But it might be argued on the contrary that what Austen borrows from conservative fiction remains as politically resonant as her subversive gestures towards it: that a conventional plot development, like marriage to a rich man, does not automatically lose its ideological potency because the courtship narrative has revealed problems in the conservative ideal of marriage. This becomes a problem whenever the question of social rank comes up. For of course the post-1789 reaction was not only about defending a gender hierarchy; it was about defending a social hierarchy based on inherited land as the basis of political power. On Johnson's view, *Emma* appears as something of a female utopia, in which (Knightley aside) women are in charge: not only Emma, but also Mrs Elton and Mrs Churchill, are the characters who take the decisions that matter in this novel. Clearly, these women are able to do this because they are, themselves, well-off members of the propertied classes. '*Emma* is a world apart from conservative fiction in accepting a hierarchical social structure not because it is a sacred dictate of patriarchy – *Mansfield Park* had spoiled this – but rather because within its parameters class can actually supersede sex' (Johnson 1988: 127).

Note what is being implied here, if not quite spelt out: *Emma* is not a conservative novel, despite the fact that it clearly affirms the existing social hierarchy, because it affirms that hierarchy *for a different reason* from other ('conservative') writers. The latter defend rank because it makes possible the authority of men over women: *Emma* because it makes possible the opposite. But it could surely be argued that a conservative is one in favour of the established social hierarchy, whatever the reason for being so. Johnson is close here to defining 'conservative' in terms of gender politics alone, even though she begins her book with a definitive account of the part played by gender in a wider political scene. Emma indeed comes to consciousness of the provisional and precarious nature of rank in her consideration of the gap in self-determination between Mrs Churchill and Jane Fairfax, and thus to a sense of solidarity with other women across this (comparatively narrow) status divide.

> By preferring to read Jane's story as a tale of guilty passion, Emma had maintained for herself the prerogative either of censure or of generous exoneration that placed her apart from and above Jane. As Emma herself recognises, in having done so she has 'transgressed the duty of woman by woman'.
>
> (Johnson 1988: 137)

But it remains likely that the 'woman' of this formulation remains the *polite* woman and not her proletarian sisters toiling in field or cotton-mill: Austen's politics would look very different if Emma were acknowledging a duty towards *them*. This overcoming of status divisions on the basis of gender remains in tension with the 'superseding of sex by class' that, for Johnson, separates *Emma* from 'conservative' fiction. It is not clear that Emma, chastened, thoughtful and married to Knightley, has abandoned at the end of the novel the principle she spells out to Harriet at the beginning: 'The Yeomanry are precisely the order of people with whom I feel I can have nothing to do' (I.iv.29).

Similarly, in the case of *Pride and Prejudice*, Johnson must confront the fact that happiness for this novel's heroine is integration into the British ruling class. Elizabeth is both remarkably immodest in her honesty regarding her own desire for Darcy and defiant in the face of a social hierarchy (represented by Lady Catherine de Bourgh) that wants to keep her in her place: we have seen that Butler has a hard time fitting *Pride and Prejudice* into her conservative model. But however Elizabeth's desire may be legitimated by the novel in this radical way, it remains desire for a rich landowner from an ancient family: female desire appears here as a support, rather than a threat, to the existing order.

> In fact, the 'conservatism' of *Pride and Prejudice* is an imaginative experiment with conservative myths, and not a statement of faith in them as they already stood in anti-Jacobin fiction. To be sure, by using these myths, even to hedge, qualify, and improve them, Austen is also, necessarily, used by them. But throughout the course of the novel those myths become so transformed that they are made to accommodate what could otherwise be seen as subversive impulses and values, and in the process they themselves become the vehicles of incisive social criticism.
>
> (Johnson 1988: 75)

But to say that Austen is 'used by' conservative myths is an odd refusal of agency to Austen in the context of a novel whose whole point, according to Johnson herself, is to make feminine agency seem to be acceptable within conservative ideology. The role given female desire in legitimating social hierarchy will tend to reconcile conservatives to a wider scope being given to the female voice within the culture as a whole, but it will also tend to reconcile propertied women to the existing social hierarchy. There is no reason to take Austen's commitment to anti-revolutionary *social* politics as any less voluntary than its commitment to this type of feminism: in *Pride and Prejudice*, they are *mutually* legitimating.

Austen, empire and nationality

Slavery in *Mansfield Park*

On two occasions in recent decades has a critical reading of Austen escaped the confines of the universities and caught the attention of the wider media. One was Eve Sedgwick's suggestion, discussed above [see **pp. 111–12**], that heterosexuality might not be the only type of sexual identity available in Austen's fiction. The other was Edward Said's suggestion, in *Culture and Imperialism* (1993), that *Mansfield Park* implicated Austen in slavery (an earlier version of Said's discussion of this novel appeared in 1989). Said's book is an examination of the way in which the core cultures of the great empires of the nineteenth and twentieth centuries imagined the countries that they ruled and exploited, and imagined them in ways which legitimated that rule and that exploitation. It also examines the forms taken by resistance to this cultural domination on the part of the ruled and exploited themselves. It is a little anachronistic to talk of 'imperialism' in Austen's period: Britain's various trading networks, forts, settlements and slave plantations clearly constituted an empire, but had not yet been conceptualised as a general *project* that might be called 'imperialism'. And references to Britain's overseas territories in Austen's novels are few and far between. Yet Austen plays an important role in the first part of Said's book, because these few references seem to acknowledge the role of colonies in supporting the social order that she chronicles at home. To understand this, Said suggests, requires thinking about a novel like *Mansfield Park* in terms of the way it represents space, as well as the way that its narrative organises time.

Much of Fanny's sense of herself in the Bertram household is determined by the spaces she is allowed to make use of (her bedroom, the old schoolroom). The misuse of domestic space for theatrical performance is a spatial transgression making possible the moral dangers of the play itself; and when she returns to Portsmouth in III.vii–viii, the narrow moral and emotional life of her family is both reflected in, and the product of, the narrowness of their house. Said argues that making increased *domestic* space a condition of Fanny's moral and intellectual development finds a parallel in the extension of the Bertram property into the West Indies, where Sir Thomas owns a plantation. He suggests that this plantation, operated with slave labour, is the source of the money that makes possible the leisured lifestyle enjoyed by the younger Bertrams, and in which Fanny participates. This parallel is given force by the moral agreement of Sir Thomas and Fanny over the theatricals which becomes apparent on his return from Antigua: 'Austen sees what Fanny does as a domestic or small-scale movement in space that corresponds to the larger, more openly colonial movements of Sir Thomas, her mentor, the man whose estates she inherits. The two movements depend on each other' (Said 1993: 106). Fanny's moral restoration of the Bertram household at the end of the novel is then the domestic equivalent of Sir Thomas restoring order among his slaves and their overseers; and it is the money from the latter that makes the former possible. This gentry family is renewed, financially and morally, by its taking within itself two 'properties' from outside, 'the wealth of Antigua and the imported example of Fanny Price' (109). And because the latter importation occurs as the happy ending to a love story, the former is made by association equally right and natural. '[T]he morality in fact is not separable from its social basis: right up to the last sentence, Austen affirms and repeats the geographical process of expansion involving trade, production, and consumption that predates, underlies, and guarantees the morality' (Said 1993: 111).

That one of those vast areas of human experience that Austen seems to largely exclude from her fiction should in fact turn out to have a crucial role in its meaning should not by now be any surprise. Austen has often been criticised for making no mention of the French Revolution and little of the wars that followed, yet, as we have seen, her novels are saturated in the political debate that they generated. And just as Austen's very concentration on the local, the rural and the domestic, to the exclusion of the state-political, is itself a political gesture in the context of that post-revolution debate, so the very slightness of her references to slavery in the West Indies constitutes for Said another aspect of Austen's 'implication' in imperialist expansion (100). For it reduces the colonial experience to the marginal, the subsidiary, of interest only in so far as it makes possible, disrupts or otherwise impinges on the lives of those in the imperial centre.

Said was certainly not the first critic to notice that the Bertrams are slave owners. Avrom Fleishman, in *A Reading of Mansfield Park* (1967), and Tony Tanner, in an essay first published in 1966 (Tanner 1986: 142–75), both draw attention to this fact. But Said's discussion of *Mansfield Park* is in the service of a wider project, a reassessment of British and French cultures in the nineteenth and twentieth centuries to show how those cultures were shaped by the experience of empire just as surely as the cultures that they colonised. This project can be understood as one version of the 'postcolonial' revision of culture generally, and *Culture and Imperialism* as a contribution to postcolonial literary criticism. This specific focus on the culture of imperialism, apparently beyond the horizon of what most readers thought of as Austen's 'world', contributed to the public impact of Said's analysis that we began by noting. This focus was maintained, however, by Said's ignoring those already published analyses of *Mansfield Park* that had paid attention to slavery in relation to the novel's critique of *gender* relations. Margaret Kirkham's chapter on *Mansfield Park* in *Jane Austen, Feminism and Fiction* (1983) [see pp. 127–30] points out that the very name of the Bertrams' estate in *Mansfield Park* evokes the 'Mansfield Judgment', the decision in 1772 by Lord Mansfield, the Lord Chief Justice and England's highest judge, that slavery was legally impossible on the territory of England itself, whatever its status in Britain's overseas possessions. A slave brought to England from the West Indies (the case in point in the courts) was by that token henceforth free. Precedent had been set by an earlier ruling that 'England was too pure an air for slaves to breathe in' (quoted by Kirkham 1983: 118) and this provides a context for Fanny's longing for fresh air that we find referred to repeatedly in *Mansfield Park*.

Similarly, in a 1991 essay Moira Ferguson, like Said, identifies Fanny as equivalent within the novel to the slaves at its margins. But where Said argues that the novel represents both colonial wealth and the poor relation being happily incorporated in a reformed imperial order, Ferguson sees Fanny as linked to Sir Thomas's troublesome slaves by her rebellion against the patriarchal neglect and oppression suffered by the women at Mansfield Park when she refuses to marry Henry Crawford. The white women 'mark silent African-Caribbean rebels as well as their own disenfranchisement, class and gender victimization' (Ferguson 1991: 118). However, these remain 'muffled' rebel voices, and *Mansfield Park* refuses to mount an 'audible' critique of slavery (118, 135). Suvendrini Perera's comments on Austen in *Reaches of Empire* (1991) develop Kirkham's point about 'fresh air' by examining the dialogue of spatial confinement and release characteristic of Austen's later novels. This she links to the wider geography of global conflict and empire, to identify the connection between the domestic sphere and its national and imperial horizons, as figured in the role of the navy in both *Mansfield Park* and *Persuasion*. In the latter novel, sailors, in both the Wentworth and Croft families, are characterised as good home-makers, and Anne finds a sort of home in the navy itself. This 'demonstrates the reciprocity between the domestic and national realms, the one underwriting the continuity of the other' (Perera 1991: 46). I shall shortly return to the question of the 'national' in Austen's writing. For Perera, in any case, the heroine's imperial 'Englishness' in these stories is 'double-edged . . . confining as it affirms, imprisoning as it expands' (46).

Carl Plasa has recently brought this debate full circle by returning to a more developed version of Said's position. He agrees with Kirkham and Ferguson that the novel asserts an equivalence between English gentry women and slaves. However, while the discourse of slavery is utilised by this novel to mount a critique of gender relations among the English gentry, this does not also constitute an implicit critique of slave owning itself. Rather, this use of the slave issue to talk about something very different is precisely the mechanism by which the novel avoids having to address slavery overtly. Plasa argues that several aspects of the novel act out this tactic of displacement and evasion. For example, Edmund's censure in I.vii.60–1 of Mary Crawford's open mockery of her uncle in the previous chapter expresses within the novel the censoring that *Mansfield Park* imposes on itself in the matter of slavery (Plasa 2001: 40) [see p. 68]. Slave rebellion is imaged, not in Fanny's refusal of Henry Crawford, but in the 'barbarism' of Maria Bertram's adulterous sexuality (42) which the novel punishes rather than rewards. This point is lent force by Maaja Stewart's observation, in *Domestic Realities and Imperial Fictions* (1993), that the Caribbean plantations were the site of quite specific worries about female sexuality: about the dependence of slave owners on the fertility of slave women to renew the supply of labour once the slave trade was abolished, and about the collapse of sexual morality in a society where white slave masters routinely kept black mistresses. Further, the ownership of the plantations by absentee landlords who remained in Britain was identified as the cause of their bad management generally. Sir Thomas's failure in regard to his own family is the failure to control female sexuality, exactly the problem ascribed to plantation owners in general at the time.

On the other hand, many critics have seen *Mansfield Park*'s linking of women to slaves in more positive terms. Joseph Lew sees Fanny's resistance as making more noise than Ferguson allows, for example: her refusal of Henry Crawford is 'an act of rebellion, endangering a system based upon the exchange of women between men as surely as a slave's refusal to work' (Lew 1994: 291). Susan Fraiman, in a discussion of Said first published in 1995, takes issue with many of Said's assertions. Sir Thomas's values are *not* those ultimately affirmed by the novel, as Said suggests. If his restoration of order at Mansfield Park is a repetition of his intervention in Antigua, as Said suggests, they are also a total failure, as the 'moral blight' infecting Mansfield remains after his return (Lynch 2000: 208). Fraiman accepts that generally Austen is one of those who 'made colonialism thinkable by constructing the West as center, home, and norm' (209). But slavery here 'is not a subtext wherein Austen and Sir Thomas converge' but is used by Austen 'to argue the essential depravity of Sir Thomas's relations to other people' (213). *Mansfield Park* thus 'challenges the ethical basis' of the English landowner's authority 'both at home and, by implication, overseas' (211). Said ignores the extent to which Austen, rather than sharing in this authority, enjoys only 'the anxious and impaired authority of the female writer' (215). Fraiman goes on to suggest that the prominence Said gives to Austen as a representative of the culture of the coloniser must itself be understood in terms of the inter-relation of imperialism and gender categories. The rhetoric of empire genders the colonising society as masculine (active, powerful) and the colonised as feminine (passive, dependent). Said's choice of Austen can be seen as a reversal of this equation, making a feminine fiction stand for the coloniser in opposition to the male anti-colonial writers whom he goes on to discuss, thus 'remasculinizing' the colonised male, writer and critic alike (218).

The very breadth of *Culture and Imperialism* requires Said to generalise an imperial project that remains essentially the same throughout the nineteenth century, making Caribbean slavery in *Mansfield Park* representative of colonial enterprise generally, and Austen's historical moment at the start of the nineteenth century indistinguishable from the confident, aggressive imperialism of the later reign of Queen Victoria. In the decade since Said's book appeared, several critics have filled in some of the specifics that Said necessarily omits. So Brian Southam, in an essay first published in 1995, picks up and expands on Moira Ferguson's precise dating of the action of *Mansfield Park* to 1810–12. Great Britain made the trade in slaves illegal in 1807; slave trading was made a felony in 1811, and this increased the legal penalties for those convicted. For Said, the 'dead silence' that meets Fanny's question about the slave trade to Sir Thomas suggests that 'one world could not be connected with the other since there simply is no common language for both' (Said 1993: 115). And yet Edmund tells Fanny that 'It would have pleased your uncle to be inquired of farther' on this matter: the 'silence' is that of the Bertram children who Fanny expects to pick up this topic of conversa-tion, but who are too ignorant, or morally indifferent, to do so (II.iii.184). Southam points out that, living at the end of a noisy twenty-year campaign for its abolition, the characters of *Mansfield Park* can hardly lack a language for the discussion of the slave trade. For Austen's first readers, Fanny's question would clearly identify her as in favour of its abolition, and, as this was a hugely popular cause in which women had a prominent role, they would most likely have approved of her stand (Southam 1998: 498). The moral problem here is not the silence of the culture as a whole, but the decadence of these particular members of the gentry.

Critiques of postcolonial readings of Austen

More recently, however, analysis of the historical context, and close attention to information given in the novel itself, have called into question Said's account of a Mansfield estate materially sustained or made possible by the income from the Antigua plantation (Said 1993: 102, 112), an account accepted as a starting point by most later accounts of the novel. Franco Moretti, in *Atlas of the European Novel 1800–1900* (1998; first published in Italian in 1997), was perhaps the first to do so (Moretti 1998: 24–9). Trevor Lloyd, in a 1999 article, assembles the evidence from various historical sources, and collates this with the novel's own, quite precise, description of the economics of Mansfield Park. His conclusion is that the slave plantation seems to be generating about 10 per cent of Sir Thomas's total income, and he comments that this seems to be typical for members of the English gentry who owned plantations (Lloyd 1999: 70). Lloyd points out that the main source for identifying the trouble in Antigua as a potential crisis in Sir Thomas's finances is Mrs Norris, and she is hardly a reliable witness to anything.

John Wiltshire continues this work of attention to historical and textual detail to undermine the idea that slavery is the 'key to this famously difficult text' (Wiltshire 2003: 303). The parallel between women and slaves was a common one at the time, but not because there was any real resemblance between well-off, leisured English women and Caribbean slaves: one glance at accounts of how slaves were actually treated renders such an equation morally absurd (308–9). Rather, it was an equation made by the likes of Mary Wollstonecraft and Hannah More in their (very different) campaigns against women's subordinate status, as a way of tapping into the much more general outrage felt against the slave trade at the time (309). Moreover, some slave *owners* managed to be against the slave *trade*, imagining that improvement of the conditions in which slaves were held, and especially the introduction of marriage as an institution among them, would end their reliance on constant infusions of new slaves from Africa to maintain their labour force. There is no reason to suppose that Sir Thomas is not one such (311, 313). Fanny's question to him, as noted above, is about the slave trade and not slavery as such: hence his readiness, ignored by Southam, to answer (315–16; these points are well made by Jon Mee in Park and Rajan 2000: 85). His hazardous trip across the Atlantic during a war to a disease-ridden Caribbean, rarely undertaken by those who owned estates there, suggests a sense of responsibility that also fits with such a surmise, and those campaigning for the abolition of the slave trade had identified Antigua, where improvements in the slaves' conditions had increased their productivity, as an exception to the general West Indian rule (Wiltshire 2003: 312). It is possible, then, that while *Mansfield Park* briefly utilises the controversy over the slave trade to highlight the moral differences between the characters, it does not identify slave holding itself as particularly morally problematic.

Wiltshire's account of *Mansfield Park* asks us to consider the 'demand' of postcolonial critics that slavery 'play a major role' in the novel as 'an articulation of modern political need' (317) rather than telling us anything about the novel itself. He asks instead that we consider *Mansfield Park* as an autonomous work of art, indifferent to present-day anxieties about race (313, 318). One might accept his criticism of too easy moral assumptions on the part of other critics, and still counter that *any* reading of a text from the past, however closely it attends to its historical and textual specifics, is bound to be informed by some contemporary need, however unconscious or covert, that might be called 'political' in the widest sense. It could be argued that the problem with postcolonial criticism of Austen is not that it is politically motivated, but that it generates its own 'dead silence' on other political problems in Austen's society. Too often, it makes a connection between women and slaves on the basis of their shared 'oppression', and this oppression needs nothing more than the greed of individual white men to explain it. As a result, such criticism ignores the one social framework within which both Caribbean slave holding and early nineteenth-century patriarchal marriage arrangements have their meaning: the economic relations of a capitalism already, in Austen's time, becoming a global system. Without being mediated by this context, a connection between the conditions of women and slaves will always appear arbitrary, with one category being used as no more than a metaphor for the other. Moreover, the critical focus on slavery tends to isolate it as an issue from the capitalism that makes it possible, and thus generates its own ideological blindness in our time. For while slavery as an institution has been largely abolished, global economic exploitation has not gone away. In a university class in Europe or North America, teachers and students may shake their heads at Sir Thomas's wickedness, at Austen's complicity in slavery, while sipping coffee grown by farmers whose income has been driven down to starvation levels by the policies of the World Bank, and while wearing trainers made on machinery that mutilates its exhausted Third World workers because their western-backed governments will not allow trades unions. *Mansfield Park* provides us with a way of thinking about the interpenetration of global economic relations with everyday life. A postcolonial approach to this text could remind us of our ongoing implication in those relations. A narrow focus on a long-abolished slavery could be helping us to forget.

Hence the value of essays such as Fraser Easton's 'The Political Economy of *Mansfield Park*: Fanny Price and the Atlantic Working Class' (1998). The objects of Austen's critique here are 'the social costs of economic modernization' in general, and Easton sees the novel's accounts of slave owning and gender politics as elements of a broader social critique. Lord Mansfield, remembered by post-colonial critics only as the judge in the slavery case, was 'a key legislative supporter of economic modernization' such as the appropriation and enclosure of communal land by landowners (Easton 1998: 459). And Northamptonshire, where Austen locates Mansfield Park, was the scene of both rapid enclosure and marked labouring-class resistance to it (467). This makes sense of Austen's request to her sister Cassandra to find out 'whether Northamptonshire is a Country of Hedgerows' (29 January 1813; Le Faye 1995: 202). Hedgerows were what physically 'enclosed' the enlarged fields produced by the capitalisation of agriculture [see pp. 20–1]. Naval dockyards such as Portsmouth, the novel's other main location, were the site of 'the greatest concentrations of labour in England', and the scene of some of the bitterest battles over the rationalisation and mechanisation of the workplace (476). Critics have traditionally seen the pairing of Mansfield Park and Portsmouth as expressing an opposition, between order and chaos, between Fanny's past and her future. But Henry Crawford's discussion with Fanny of his responsibilities as a landowner takes place in the dockyard at Portsmouth, suggesting that the same issues are at stake in industry as on the land and indeed in the West Indies.

This is not to claim that Austen was in any sense a radical: as Easton observes, 'a conservative orientation is not necessarily a submissive one' (1998: 461), and labouring-class resistance to rationalisation was usually in defence of rights accorded them by the old order, rather than in the name of rights aspired to in a democratic future. In her essay 'Domestic Retrenchment and Imperial Expansion' (Park and Rajan 2000: 93–115) Clara Tuite, like Easton, looks for a common ground for postcolonial and feminist accounts of *Mansfield Park* by describing the novel's account of 'improvement and investment' generally (100). But where

Easton finds this in the novel's echoes of specific historical circumstances, for Tuite the novel's politics are expressed through its use of particular genres of writing. For example, 'liberal feminist' critics like Fraiman, discussed above, take the novel's criticism of Sir Thomas as criticism of his class and thus as part of Austen's 'structural critique' of her society. But Tuite argues that Austen is writing satire here, 'a conservative, diagnostic and recuperative genre'. That is, Sir Thomas is criticised for failing to fulfil the duties of his class, and the novel shows him being restored to his proper role by Fanny as a way of strengthening and continuing the social hierarchy to which he belongs. 'Austen's satire is not engaged in an outright denunciation of these institutions of empire and aristocracy . . . but is an attempt to renovate them' (Park and Rajan 2000: 97). That is, *Mansfield Park* is itself committed to the agenda of 'improvement', of modernisation, that Fraser Easton sees it as questioning.

Domesticity and empire

Alongside genre, the *nation* appears in Tuite's argument as the category that links the gender politics of *Mansfield Park* to its imperial horizons. As part of her extended critique of Said, Tuite notes that the 'dead silence' of the Bertrams over the slave trade appears in the text less as a signal of their moral attitudes to slavery than as a moment in the ongoing drama of Fanny's relation to her uncle and his daughters: this is the context in which Fanny and Edmund understand it in the dialogue in which that silence is reported. 'In this way, this momentary gesture of outward-looking, worldly, colonial critique is subordinated to and chastised by the impulses of domestic drama. . . . The world of the colonies is represented or subsumed by the terms of representation by [*sic*] the other world of the domestic' (Park and Rajan 2000: 104). And the 'domestic', now understood as 'subsuming' the imperial within itself, no longer names the interior world of the home, but the home *nation*, England. England's status as a nation is imagined in terms of its reconfiguration as an island, self-sufficient because what was outside its territory (the slave plantations of the Caribbean) is reconceived as already inside itself. The interior of that nation is imagined as a 'green core' ruled by reformed gentry like Sir Thomas, while 'Fanny and William figure the lower classes as the outer periphery' that protects them (110).

Tuite's argument develops and expands points originally put forward by Maaja Stewart in *Domestic Realities and Imperial Fictions* (1993). For Stewart, the subsuming of stories of empire into domestic narratives that Tuite describes in *Mansfield Park* is also a feature of *Sense and Sensibility* and *Persuasion*. This recurring pattern makes the domestic sphere complicit in empire but 'the domestic sphere' and 'empire' are not so much locations as genres of narrative:

> The separation of violence intrinsic to imperial power from the metropolitan and domestic realm is part of the ideology of imperialism. Austen enforces this separation in *Mansfield Park* with a recurrent textual subordination of male reality and men's stories to the reality and stories of women.
>
> (Stewart 1993: 123)

So that, in each of the three novels, the heroine's power to morally renew decaying gentry families is linked to a man who comes back to England from some sort of imperial or military experience abroad: Elinor Dashwood with Colonel Brandon in *Sense and Sensibility*, Fanny with Sir Thomas, and Anne Elliot with Captain Wentworth in *Persuasion*. Each of these women is able to 'secure, stabilize, and assure the unstable psychological and ethical capital that is created in conjunction with the insecure financial capital of imperial endeavours' (Stewart 1993: 8). That is, the profits of the modern military/mercantile empire can only be put to use in renovating Britain's social order through the figure of the domestic woman. And they do this through listening to the stories that the male adventurers can tell.

In the case of *Sense and Sensibility*, Stewart focuses on that narrative of Colonel Brandon's that is also central to Claudia Johnson's discussion of the novel [see **p. 131**]. Stewart argues that Brandon's imposition of the archetypes of sentimental fiction on the three women victims of his narrative (the two Elizas, mother and daughter, and Marianne) is the characteristic act of a man returning from the scene of imperial suffering and violence (Brandon chooses a dangerous posting to the West Indies when the first Eliza, his lover, marries his brother instead). Brandon needs to find in Marianne the tamely domestic woman that the first Eliza should have been as a way of recovering 'home' (his own home, but also Britain) as a refuge both from the emotional turmoil from which he escaped, and from its physical equivalent, the disease and horror that he then found in the Caribbean. His narrative thus sets up Marianne's recovery and reformation as necessary to put distance between himself and his colonial experience and its causes: but only Elinor can bring this reformation about. Imperial adventurer and domestic woman thus act in concert to produce the 'home' which sets itself apart from imperial activity, but whose meaning remains determined by that activity, as mediated by the stories told of empire within the home.

Note how the position of the heroine as audience for these stories of empire might relate to the position of the female reader of novels generally. In *Mansfield Park*, the stories that William Price tells of his adventures in the navy (in the Mediterranean as well as the West Indies) are consumed by his sister Fanny as artefacts, souvenirs from exotic elsewheres; they are the narrative equivalents of the shawls that Lady Bertram asks William to bring back from India (II.xiii.282). Male experience at the imperial margins becomes itself a source of pleasure for female consumers at the imperial centre. The problem is not, as Said would have it, that stories of empire cannot be told at the Mansfield dinner table. It is rather that the context of their telling domesticates them, removes them from the political and moral realm where the horrors they describe might demand a moral and political response, by turning them into aesthetic objects for feminine consumption: turns them, that is, into something like novels.

Austen and English nationalism

In Part 1 we saw that the rise of women's moral authority over the household increases (while in some ways it also limits) their cultural authority as writers in the course of the eighteenth century [see **p. 11**]. We saw also that these forms of authority are consolidated by a new English or British nationalism that emerges in the course of that century's wars, especially the war with revolutionary France in the 1790s, a nationalism that includes and legitimates an important place for women in the life of the nation [see pp. 25–6, 35–6]. It is in this context that Jon Mee places Austen's work in 'Austen's Treacherous Ivory: Female Patriotism, Domestic Ideology, and Empire' (Park and Rajan 2000: 74–92), an essay in the same valuable collection as Clara Tuite's, discussed above, *The Postcolonial Jane Austen* (2000). But Mee's essay includes a slightly different account of how this new version of the nation is related to empire. Mee identifies Fanny's 'Englishness' with her emotional response to rural landscape, and particularly the avenue of oak trees that Mr Rushworth wants to chop down, images of a national identity that is both old and an organic growth from English soil [see pp. 116–17]. Mee is in accordance with both Tuite and Maaja Stewart on many points: the identification of England with its landscape (81–2), the 'sublimation' of the issue of slavery 'into the issue of female participation in the nation' (85), and the way in which Fanny and William 'insulate Mansfield Park from . . . a larger, more uncertain, and un-English world. An ideal of female agency in the novel comes, we might say, with an ideal of English autonomy' (87). But he sees the novel as sharing the period's distinctive anxieties about Britain's imperial role: Austen's 'female patriotism' is in a state of 'uneasy tension' with the new realities of 'imperial expansion' (86). In Mee's view, the retreat into an England imagined as a series of country estates ruled by benevolent gentlemen is just that, a retreat from the outside world, and not the positive 'domestication' of empire within the nation that Stewart and Tuite perceive in Austen's novels.

Perhaps the most striking evocation of an English nation identified with its countryside comes, not in *Mansfield Park*, but in Austen's next novel, *Emma*. From Mr Knightley's manor, Donwell Abbey, Emma looks over the country-side and sees 'a sweet view—sweet to the eye and mind. English verdure, English culture, English comfort, seen under a sun bright, without being oppressive' (III.vi.338). Mee notes the implicit contrast with the oppressive sun of tropical colonies that leaves Sir Thomas 'burnt' on his return from Antigua (Park and Rajan 2000: 81). But implicit here also is a version of England defined by its unique balance of old and new. The medieval Donwell Abbey, owned by a man whose very name suggests medieval aristocracy, speaks of a deep continuity in English life and institutions (in contrast to the new political institutions of France or America). On the other hand, 'culture' here clearly means 'agriculture', and if this is distinctively English, it is not because it is old, but because it is new: an improved, rationalised agriculture capable of generating the 'comfort' that contrasts more broadly with peasant agriculture on the continent.

For Miranda Burgess, in *British Fiction and the Production of Social Order* (2000), this combination of an evoked national past with an acknowledgement of the modernity which makes that evocation possible is the distinctive feature of novels in the later eighteenth and early nineteenth centuries. Such novels take the form of 'romances' to the extent that they tell stories in which continuity is asserted between an English (or Scottish, or Irish) past and an English (or British) present: lost heirs are restored to their estates, new blood is incorporated with the old gentry stock through marriage and so on. But at the same time, the novels that told these stories were themselves, very obviously, commodities in a distinctly modern sense: produced as a speculation by enterprising booksellers for sale on the open market in the hope of a profit [see pp. 12–13]. This market for books was largely a national one: indeed, the nation could begin to be defined as a set of families reading the same books. In consequence, novels like Austen's make the consumption of books central to their stories, and in doing so define the nation in terms of its literature.

> For Austen and Scott, romance and the systems that circulated it – the emerging means of cultural production – provided ideological founda-tions and practical infrastructure for an explicitly national unity in which political economy played no role. Austen founded her Britain on engaged reading and commentary among family members living within a private but consuming household, a code of conduct that her fictions and others were expected to reproduce wherever distribution systems took them.
>
> (Burgess 2000: 24)

Among Austen's novels, romance, the relation of modernity to the past, and reading are all themes most conspicuously highlighted in *Northanger Abbey*. For Burgess, Henry Tilney's crucial intervention with Catherine Morland is not to close down the feminine autonomy of her imagination, as feminist critics such as Margaret Kirkwood and Claudia Johnson would argue [see pp. 127–34]. Rather, Henry confronts Catherine with the status of the books she reads as commodities: as 'three duodecimo volumes, two hundred and seventy-six pages in each' (I.xiv.108), produced, distributed and consumed in a national context. Henry's disillusioning of Catherine with her Gothic fantasies at the end of II.ix is striking for Burgess for its evocation of a nation composed not of 'voluntary spies' [see p. 93] but of *readers*: 'Remember that we are English. ... Could they [Catherine's imaginary atrocities] be perpetrated without being known, in a country like this, where social and literary intercourse is on such a footing ... where roads and newspapers lay every thing open?' (II.ix.186). And this concep-tion of England is Austen's own, in her closing address to 'whomsoever it may concern' (II.xvi.235), which places her book in an 'encounter with a faceless literary marketplace and its subjection to unknown critics and readers' (Burgess 2000: 173). The 'Gothic' England that Catherine both imagines and encounters is revealed to be a product of a modern capitalist economy, not its opposite and antidote. Yet in so far as this invented idea of tradition works to produce the national coherence and social order celebrated by Henry in that speech, its artificiality is no objection to it. 'Englishness' is not a fact of nature, but it is necessary for all that.

> Having discredited the naturalness of English Gothic, Henry takes up, makes explicit, and politicizes the submerged artificiality in the Gothic revival's celebration of canon and tradition, emphasizing the role of print production in producing a modicum of social order.
>
> (174)

One might summarise this by saying that, in Austen as in other novelists in her period, the national appears not as a political category, but as an aesthetic one: the nation is defined by its production and consumption of particular types of art, of literature above all, rather than by its political institutions. We have already encountered this idea in the discussion of *Pride and Prejudice* in Part 2 [see pp. 60–2]. In the discussion of Duckworth above [see pp. 116], we noticed that Burke's admitted transformation of politics into a branch of aesthetics might be seen behind the work of landscape in *Mansfield Park*. And in our discussion of Maaja Stewart we have just seen a parallel process at work in the aestheticisation of empire [see pp. 141–2].

These accounts all argue that the novel has a unique role to play in producing and maintaining 'England' as a unified whole: a whole composed, not of subjects or citizens, but of *readers*. Janet Sorensen, in *The Grammar of Empire* (2000), notes that one of the ways in which the novel does this is by propagating a newly standardised version of English as a national language (and while the language is English, the 'nation' invoked here is usually Great Britain rather than England: a common language is required as a unifier of the various nations of the UK as well as a unifier of England itself). As long ago as 1939 Mary Lascelles noted that all of Austen's characters are identifiable by fairly minor deviations from a polite linguistic norm [see pp. 94–5]. None of them speaks in dialect or jargon, for example. This is the other context in which we can understand Henry Tilney's disciplining of Catherine Morland's language in *Northanger Abbey* [see p. 141] or the politics of language in *Emma* [see p. 123]. Henry is not only bringing Catherine into line with the standard practice of polite society. He is also bringing her into line with a *national* standard. That this type of language must function to define both a nation, and a particular group within that nation (the 'polite' classes), is not necessarily a paradox. On the one hand, this group takes itself as representing the nation as a whole, on the grounds that the interests of property owners just *are* the interests of the nation (a familiar argument even today). On the other hand, this is a type of language which will be spoken by any member of the polite classes wherever in England (and indeed Britain) they come from. It is not marked as tied to any particular locality in the way that labouring-class speech is. And we should not lose sight of the fact that the language in question here is that of everyday social intercourse, a common or plain style of speech, unadorned and unselfconscious. It is thus that 'Austen endows the ephemeral with significance beyond its own particular space and time, and it is that perceived ability – to make the shreds and patches of everyday life speak to a larger national experience ... that is the basis of nationalist ideology' (Sorensen 2000: 204).

Indeed, for Franco Moretti, the eighteenth century's new literary form, the novel, is closely related to its new socio-political form, the nation-state. This is precisely because the novel is able to describe how local loyalties are absorbed within a larger, national, identity. The novel, argues Moretti in *Atlas of the European Novel*, is 'the only symbolic form that could represent' this new type of identity, make it imaginable and thus a lived reality for readers. And unlike the other versions of nationality in Austen that we have considered, Moretti's places the marriage plot itself at centre-stage. His point may seem an obvious one, but its implications are important. The Austen heroine and her destined husband tend to come from different places:

> the distance between them means that Austen's plots join together – 'marry' – people *who belong to different counties*. Which is new, and significant: it means that these novels try to represent what social historians refer to as the 'National Marriage Market': a mechanism that crystallized in the course of the eighteenth century, which demands of human beings (and especially of women) a new mobility: physical, and even more so *spiritual* mobility. Because it is clear that a large marriage market can only work if women feel 'at home' . . . not only in the small enclave of their birth, but in a much wider territory.
>
> (Moretti 1998: 14–15)

And that territory of potential matrimonial settlement constitutes the nation. In Part 1 we noted the political importance of marriage in integrating the newly wealthy classes into the old landowning classes [see **pp. 8–10**]. Moretti's point is the one we made about *Pride and Prejudice* in Part 2, that such marriages can also unite those whose power extends only over the neighbourhood or county with those used to exercising power in London, at court or in parliament [see **pp. 60–2**]. That is, they unite 'a *local* gentry' such as the Bennets, with 'the *national* elite of Darcy and his ilk' (Moretti 1998: 18). Thus, while the novel is the 'symbolic form of the nation-state', it is 'a form that (unlike an anthem, or a momument) not only does not conceal the nation's internal divisions, *but manages to turn them into a story*' (20). Like Miranda Burgess, Moretti sees narrative as essential to the production of modern nationhood. But where for Burgess narrative overcomes a distance in time between past and present, for Moretti it overcomes (in Austen, at least) a distance in space, between province and metropolis, between county and county.

If Austen had a central role in producing this kind of 'Englishness' at the start of the nineteenth century, it remains an important context in which she is read and enjoyed today. If her novels, as has been suggested, understand 'being English' in terms of a particular class, in terms of certain kinds of literature and landscape, and in terms of the uniquely English continuity with the past that these represent, then one can begin to understand the immense comfort that many, particularly English, readers find in her fiction. Roger Gard's book, *Jane Austen's Novels: The Art of Clarity*, is evidence of the continuing identification of Austen with the English nation. Gard's book is a defence of 'the reading public', 'the common reader' who appreciates the absolute clarity of Austen's meanings independently of the obscure jargon of the 'historical and theoretical specialisms' with which this part of my book has mostly been concerned. But Austen's clarity is only available to native speakers of English. '[F]oreigners, whether reading in translation or in the original, see little or nothing' of her true brilliance (Gard 1992: 14). And this is not only a matter of their limited linguistic competence: 'the *feel* of Jane Austen – so far as we can imagine it dissociated it [*sic*] from her language' is 'still . . . peculiarly English'. The reason for this turns out to be revealed by the contrast between Austen and the great French and Russian novelists of the nineteenth century. Their concern with the institutions of the state 'may well reflect European life'. Austen, on the other hand, is 'remarkably unpolitical for a novelist' (15):

> But *equally* unpolitical, I think, is a dominant part of Anglo-Saxon culture. . . .
>
> . . . it is my impression that modern Anglo-Saxon civilisations . . . are historically very unusual in being peopled with those who, even during continental or world wars, on the whole contrive to evince a *positive* disregard for politics and power. . . . I think this is because of the loss of a habit of fear. Politics, with its associated ambitions and trepidations, is not allowed to impair or cramp the moral style. . . .
>
> It is significant that Jane Austen's own class and the one she writes about – the upper range of the middle – is the one most associated with the capture of executive power from aristocratical oligarchy in England in the eighteenth century. . . . The security thus generated allowed to the majority not actually involved . . . a consequent disregard of direct political power in everyday life (underlying economic power and influence is a different matter, and for once not to the point here). . . .
>
> This is a reason, to put beside the fineness of her language, for our feeling that Jane Austen is especially, and congenially, English. She writes from and into a spiritual atmosphere which, by means of a positive absence of perceived restraint, is a real presence in English culture and those related to it. Unpolitical, she is *therefore* the realistic novelist of an evolving national democracy.
>
> (15–17)

In some ways, Gard is simply reproducing the definition of 'England' that Austen offers as if it was no more than the truth. England is identified here with those granted 'security' under the eighteenth century's political settlement (that is, the propertied minority); morality is a matter of 'style', liberated from the need to find expression in political action [see pp. 15–16]. However, Gard is also putting this England to work in a distinctly twentieth-century political rhetoric. Austen died fifteen years before the Great Reform Bill that extended the vote in very limited ways, and nowhere in her novels or letters is England imagined as 'evolving' towards democracy of any kind. And while her novels certainly define England in opposition to 'the continent', they do not remove England from 'Europe' and absorb it into an 'Anglo-Saxon culture' which also, it seems, includes the United States. In the critical discourse of the universities, Austen has been read as a proto-Marxist critic of her society [see pp. 120–4], as sympathetic to the campaign to abolish the slave trade [see p. 138], and, much more often, as a feminist [see pp. 126–7]. Gard's book demonstrates that it is possible for her to be read as a late twentieth-century British Conservative as well. However, to properly address the place of Austen in contemporary culture, we need to turn to the film and television adaptations of her work which have done so much to shape its popular reception, both in Britain and the United States, and indeed among foreigners.

4

Austen on screen

Introduction

A selection of the film and television adaptations of Austen's novels are listed in the bibliography [see p. 167]. The most useful sources of criticism of these adaptations are three collections of essays: *Jane Austen in Hollywood* (1998) edited by Linda Troost and Sayre Greenfield; *Jane Austen and Co.* (2003) edited by Suzanne Pucci and James Thompson; and *Jane Austen on Screen* (2003) edited by Gina and Andrew Macdonald. The discussion below draws on these collections but also on many other books and journals. The most comprehensive critical survey of all the film and television adaptations of Austen's novels (nearly thirty to date), taking each novel in turn, is Sue Parrill's *Jane Austen on Film and Television* (2002). Note that in what follows 'film' is often used to mean any screen adaptation, whether for the cinema or for television, simply being the most convenient term.

Adaptation: from page to screen

At the beginning of Part 3, we saw that early twentieth-century criticism of Austen often appears worried by her continuing commercial success. Underlying this anxiety seems to be the assumption that really great writers are difficult in a way inconsistent with widespread popularity. In the 1990s, Austen's popularity was manifested and disseminated in a particularly striking manner by a series of very successful film and television adaptations of her novels. These are fascinating versions of her stories for a number of reasons. The translation of a novel from prose narration to cinematic imagery can, for one thing, tell us a lot about the original text, even if only by highlighting what has been lost in the process. It can tell us a lot about the possibilities of cinema, too, as filmmakers struggle to find visual or dramatic equivalents for effects achieved in the novel by words on the page. But above all such adaptations can suggest much about why, exactly, Austen remains popular today. The types of pleasure gained by the non-specialist reader of Austen necessarily appear in specialist criticism (when they are mentioned at all) as the objects of speculation and hypothesis. As we have seen, when such pleasure is mentioned by critics, it is usually only to be denigrated in contrast to the intellectually rigorous response of the critics themselves. However, screen adaptations provide something more than speculation on which such discussion can be based. Screenwriters and directors working within the commercial demands of the television or movie industries must produce a commodity which will sell to a wide audience if the huge production costs are to be recouped and a profit generated for investors. And as John Wiltshire comments, in doing so they are themselves working as readers of the text, interpreting and understanding it in particular ways. There is no essential difference, he suggests, between this and the process of reading the novel in private, except that this reading is made public (Wiltshire 2001: 5). Indeed, one might add, the very commercial constraints within which filmmakers work demand a certain sensitivity to the way in which Austen is enjoyed by those existing fans who could thus be tempted into the cinema. On the other hand, by introducing Austen's work to cinemagoers who have not read the novels, the interpretations offered by these films provide the framework in which the novels will be first enjoyed by a new generation of readers. Much of our discussion in the previous part has concerned the relation of Austen's work to her society. As public versions of a contemporary, popular Austen, these films give us material through which to think about the place of Austen in our own.

However, to think of a film adaptation as just one more interpretation of the text, equivalent to that of any reader in our own time or in Austen's, might be to ignore the particular demands that cinema as a medium places on such an interpretation. Accordingly, some literary critics approach film adaptations of Austen's work in a spirit of mourning for the violence necessarily done in reducing an intricate work of verbal art to source material for a visual entertainment. Jocelyn Harris, in her essay in *Jane Austen on Screen* (Macdonald and Macdonald 2003: 44–68), catalogues the reasons why a 'faithful translation' of an Austen novel to the screen is an impossibility. To take a particularly marked example, it is very difficult to find a cinematic equivalent for the ironic narrative voice of the original texts [see pp. 96–100]. This difficulty is explored by several critics including Nora Nachumi in her contribution to *Jane Austen in Hollywood* (Troost and Greenfield 1998: 130–9) and Jan Fergus (Macdonald and Macdonald 2003: 67–89). In consequence of dispensing with this ironic distance, the 1995 film of *Sense and Sensibility*, for example, 'glorifies the romantic conventions that Austen deflates' in the novel (Troost and Greenfield 1998: 132–3). Interestingly, both Nachumi and Fergus praise the film that most radically transposes an Austen novel into the present day. Amy Heckerling's *Clueless* (1995) reimagines *Emma* in a 1990s Beverly Hills high school, its heroine the spoilt and shallow but ultimately good-hearted Cher Horowitz. *Clueless* retains Austen's irony in the form of a voice-over commentary on events from Cher herself. This reveals to the audience her misreadings of the world around her just as free indirect discourse exposes Emma Woodhouse's faulty perspective in the novel [see pp. 72–5]. However, voice-over is not used by any of the films that try to recreate Austen's own period in the name of 'faithful translation'.

An alternative approach is to think about the specific artistic resources available to the filmmaker but not to the novelist and examine how these films utilise them. The most obvious difference between novel and film is of course that in the novel we do not actually *see* anyone or anything. The two forms may share narrative structure and dialogue, but the dominant visuality of cinema can be thought of as supplementing, or enclosing, or simply competing for our attention with, these other elements. Julianne Pidduck's essay 'Of Windows and Country Walks' looks at the 1995 *Sense and Sensibility* and the BBC TV productions *Pride and Prejudice* and *Persuasion*, made in the same year, from this perspective. Pidduck points out a number of ways in which women are characteristically pictured in these films, for example at a window, looking out from inside a house, or walking in a country landscape. She suggests that the combination of the first two suggest a 'liberal-feminist mode of thought' at work in the film, which symbolises 'social constraint and repression' in the first, while the second 'wishfully projects the female body into motion' as an image of social liberation (Pidduck 2000: 126, 124).

The most sophisticated discussion of the issue of these films' 'fidelity' (to the novels, to the period they represent, or to an abstract idea of 'Jane Austen') is Mary Favret's essay 'Being True to Jane Austen' (2000), and the defining role of movement in film is central to her argument. Favret uses Fredric Jameson's idea in *Signatures of the Visible* (1990) that film's moving images resist the tendency of still photographs to fix the world represented in a dead past, offering instead a world where change and agency are still possible. She then links this to the place of the past in the stories that these films tell. These are stories of women mourning or transfixed by the past: the past represented by the mourned father of the Dashwood girls in *Sense and Sensibility*, or the lost love of Anne Elliot in *Persuasion*. The fidelity of these women to the past thereby becomes the way in which these films address as a theme their own relation (of various degrees of fidelity) to the novels on which they are based. Favret argues that the 1995 *Sense and Sensibility* is in fact more like Jameson's description of the photographic still than a movie in this regard, as Elinor and Marianne are represented there as captured in 'a daughter's death-dealing love for the paternal' (Favret 2000: 70). The 1995 *Persuasion*, on the other hand, features (for example) wandering camera-angles that represent Anne's unexpressed desire even where she herself appears static (75) and alludes to other films set in later ages. It ends with a public kiss that, in its very impossibility for the period, draws our attention to film as 'a sort of fantastic spectacle', liberated from the deadening fidelity to the past by which Anne herself had been crushed earlier in the story.

This raises the important point that among the things that we necessarily see in films but which remain invisible in the novels are human bodies [see pp. 112–14]. The BBC *Pride and Prejudice*, eager to stress the extent to which sexual desire is the motor of the novel's plot, caused some controversy with its emphasis on the physicality of the story's young people, and of Darcy in particular. In one particularly notorious scene, Darcy arrives unexpectedly at Pemberley and, heated by his long ride, strips to his shirt for a swim in the lake, from which he emerges, wet linen clinging to his muscular frame, to encounter a startled Elizabeth. But more subtly, Pidduck observes, the confident bodily carriage, physical manner and gestures of Jennifer Ehle, the actress playing Elizabeth Bennet, are those of 'a late twentieth-century western corporeality' (Park and Rajan 2000: 126). These films thus take a certain kind of feminine physical freedom with which we are now familiar, represent it as at least possible in Austen's time, and use it to symbolise the social freedoms that Austen, it is implied, imagined as potential for her women characters. As a reading of the novels, this is of course perfectly in tune with that prominent strand of literary criticism that understands Austen as herself a liberal feminist [see pp. 126–34]. On a slightly different tack, Penny Gay praises Ang Lee's 1995 *Sense and Sensibility* for offering its audience an implicitly feminist narrative 'of the characters' experiences as *bodies*' as a cinematic equivalent for the novel's narrative of feminine subjectivity (Macdonald and Macdonald 2003: 93). Deidre Lynch similarly notes how, in the 1995 *Persuasion*, a close-up of the ladies' tiny shoes as they slither around the breakwater at Lyme Regis provides 'vivid documentation of the material constraints on the nineteenth-century lady's mobility' (Pucci and Thompson 2003: 86), and in doing so offers resources for teaching feminist history beyond those available in written texts.

We will return to the question of the feminist potential of these films in a moment. In the meantime, we can note that, along with this visual representation of the characters' bodies, the translation to film also seems to demand that their inner life be made visible as well. If Austen's novels are understood as primarily about the privacy of thought and feeling, this requirement of the cinematic form seems to entail abandoning important aspects of the novels' content. For example, Rebecca Dickson sees the 'strong and self-sufficient Elinor' of Austen's *Sense and Sensibility* reduced to 'a girl woman with unexpressed emotions who must learn to demonstrate them' in the 1995 film (Troost and Greenfield 1998: 56), undermining the novel's 'quiet feminist force' for purely commercial reasons (44). Julian North similarly points out that this 'dramatization of Elinor's inner life' erodes the contrast between her and Marianne that is at the heart of the novel (North 1999: 46).

One could argue against Dickson that 'learning to demonstrate emotions' is not just what Elinor does in the 1995 film: it is what all Austen characters must learn to do in their journey from page to screen. Once voice-over has been rejected as a technique, cinema tends to rely on look, gesture and movement to express non-verbalised thought and feeling. This demands that all characters become physically and transparently expressive in a way that only problem cases such as Marianne Dashwood indulge in the novels. This pressure is particularly noticeable with male characters, whose subjectivities are hardly ever the focus of Austen's narratives in the first place. Cheryl Nixon suggests that Darcy's famous swim, for example, functions as a promise that Darcy could be emotionally, as well as physically, uninhibited, that there are depths to his character waiting for the opportunity to show themselves (Troost and Greenfield 1998: 22–43). On the other hand, Dickson may have a point that easily understood emotion is made necessary, not by film as such, but for 'commercial reasons' in films aimed at the widest possible audience. John Wiltshire observes that Amanda Root, the actress playing Anne Elliot in the 1995 BBC *Persuasion*, offers only the slightest facial expression and physical gesture: the viewer must intuit her inner life from this, in the context of situation, music, lighting and the movement of the camera. '[H]er pale countenance, though focused on, is represented as blank. . . . Out of this [other] sensory information the viewer here generates what he or she might call a knowledge of Anne's "character" ' (Wiltshire 2001: 95). But then *Persuasion* was not aimed at big box-office success in the same way as *Sense and Sensibility*. The latter was co-produced by Hollywood studio Columbia, the former by a publicly funded state broadcaster and its up-market Boston associate WGBH, designed for television in the first instance, and with a theatre release restricted to art-house cinemas in the US. A film that must recoup *Sense and Sensibility*'s $15 million budget perhaps cannot afford to make demands on the interpretative skills of its viewers in the way that Wiltshire describes *Persuasion* as doing.

Films and feminism

Julianne Pidduck is not the only critic to identify a feminist element in the 1990s screen adaptations. Devoney Looser suggests that the films' portrayal of intelligent, physically and socially active women, and in particular the importance they accord supportive relationships between women, is an example of the way in which feminist ideas, once perceived as dangerously left-field, had been 'mainstreamed' in late twentieth-century culture (Troost and Greenfield 1998: 159). The films' relation to a more radical twentieth-century feminist agenda thus echoes Austen's own 'de-polemicizing' of the feminism of Mary Wollstonecraft (Troost and Greenfield 1998: 173) [see p. 132]. However, many other commentators on these films are less confident than Pidduck and Looser concerning their feminist potential. Kristen Samuelian identifies the 1995 *Sense and Sensibility* as reflecting a 'postfeminist' position, in that it first protests at patriarchy's oppression of its heroines, then assures us that they can live happy lives despite this by marrying the right man (Troost and Greenfield 1998: 148–58). This is a critique based on an analysis of the film's manipulation of plot. Shannon Wooden (2002) identifies the same ambivalence in the visual language of the films of *Sense and Sensibility*, *Persuasion*, *Clueless* and the 1996 Hollywood version of *Emma*. All four films, she notes, pick up on the food symbolism of Austen's novels, where not eating can represent a protest by women against patriarchal control, or be a sign of their poverty (see Lane 1995: 84–6). The films, however, juxtapose food with representations or discussions of physical beauty, making a very late twentieth-century connection between not eating and feminine social and sexual success. The female viewer is thus invited to observe and internalise this connection, and judge herself as the films demand she judge Austen's characters.

Other critics see the visual effect of these films on female viewers as centring on particular types of pleasure and desire. Martine Vioret suggests that they 'cater to female desires and to the female gaze', specifically in their repeated focus on young male bodies, dressed in the close-fitting breeches and short-fronted coats of 'an era when men could still be the locus of the beautiful' (Pucci and Thompson 2003: 230). Lisa Hopkins is more ambivalent about the role of the female gaze in these films. The 1995 BBC *Pride and Prejudice*, especially, offers up the handsome Mr Darcy, embodied in the actor Colin Firth, as an object of pleasurable looking for female viewers, in a way that is more normally associated with female actors and male viewers, and indeed the British adaptations in general 'fetishize the looks of the heroes' (Troost and Greenfield 1998: 119). However, the specific fantasy that Darcy's 'look' meets in women viewers, Hopkins suggests, is that of an absolute and unconditioned male need for a woman, and this fantasy itself only makes sense in the context of a general and ongoing female powerlessness in which this sort of recognition can only appear as a fantasy. In her essay 'The Return to Repression', Virginia Blum considers the popularity of Colin Firth's Darcy with a female audience and asks what this tells us about modern sexuality in general, within the context of Michel Foucault's account of this (Pucci and Thompson, 2003: 157–78).

Englishness, 'heritage' and cultural materialism

It is noticeable that the issues we have discussed so far, the visual representation of bodies and feelings in film adaptations of Austen's novels, have evoked responses from critics that ask questions about these films', and Austen's, relative commitment to various kinds of feminism. Vioret's essay cited in the previous paragraph already asks us to think about the ways in which the representation of persons in the films is part of a wider construction of period and nation, one which requires the visual representation of buildings, clothes and landscapes as well. Among British critics, discussion of the ways in which these films represent a historically distant social order and an idea of 'Englishness' have been informed by an ongoing debate about the function of 'costume drama', particularly the adaptation of classic novels for television, in the cultural politics of the present-day UK. Such critics ask what political interests are served by these reproductions of Austen in a contemporary context, how (for example) they relate to the needs of the institutions that produce them (especially the BBC) and consume them (for example the secondary school system). In asking these questions, such critics might be understood as engaging in a critical practice often referred to as 'Cultural Materialism'. Such an approach assumes that the meaning of a text is not inherent in itself but produced in the process of its consumption and reproduction within particular contexts. Those contexts, moreover, cannot be reduced to the mental apparatus of readers understood as isolated and unique individuals; rather, meaning-giving contexts are determined by institutions (the state, media, education) which exist (materially) prior to the individual reader's (mental) response. Cultural Materialism borrows heavily from Marxist thinking [see pp. 120–4] without limiting the social meaning of a text to that which it had in the context of its original production. It has been prominent in discussions of Shakespeare, for example, as a way of thinking about the role of his plays in producing certain versions of English or British national identity, through its place in school curricula or the London stage, in the context of the Second World War, say, or Margaret Thatcher's populist-conservative governments in the 1980s.

The particular British institution with which film adaptations of Austen are most immediately linked is the so-called 'heritage industry'. This term is used to name the governmental organisations, charities and pressure groups whose aim is to conserve certain physical environments, principally old buildings and certain landscapes, in the name of a 'national heritage' which links the present generation culturally to previous ones. 'National heritage' thus constructs 'England' (or 'Britain') as continuous through historical time. However, the particular buildings and landscapes selected for preservation, for example in the hands of the not-for-profit National Trust, have tended to be country manor houses and estates, and it can be argued that it is a very particular aspect of England that is being conserved in the name of the whole. Austen can be seen to be imagining the nation in similar terms [see pp. 142–7]. By imagining the past in terms of the possessions of the ruling class, 'national heritage' imagines a past purged of political tension, and thus serves to empty current political tensions of any sense of historical importance (Wright 1985: 69–70). Accordingly, Andrew Higson identifies adaptations of classic novels which foreground the visual splendour of period costume and architectural backdrop as the 'heritage film'. Particularly in the context of the social divisiveness of the Conservative administrations of the 1980s and 1990s, Higson argues that, for example, the lush 1980s film versions of the novels of E.M. Forster represent 'a relatively conservative and nostalgic attempt to turn away from contemporary realities' towards the stability of 'an invariant and spectacular national past' (Higson 1995: 273–4).

The 1995 BBC *Pride and Prejudice* is often cited as an example of the complicity of 'heritage films' in the 'heritage industry' (Gibson 2000: 116). Previous, more cheaply produced TV serialisations depended on studio-shot interiors with relatively few external shots to set the scene: the higher budget of the 1995 version allowed extensive filming on location. Not only did this allow it to revel visually in the country houses that it used as sets, it also sparked a wave of tourist interest in these real locations, acting, in effect, as an advertisement for the owner of many of them, the National Trust. Pemberley is Austen's invention: as Mike Crang points out in a discussion of Austen and tourism, Lyme Park, the National Trust property that stood for Darcy's home in the TV version, now attracts visitors with its 'Pemberley Trail' (Pucci and Thompson 2003: 118). Accordingly it can be argued that Austen has become

> something of a conservative icon in popular culture: a canonical author whose life and work signify English national heritage and all that implies of the past as an idyll of village life in a pre-industrial society, of traditional class and gender hierarchies, sexual propriety and Christian values.
>
> (North 1999: 38)

The praise that reviewers heaped upon many of the 1990s adaptations for their 'faithfulness' could be seen as continuous with Austen's incorporation in 'national heritage' in that her novels are treated as equivalent to the old buildings in which the films were made, full of original features which need to be conserved in the face of encroaching modernity (39).

It can, however, be argued that 'national heritage' in Britain does not necessarily serve conservative political purposes. Raphael Samuel in particular has argued that the concept of 'heritage' is a democratic one, making the British past available for appropriation by all, including relatively disempowered groups in society, and thus constitutes 'a cultural capital on which all were invited to draw' in a huge variety of ways (Samuel 1994: 237–8). Andrew Higson himself has admitted that the classic adaptations he examined could be seen as serving a diversity of political positions, not just the defence of the status quo. Understood as 'women's films', for example, they could be seen as using the cultural authority of 'national heritage' to advance a feminist *critique* of the status quo (Higson

1996: 246–7). As we have seen, the 1990s adaptations of Austen's novels (which Higson does not consider directly) can be read in just this way.

Moreover, many of those adaptations of Austen seem keen to distance themselves from 'heritage culture' versions of Austen. Edward Neill's book *The Politics of Jane Austen*, which mostly makes familiar points about Austen's critique of capitalism and her ironic subversion of narrative conventions, turns in its last chapter to the ways in which screen adaptations generally ignore these radical elements in the novels. However, Neill contrasts the 1996 film of *Emma* with the ITV (British commercial television) version broadcast the same year (Neill 1999: 142–5). The latter was overshadowed by the former, a major Hollywood film starring Gwyneth Paltrow, and still attracts far less critical attention than the other adaptations. But it foregrounds the problematic class relations referred to in the novel in striking ways. Servants, invisible in the movie, are everywhere in the ITV version, their tasks often pointedly absurd; starving labourers repeatedly raid the chicken coops of the farmers; and Robert Martin remains angry at Emma's interference in his love life. In other words, the ITV account resists the tendency of 'heritage cinema' to erase social tensions from the national past, making it a hard film to recruit for a conservative vision of a lost idyll of contented social hierarchy. Similarly, Roger Sales has noted that the framing of women in the windows of country houses in earlier adaptations (as noted more recently by Julianne Pidduck, as mentioned above) undercuts the 'conservative meanings' of 'heritage images' by visualising these historic buildings as 'genteel prisons' (Sales 1994: 25). One of the most radical adaptations that remains in the period mode is Patricia Rozema's 1999 film of *Mansfield Park*, which transforms Fanny Price by giving her dialogue from, among other places, the more acerbic of Austen's private letters. In doing so, notes Mireia Aragay, the film refuses the heritage Austen, 'a synonym for gentility, decorum, domesticity and quietism' and evokes instead the 'proto-feminist social commentator' discovered by many of the literary critics discussed in the previous part (Aragay 2003: 177).

However, even adaptations that thus distance themselves from a heritage version of Austen usually share with heritage cinema a concern to construct a visually detailed and convincing impression of her historical era. We have already noted that film demands the visualisation of bodies and expressions, and in doing so tends to collapse any difference between early nineteenth-century manners and those of our own period. But at the same time film also demands the visualisation of dress, interior design and architecture, and in this case tends to emphasise the *difference* between the period represented and our own. In one of the most consistent and comprehensive Cultural-Materialist approaches to the Austen adaptations (although it calls itself a specifically Marxist one), Moyra Haslett points out that, in fact, the more attention the camera lavishes on the 'authentic' re-creation of 'period detail', the more our perspective remains rooted in the present. For a contemporary of Austen's, Regency china or an Empire-cut dress was not 'period detail', it was just a cup or a frock, without the function of signifying an entire era. But for us, 'these artefacts mean very differently indeed. Even the everyday object becomes glamorised as an antique'. This is a 'fetishisation' of the past 'rather than a replication, because the re-creation is done to current tastes, while masquerading as "authenticity" ' (Haslett 2000: 205,

210). Even attempts to draw attention to less attractive aspects of Austen's period are bound to fall into this trap. Jocelyn Harris points out that Roger Michell's 1995 *Persuasion* was praised for the 'realism' of its muddy boots and clothes, unwashed hair and poorly lit interiors, as if the material discomfort in which the characters lived 'guaranteed their "real" existence' (Macdonald and Macdonald 2003: 47). But nobody in the early nineteenth century felt their reality guaranteed by an absence of electric lighting or running hot water. Such details signify 'reality' in their contrast to other, more idealising, film versions of the period, not by virtue of their fidelity to what it was actually like at the time. For Harris, as for Edward Neill, the 'sheer materiality' (Macdonald and Macdonald 2003: 46) of the 1995 BBC TV production *Sense and Sensibility*, the 'semiotic prominence' of its 'props, properties and appurtenances' (Neill 1999: 138), tends to drown out the elements of the films that have been drawn from the original novel (see discussion of Favret 2000 above for another take on 'fidelity' in *Sense and Sensibility* and *Persuasion*).

Austen, consumption and history

On the other hand, there might be one sense in which the clothes, furniture and houses of these films have a similar meaning for their audience and for Austen's contemporaries, and that is the sense in which these are expensive commodities, designed to impress the viewer with their splendour. Moyra Haslett observes:

> The sumptuousness of Austen's settings are, of course, implicit in all of her novels, for they are all peopled by gentry families whose aspirations to gentility are measured in conspicuous consumption and the trappings of wealth, whether land, property or the latest fashions.
>
> (Haslett 2000: 214)

As a result, we find ourselves in the position of Austen's less well-off characters, themselves a type of tourist, in our 'vicarious snooping on the houses and life-styles of the wealthiest estates in England'. To take the obvious example, there is a 'complicity between Elizabeth Bennet's and our pleasure in the prospect of Pemberley' in the 1995 *Pride and Prejudice* (Haslett 2000: 223, 234), a point also made by H. Elisabeth Ellington in her essay 'Pemberley as Fetish and Commodity' (Troost and Greenfield 1998: 91). More broadly, what we have in common with Austen's period (or at least, with the social strata her characters represent) is precisely the culture of consumer capitalism. So Deidre Lynch suggests that 'the spectacle of Regency dresses and furnishings makes the privatised sphere of consumerism into the primary ground of historical continuity' between then and now (Pucci and Thompson 2003: 73).

Now, Fredric Jameson has argued that that the culture of consumer capitalism is in fact destructive of a sense of 'historicity'; that is, of a sense of the present as a historical epoch, distinct from past historical epochs, but available for analysis in similar terms (Jameson 1983, 1991). He suggests that consumer goods reduce the past to a storehouse of styles and artefacts that can be mixed and recycled in the present, stripped of the context in which they were first produced. The present, thus emptied of any style that can be called its own, then appears a quite different place from previous eras. It is not, for one thing, a place in which effective political action can be imagined. Both the Lynch essay just cited ('*Clueless*: About History' in Pucci and Thompson 2003: 71–92) and Esther Sonnet's earlier 'From *Emma* to *Clueless*: Taste, Pleasure and the Scene of History' (Sonnet 1999: 51–62) engage with Jameson to think about the meanings of Amy Heckerling's recycling of *Emma* in terms of the frantically consumption-driven lifestyles of her rich Californian teenagers. For Lynch, the high school setting of *Clueless* is important, as the education system has traditionally been charged with drawing the boundary between 'real history' and its commercially driven appropriation as 'fashion' (74: the film's other main location is the shopping mall). Lynch suggests that we understand 'fashion', as represented in *Clueless*, as a tactical appropriation of the past by women (in particular) for particular purposes, and not merely as a sign of Cher's mental limitations. Sonnet develops a similar point in terms of class rather than gender, using Pierre Bourdieu's theory of cultural consumption as a marker of status positions in society (Bourdieu 1984). Branded consumer goods obviously function as markers of status in *Clueless*. More subtly, Sonnet argues, different types of cultural knowledge (the ability to quote Shakespeare, for example) serve a similar role, and the ability to understand a literary or other cultural reference distinguishes two groups of characters in the film. To be able to deploy this sort of cultural knowledge is to lay claim to a certain kind of class 'distinction', in Bourdieu's terms, and (to revert to the British context) the whole 'heritage industry' could be seen as in the business of producing 'distinction' in this sense. Sonnet uses these ideas to think about our position as viewers of *Clueless* or indeed of *Emma*, popular, commercial films whose audience is nevertheless divided into those who 'get' their reference back to Austen's novel and those who do not (Sonnet 1999: 55; see also Wiltshire 2001: 52–3). In this sense, such films are not really about historical understanding in Jameson's terms, but rather 'perform *contemporary* social and economic power relations' (Sonnet 1999: 56).

The point that Austen is used to exhibit a certain sort of 'cultural capital' (Bourdieu's term) is one made by several critics. For example, Harriet Margolis suggests that, within the US television industry, the association of PBS (the American public-service broadcaster) and niche producers like WGBH Boston with British-based Austen adaptations is a means of asserting their cultural superiority over the big commercial networks (Macdonald and Macdonald 2003: 26); Erica Sheen makes a similar point in the case of the BBC itself (Sheen 2000: 15–16). This allows observers frequently to comment that 'Jane Austen' is now effectively, among other things, a brand name for marketing purposes (for example Wiltshire 2001: 8) or a 'cultural commodity' (for example Rachel Brownstein in Troost and Greenfield 1998: 9; Aragay 2003). Yet at the same time, it can be argued that the success of this 'brand' is due not to its high-cultural credentials alone, but to its combination of these credentials with a mass-market appeal. And this mass appeal can be credited to the perceived continuity between Austen's fiction and a popular or 'low-cultural' genre, the pulp period romance published by Harlequin, Silhouette or Mills and Boon. Critics sometimes complain that film adaptations engage in a 'harlequinization' of Austen's novels, reducing them to the elements they have in common with popular romance as a way of appealing to a mass (female) audience (the term is Deborah Kaplan's in Troost and Greenfield 1998: 178).

But the sharp distinction that we make now between novels that are 'literature' and novels that are popular culture is one that was only emerging in Austen's own time, as novels of any kind had little in the way of cultural prestige [see pp. 16–18]. Barbara Benedict observes that Austen's work is listed by the circulating libraries that were a large part of her market alongside much that would now count as mere 'popular fiction', the ancestors of today's Mills and Boon romance, without any marker of her difference from them (Lynch 2000: 63–86). Margolis suggests that if these films harlequinise Austen, it is because continuities between the concerns of Austen's fiction and those of popular romance are really there (see also James Thompson's point on this in Pucci and Thompson 2003: 21). Critics determined to defend Austen's difference from popular fiction are in danger of repeating the denigration of 'romance' by critics in Austen's own time [see pp. 17–18], one that was also a denigration of women writers and women readers (Macdonald and Macdonald 2003: 24). Paulette Richards points out that even an adaptation as self-consciously 'gritty' as the 1995 *Persuasion* will be interpreted by audiences within a set of expectations shaped by popular Regency-set fictions among other types of text (in Macdonald and Macdonald 2003: 111–26). For both Margolis and Erica Sheen (2000), claims to 'authenticity' or 'faithfulness' to the original text are the way in which television networks and film studios can maintain 'a high cultural status while achieving mass popularity' and thus commercial success. And ultimately, 'once culture takes on an economic role, distinctions between high and low culture grow difficult to maintain' (Margolis in Macdonald and Macdonald 2003: 31).

Austen in American culture

To consider the way that Austen is interpreted in relation to the commodity culture of consumer capitalism, as we have in the last five paragraphs, is to think about Austen in a global context. Previously we discussed the issues raised by the Austen adaptations in the specifically British context of 'heritage culture'. But many critics have also addressed the specific meanings that Austen's work takes on in the United States, which remains the most commercially important market for these films. One of the things at stake in the American reception of Austen is bound to be the national question itself, the way in which Americans imagine England and why they do so. For example, Ellen Belton argues that the earliest Hollywood version of an Austen novel, the MGM *Pride and Prejudice*, mutes the novel's portrayal of social hierarchy. Pemberley is never portrayed, Lady Catherine de Bourgh is turned into a benign match-maker, and Darcy's snobbery thus becomes a personal flaw rather than the expression of an entire social system. Instead, the film emphasises a 'middle-class family solidarity' that it bestows upon the Bennets (Macdonald and Macdonald 2003: 183). The effect is to make a 'lost and lovingly remembered world' more sympathetic to viewers imbued with the democratic values of the US (178). And this, Belton suggests, was designed to meet a clearly identifiable political need. This film was made in 1940, and released during the Battle of Britain, when the UK was under aerial bombardment and the threat of invasion by Nazi Germany. 'By stressing the common values of US and British society, the 1940 film implicitly encourages US support for the British war effort' (186).

In the US, as in Britain, the rise in Austen's popularity in the 1980s and 1990s was identified with a conservative cultural agenda, although, according to Devoney Looser, only the Austen adaptations were read in this way, rather than being lumped in with the films of E.M. Forster and Henry James novels as they were in Britain under the category of 'heritage cinema' (Troost and Greenfield 1998: 160). However, in 1995 as in 1940, Americans cannot simply embrace the vision of social hierarchy that Austen's novels offer. This is not, however, because the United States has no social hierarchy of its own. For Carol Dole in her essay 'Austen, Class and the American Market', the appeal of the Austen films lies precisely in their direct confrontation with the topic of class, one 'which American films in particular have resisted confronting openly', propagating instead a 'myth of classlessness' (Troost and Greenfield 1998: 58). One of the genres of film that addresses class *in*directly is the high-school movie, where hierarchies of 'cool' or intelligence substitute for the racial or economic hierarchies in the world outside, in a setting where most Americans have their only prolonged social interaction with members of other classes. Hence the success of *Clueless* in translating the class boundaries of *Emma* into an American context is achieved at the expense of ignoring or disguising the class divisions that exist, vestigially, even in a Beverly Hills high school. Contrastingly direct in its approach to class is Whit Stillman's 1990 film, *Metropolitan*. This too is set among late twentieth-century hyper-privileged young Americans, but this time they are the children of older-established money in New York, and are anxiously self-conscious about their privilege in a way totally alien to the carefree Californians of *Clueless* (Troost and Greenfield 1998: 66; Wiltshire 2001: 52). The narrative of *Metropolitan* is only very loosely based on an Austen novel, *Mansfield Park*. Its stroke of genius is to make its characters discuss, not only *Mansfield Park*, but Lionel Trilling's essay on *Mansfield Park* [see pp. 108–9]; see Caroll (2003) for more on this. Quite apart from the connections that they and the film make between these texts and their own lives, the fact that they hold Austen in common itself functions to mark them as belonging to a particular, and particularly American, class: the white Anglophile East Coast elite. Austen is an element in their 'cultural capital', mirroring on screen the situation of any viewer of the film who can pick up precisely these references. A comment of Trilling's in his other essay, the one on *Emma*, is relevant to the role of Austen in their lives: 'not to like Jane Austen is to put oneself under suspicion . . . of a want of breeding' (Trilling 1967: 44).

I said that Stillman's characters belong to a *white* Anglophile class. One of the appeals that Austen may offer to white conservatives in the US is precisely a dream of a racially homogeneous society, allowing James Thompson to assert that 'Austen is the very embodiment of a white Englishness, especially for an Anglophile American audience' (Pucci and Thompson 2003: 23). Mary Favret, in her essay 'Jane Austen in America', observes that the 1940 *Pride and Prejudice* brings forward the period in which the action is set to the mid-nineteenth century. The usual explanation for this is that the actress playing Elizabeth Bennet, Greer

Garson, thought that high-waisted Regency dresses did not suit her figure. But Favret observes that the effect is to make the film strongly reminiscent visually of the massive cinema hit of the previous year, *Gone with the Wind*, a melodrama of the American Civil War told from the perspective of the white Southern slave owners (Lynch 2000: 181). The social idyll of a lost pre-industrial England that Austen often represents for conservatives is here aligned with a similar idyll imagined in the pre-Civil War Southern states. The slave labour on which the latter was based is conveniently erased by the adoption of a narrative by Austen which allows farm labour of any kind to be made invisible. In this context, Patricia Rozema's 1999 version of *Mansfield Park* is once again provocative in its insistence on the exploitation by the Bertram family of plantation slavery in Antigua. More generally, the visual emphasis on material luxury, and the general invisibility of servants, in films such as the Miramax *Emma* tend to assimilate an alien hierarchy based on birth and land to one more recognisable to modern Americans, namely a hierarchy of leisure and consumption (Carol Dole in Troost and Greenfield 1998: 70) or 'class as "status conferred by money" ' (Neill 1999: 137).

However, we should not be too quick to attribute the success of the Austen adaptations in the US to an implicitly racist Anglophilia. Favret points out that the first wave of enthusiasm for Austen's novels in the US came in the late nineteenth and early twentieth centuries, as part of a great debate on the identity and future of American literature.

> Austen does and does not become something altogether new when she hits these shores. . . . [T]o some readers on this [American] side of the Atlantic, she no longer looks English, nor are her novels naturally rooted in a Great Tradition of British Literature. Rather than simply adopting Austen as a means of acquiring cultural capital (though that surely has happened), readers performed their American-ness by accepting Austen as one of their own.
>
> (Lynch 2000: 167)

Gayle Wald, in her essay '*Clueless* in the Neocolonial World Order', suggests that this film is engaged in just this utilisation of Austen to construct an American nationality. It does this through its exploitation of that which the late twentieth-century United States has in common with the early nineteenth-century United Kingdom: commodity consumption based on dominance of a global trading system. In Austen's England this was discussed in terms of empire: in *Clueless* it appears in the presence of the 'Third World' as a topic for classroom discussion, on rolling TV news, and in the Horowitzes' El Salvadorean maid. These elements undermine 'the film's narrative of a "multicultural" and class-transcendent American nation' by being 'not easily assimilable to it' even while America is defined in opposition to the Third World they represent (Wald 2000: 227). But ultimately the film turns away from and silently absorbs these elements by finding its narrative resolution instead in Cher's identification of her own personal interests in marrying Josh (228–9). Just as in Austen's novels, nationality is constructed, and social conflict resolved, in the happy ending of the romance plot.

Chronology

Bullet points are used to denote events in Jane Austen's life, and asterisks to denote historical and literary events.

1775
- Jane Austen born (16 December) at Steventon, Hampshire, to Revd George Austen and Cassandra Leigh Austen
* Battles of Lexington, Concord and Bunker Hill in the American War of Independence

1776
* American Declaration of Independence (4 July); Adam Smith, *An Inquiry into the Nature and Causes of the Wealth of Nations*

1778
* Frances Burney, *Evelina*

1781
- Eliza Hancock, Austen's cousin, marries Captain J.-F.C. de Feuillide, a French army officer.
* Jean-Jacques Rousseau, *Confessions* (published posthumously)

1782
* Burney, *Cecilia*; William Cowper, *Poems*

1783
- Austen with her sister Cassandra at Mrs Cawley's school at Oxford and Southampton
* Peace of Paris ends American war; Hugh Blair, *Lectures on Rhetoric and Belles-Lettres*; William Blake, *Poetical Sketches*

1784
* Charlotte Smith, *Elegiac Sonnets*

1785
- Austen with Cassandra at the Abbey School, Reading

1786
- Austen and Cassandra leave the Abbey School; their brother Frank enters the Royal Naval Academy, Portsmouth

1787
- Austen probably writing the surviving early stories and verses (the 'Juvenilia') from this year

1788
- Austen's brother Henry enters Oxford University; Frank sails to the East Indies

1789
* The French Revolution: the Third Estate declares itself a 'National Assembly' (17 June); a Paris mob storms the Bastille prison (14 July); the National Assembly approves the 'Declaration of the Rights of Man and Citizen' (26 August); Blake, *Songs of Innocence*

1790
* Edmund Burke, *Reflections on the Revolution in France*; Mary Wollstone-craft, *A Vindication of the Rights of Man*; Ann Radcliffe, *A Sicilian Romance*; Blake, *Marriage of Heaven and Hell*

1791
- Austen's brother Charles enters the Royal Naval Academy, Portsmouth
* Louis XVI flees Paris and is captured at France's northern border (20 June); on his return, he is forced to sign the 'Declaration of the Rights of Man and Citizen'; Thomas Paine, *The Rights of Man*, vol. I; Elizabeth Inchbald, *A Simple Story*; Radcliffe, *The Romance of the Forest*

1792
- Austen completes 'Catharine, or the Bower'; her brother James marries and becomes curate at Deane
* Prussia and Austria invade France, repulsed; Robespierre's Jacobin party seizes power; the royal family is imprisoned (10 August); monarchy abolished and a republic declared (21, 22 September); Louis XVI put on trial and convicted (December); Paine, *The Rights of Man*, vol. II; Wollstonecraft, *A Vindication of the Rights of Woman*; Thomas Holcroft, *Anna St. Ives*

1793
- Austen's brother Henry joins Oxfordshire Militia
* Louis XVI executed (21 January); French Republic declares war on Britain (1 February); the Terror, Jacobin execution of their enemies, begins; execution of Queen Marie Antoinette (16 October); radicals tried for treason in Edinburgh; William Godwin, *Political Justice*; Hannah More, *Village Politics*

1794

- Captain de Feuillide guillotined in Paris; Austen begins drafting 'Lady Susan'; brother Charles joins his first ship
* The Terror ends after the execution of Robespierre (28 July); Godwin, *Caleb Williams*; Radcliffe, *The Mysteries of Udolpho*; Blake, *Songs of Experience*

1795

- Austen writes 'Elinor and Marianne' (later revised as *Sense and Sensibility*); her first serious flirtation, with Tom Lefroy, begins
* Bad harvest leads to scarcity and social unrest in Britain; parliament passes Seditious Meetings Act and Treasonable Practices Act (the 'Two Acts'); More, *Repository Tracts*

1796

- Austen begins writing 'First Impressions' (later revised as *Pride and Prejudice*)
* Burney, *Camilla*; Mary Hays, *Memoirs of Emma Courtney*; S.T. Coleridge, *Poems on Various Subjects*

1797

- George Austen, Jane's father, submits 'First Impressions' to publishers Cadell and Davies: they reject it without reading it; Austen begins turning 'Elinor and Marianne' into *Sense and Sensibility*; her brother Henry marries Eliza de Feuillide
* Mutinies in the British navy; death of Wollstonecraft; *The Anti-Jacobin* (reactionary journal) begins publication; Radcliffe, *The Italian*

1798

- Austen possibly begins 'Susan' (later *Northanger Abbey*)
* Rebellion of 'United Irishmen' in Ireland defeated with much bloodshed; Admiral Nelson destroys the French fleet at the Battle of the Nile; Godwin, *Memoirs* (of Wollstonecraft); Wordsworth and Coleridge, *Lyrical Ballads*; Thomas Gisborne, *An Enquiry into the Duties of the Female Sex*

1799

- Austen completes 'Susan'
* Suppression of radical societies and trade unions in Britain; in France, Napoleon becomes First Consul; Godwin, *St. Leon*; More, *Strictures on the Modern System of Female Education*

1800

* Irish parliament abolished by Act of Union; Maria Edgeworth, *Castle Rackrent*; Elizabeth Hamilton, *Memoirs of Modern Philosophers*

1801

- Henry resigns his commission in the Oxfordshires and sets up as banker in London; George Austen retires and moves the Austen family to Bath
* Edgeworth, *Belinda*

1802

- Harris Bigg-Wither proposes marriage to Austen; she first accepts, then withdraws; she revises 'Susan' for publication
- * Peace of Amiens (March): a pause in the war; Napoleon Bonaparte made First Consul for life; *Edinburgh Review* begins publication; Jane West, *The Infidel Father*

1803

- Austen sells copyright for 'Susan' to Crosby & Co. for £10; it is advertised but not published; Henry and Eliza nearly trapped in France by resumption of hostilities
- * War resumed (May)

1804

- Austen begins drafting 'The Watsons'
- * Napoleon crowns himself emperor of France

1805

- Death of George Austen (21 January)
- * British naval victory at Trafalgar under Nelson; Napoleon crushes Austrians and Russians at Austerlitz; Walter Scott, *The Lay of the Last Minstrel*

1806

- Austen, her mother and sister Cassandra move in with brother Frank and his wife Mary in Southampton
- * Napoleon defeats Prussians at Jena; Sydney Owenson, *The Wild Irish Girl*

1807

- * British Parliament passes Act abolishing the slave trade; France invades Spain and Portugal; Wordsworth, *Poems in Two Volumes*

1808

- * British troops in Spain under Sir John Moore; Scott, *Marmion*

1809

- Austen writes to Crosby to demand that they publish 'Susan'; the Austen women move to Chawton, on the second son Edward's large estate in Hampshire
- * Moore on retreat in Spain, is killed at Corunna; Arthur Wellesley, later Duke of Wellington, in command in Portugal; *Quarterly Review* begins publication; More, *Cœlebs in Search of a Wife*

1810

- *Sense and Sensibility* accepted for publication
- * Siege of Lisbon

1811

- *Sense and Sensibility* published by Egerton; Austen reworks 'First Impressions' into *Pride and Prejudice*; begins writing *Mansfield Park*

*   George III declared insane, Prince of Wales now Regent in his place (i.e. the 'Regency' begins); Luddite anti-factory riots in the Midlands

1812
- Austen sells copyright of *Pride and Prejudice* to Egerton
- *   US declares war on Britain; Napoleon invades Russia; his massive army is destroyed in a winter retreat; Lord Byron, *Childe Harold*, cantos I and II

1813
- *Pride and Prejudice*, and a second edition of *Sense and Sensibility*, published; *Pride and Prejudice* goes to a second edition
- *   Wellington victorious in Spain; Prussians defeat Napoleon at Leipzig, French driven from Holland, Italy and Switzerland; Byron, *The Giaour*; Percy Shelley, *Queen Mab*

1814
- Austen begins *Emma; Mansfield Park* published
- *   Allies take Paris: Napoleon abdicates and is exiled to Elba; the victorious powers meet in the Congress of Vienna to restore monarchical European order; Burney, *The Wanderer*; Scott, *Waverley*; Wordsworth, *The Excursion*

1815
- Austen begins *Persuasion; Emma* published by John Murray
- *   Napoleon escapes exile: is finally defeated at Waterloo; restoration of monarchy in France; Scott, *Guy Mannering*; Wordsworth, *Poems*

1816
- Murray brings out second edition of *Mansfield Park*: it loses money; first signs of illness in Austen; 'Susan' bought back from Crosby; Austen finishes *Persuasion*; Henry's bank fails
- *   Severe economic depression and riots in Britain; Byron, *Childe Harold*, canto III; Coleridge, *Christabel, Kubla Khan*; Scott, *The Antiquary, Old Mortality*; Percy Bysshe Shelley, *Alastor*

1817
- Austen begins *Sanditon*; she dies on 18 July; Henry publishes 'Susan' as *Northanger Abbey* together with *Persuasion* and his own 'Biographical Notice of the Author'
- *   Detention without trial introduced; Seditious Meetings Bill outlaws pro-democracy societies; Byron, *Manfred*; John Keats, *Poems*

Bibliography

Editions

This book refers throughout to the most recent, 2003, reprints of the Penguin Classics editions of Austen's novels: *Northanger Abbey* edited by Marilyn Butler; *Sense and Sensibility* edited by Ros Ballaster; *Pride and Prejudice* edited by Vivien Jones; *Mansfield Park* edited by Kathryn Sutherland; *Emma* edited by Fiona Safford; and *Persuasion* edited by Gillian Beer. This reprint includes an updated bibliography, and *Sense and Sensibility*, *Pride and Prejudice* and *Mansfield Park* include Tony Tanner's introduction to the original 1960s Penguin edition of each as an appendix (these introductions formed the basis of Tanner 1986 listed below). All of the novels are also available in the World's Classics series published by Oxford University Press, and in the Everyman Library, with a similarly distinguished list of editors and commentators.

Two other series are worth mentioning that offer more than a scrupulously edited text and informative introduction. The Norton Critical editions include a very useful selection of up-to-date critical material, drawn from many of the sources discussed in Part 3 above: *Northanger Abbey* edited by Susan Fraiman (2004); *Sense and Sensibility* edited by Claudia Johnson (2001); *Pride and Prejudice* edited by Donald J. Gray (third edition 2001); *Mansfield Park* edited by Claudia Johnson (1998); *Emma* edited by Stephen M. Parrish (third edition 2000); and *Persuasion* edited by Patricia M. Spacks (1995). The Broadview Classics editions, on the other hand, include a range of documents from Austen's own time, drawn from many of the sources discussed in Part 1 above: *Northanger Abbey* edited by Claire Grogan (second edition 2002); *Sense and Sensibility* edited by Kathleen James-Cavan (2001); *Pride and Prejudice* edited by Robert P. Irvine (2002); *Mansfield Park* edited by Jane Sturrock (2001); *Emma* edited by Kristin F. Samuelian (2004); and *Persuasion* edited by Linda Bree (1998).

Film and television

This is a selective list, by date, covering the adaptations discussed in Part 4 above.

Pride and Prejudice (feature film, MGM, 1940). Director Robert Z. Leonard; screenplay Aldous Huxley and Jane Murfin. Starring Laurence Olivier (Darcy) and Greer Garson (Elizabeth).

Emma (TV series, BBC, 1972). Director John Glenister; screenplay Denis Constanduros. Starring Doran Godwin (Emma) and John Carson (Knightley).

Mansfield Park (TV series, BBC, 1983). Director David Giles; screenplay Ken Taylor. Starring Sylvestra Le Touzel (Fanny), Nicholas Farrell (Edmund) and Bernard Hepton (Sir Thomas).

Metropolitan (feature film, Columbia, 1990). Director and screenplay Whit Stillman.

Clueless (feature film, Paramount, 1995). Director and screenplay Amy Heckerling.

Persuasion (TV series, BBC/WGBH Boston, 1995; released as a feature film in US). Director Roger Michell; screenplay Nick Dear. Starring Amanda Root (Anne) and Ciaran Hinds (Captain Wentworth).

Pride and Prejudice (TV series, BBC 1995/A&E, 1996). Director Simon Langton; screenplay Andrew Davies. Starring Jennifer Ehle (Elizabeth) and Colin Firth (Darcy).

Sense and Sensibility (feature film, Mirage/Columbia, 1995). Director Ang Lee; screenplay Emma Thompson. Starring Emma Thompson (Elinor), Kate Winslet (Marianne), Hugh Grant (Edward Ferrars) and Alan Rickman (Colonel Brandon).

Emma (feature film, Miramax, 1996). Director and screenplay Douglas McGrath. Starring Gwyneth Paltrow (Emma) and Jeremy Northam (Knightley).

Emma (TV series, ITV 1996/A&E, 1997). Director Diarmuid Lawrence; screenplay Andrew Davies. Starring Kate Beckinsale (Emma) and Mark Strong (Knightley).

Mansfield Park (feature film, Miramax, 1999). Director and screenplay Patricia Rozema. Starring Frances O'Connor (Fanny), Jonny Lee Miller (Edmund) and Harold Pinter (Sir Thomas).

Biographical

Austen, H. (1998) 'Biographical Notice of the Author' in L. Bree (ed.) *Persuasion.* Peterborough, Ont.: Broadview Press.

Fergus, J. (1991) *Jane Austen: A Literary Life.* New York: St Martin's Press.

Halperin, J. (1984) *The Life of Jane Austen.* Baltimore, Md.: The Johns Hopkins University Press.

Honan, P. (1997) *Jane Austen: Her Life.* London: Phoenix.

Le Faye, D. (ed.) (1995) *Jane Austen's Letters.* Third edition. Oxford: Oxford University Press.

Nokes, D. (1997) *Jane Austen: A Life*. London: Fourth Estate.

Shields, C. (2001) *Jane Austen*. London: Weidenfeld & Nicolson.

Spence, J. (2003) *Becoming Jane Austen: A Life*. London: Hambledon and London.

Tomalin, C. (2000) *Jane Austen: A Life*. Harmondsworth: Viking.

Historical context

The books listed in this section are referred to in Part 1 above, and most of them make no explicit mention of Austen.

Barker, H. and Chalus, E. (eds) (1997) *Gender in Eighteenth-Century England: Roles, Representations and Responsibilities*. Harlow: Longman.

Bond, D.F. (ed.) (1965) *The Spectator*. 5 vols. Oxford: Oxford University Press.

Burke, E. ([1790] 1968) *Reflections on the Revolution in France*, ed. C.C. O'Brien. Harmondsworth: Penguin.

Cohen, M. (1996) *Fashioning Masculinity: National Identity and Language in the Eighteenth Century*. London: Routledge.

Colley, L. (1992) *Britons: Forging the Nation 1707–1837*. New Haven, Conn.: Yale University Press.

Davidoff, L. (1995) *Worlds Between: Historical Perspectives on Gender and Class*. Cambridge: Polity.

Davidoff, L. and Hall, C. (1987) *Family Fortunes: Men and Women of the English Middle Class 1780–1850*. London: Routledge.

Gillis, J.R. (1985) *For Better, For Worse: British Marriages, 1600 to the Present*. Oxford: Oxford University Press.

Guest, H. (2000) *Small Change: Women, Learning, Patriotism, 1750–1810*. Chicago, Ill.: University of Chicago Press.

Hansard (1813) *The Parliamentary History of England, from the Earliest Period to the year 1803*, Volume XV: *1753–1765*. London: T.C. Hansard.

Hill, B. (1989) *Women, Work and Sexual Politics in Eighteenth-Century England*. Oxford: Basil Blackwell.

Hunt, M.R. (1996) *The Middling Sort: Commerce, Gender, and the Family in England, 1680–1780*. Berkeley, Calif.: University of California Press.

Klein, L.E. (1995) 'Gender and the Public/Private Distinction: Some Questions about Evidence and Analytic Procedure'. *Eighteenth-Century Studies* 29.1: 97–109.

More, H. (1799) *Strictures on the Modern System of Female Education, with a View of the Principles and Conduct Prevalent among Women of Rank and Fortune*. 2 vols. T. Cadell Jun. and W. Davies.

Perkin, H. (1969) *The Origins of Modern English Society 1780–1880*. London: Routledge & Kegan Paul.

Plumb, J.H. (1950) *England in the Eighteenth Century*. The Pelican History of England. Harmondsworth: Pelican Books.

Shevelow, K. (1989) *Women and Print Culture: The Construction of Femininity in the Early Periodical*. London: Routledge.

Stone, L. and Stone, J.C.F. (1977) *Family, Sex and Marriage in England, 1500–1800*. New York: Harper & Row.

—— (1984) *An Open Elite? England 1540–1880*. Oxford: Oxford University Press.

Trumbach, R. (1978) *The Rise of the Egalitarian Family: Aristocratic Kinship and Domestic Relations in Eighteenth-Century England*. New York: Academic Press.

Vickery, A. (1998) *The Gentleman's Daughter: Women's Lives in Georgian England*. New Haven, Conn.: Yale University Press.

Wilson, K. (1996) 'Citizenship, Empire, and Modernity in the English Provinces, c.1720–1790'. *Eighteenth-Century Studies* 29.1: 69–96.

—— (2002) *The Island Race: Englishness, Empire and Gender in the Eighteenth Century*. London: Routledge.

Wollstonecraft, M. ([1792] 1975) *A Vindication of the Rights of Woman*, ed. M. Brody. Harmondsworth: Penguin.

Theoretical perspectives

Again, most of these books make no explicit mention of Austen, but are referred to, mostly in Parts 3 and 4 above, as sources upon which various studies of Austen draw.

Bourdieu, P. (1984) *Distinction: A Social History of Taste*, trans. R. Nice. London: Routledge.

—— (1993) *The Field of Cultural Production*, ed. and intro. R. Johnson. Cambridge: Polity.

Brooks, C. (1947) *The Well Wrought Urn: Studies in the Structure of Poetry*. New York: Reynal and Witchcock.

Foucault, M. (1970) *The Order of Things: An Archaeology of the Human Sciences*. London: Tavistock.

—— (1977) *Discipline and Punish: The Birth of the Prison*, trans. Alan Sheridan. Harmondsworth: Penguin.

—— (1979) *The History of Sexuality*, Vol. 1: *An Introduction*. Harmondsworth: Penguin.

Habermas, J. (1989) *The Structural Transformation of the Public Sphere: An Inquiry into a Category of Bourgeois Society*, trans. T. Burger. Cambridge, Mass.: MIT Press.

Jameson, F. (1983) 'Postmodernism and Consumer Culture', in H. Foster (ed.) *Postmodern Culture*. London: Pluto, pp. 111–25.

—— (1990) *Signatures of the Visible*. London: Routledge.

—— (1991) 'Nostalgia for the Present', in *Postmodernism: Or, the Cultural Logic of Late Capitalism*. London: Verso, pp. 279–96.

Lukács, G. ([1920] 1971) *The Theory of the Novel*, trans. A. Bostock. Cambridge, Mass.: MIT Press.

—— (1972) *History and Class Consciousness*, trans. R. Livingstone. London: Merlin.

Marx, K. (1977) *Selected Writings*, ed. D. McLellen. Oxford: Oxford University Press.

Wimsatt, W.K. (1954) *The Verbal Icon: Studies in the Meaning of Poetry*. Lexington, Ky.: University of Kentucky Press.

Critical studies of Austen

Abrams, M.H. (1953) *The Mirror and the Lamp: Romantic Theory and the Critical Tradition*. Oxford: Oxford University Press.
—— (1971) *Natural Supernaturalism: Tradition and Revolution in Romantic Literature*. New York: Norton.
Aers, D. (1981) 'Community and Morality: Towards Reading Jane Austen', in David Aers, Jonathan Cook and David Punter (eds) *Romanticism and Ideology: Studies in English Writing 1765–1830*. London: Routledge & Kegan Paul.
Aragay, M. (2003) 'Possessing Jane Austen: Fidelity, Authorship, and Patricia Rozema's *Mansfield Park* (1999)'. *Literature Film Quarterly* 31.3: 177–85.
Armstrong, N. (1987) *Desire and Domestic Fiction: A Political History of the Novel*. Oxford: Oxford University Press.
Auerbach, N. (1978) *Communities of Women: An Idea in Fiction*. Cambridge, Mass.: Harvard University Press.
Babb, H.S. (1962) *Jane Austen's Novels: The Fabric of Dialogue*. Columbus, Ohio: Ohio State University Press.
Ballaster, R. (1992) *Seductive Forms: Women's Amatory Fiction from 1684 to 1740*. Oxford: Oxford University Press.
Barrell, J. (1983) *English Literature in History 1730–80*. London: Hutchinson.
Bilger, A. (1998) *Laughing Feminism: Subversive Comedy in Frances Burney, Maria Edgeworth, and Jane Austen*. Detroit, Mich.: Wayne State University Press.
Booth, W.C. (1961) *The Rhetoric of Fiction*. Chicago, Ill.: University of Chicago Press.
—— (1988) *The Company We Keep: An Ethics of Fiction*. Berkeley, Calif.: University of California Press.
Bradbrook, F. (1966) *Jane Austen and her Predecessors*. Cambridge: Cambridge University Press.
Brown, J.P. (1979) *Jane Austen's Novels: Social Change and Literary Form*. Cambridge, Mass.: Harvard University Press.
Brown, L.W. (1973) *Bits of Ivory: Narrative Technique in Jane Austen's Fiction*. Baton Rouge, La.: Louisiana State University Press.
—— (1973–4) 'Jane Austen and the Feminist Tradition'. *Nineteenth-Century Fiction* 28: 321–38.
Brownstein, R.M. (1982) *Becoming a Heroine: Reading about Women in Novels*. New York: Viking.
—— (1994) 'Irony and Authority', in R. Clark (ed.) *Sense and Sensibility and Pride and Prejudice*. New Casebooks Series. London: Macmillan.
Burgess, M. (2000) *British Fiction and the Production of Social Order 1740–1830*. Cambridge: Cambridge University Press.
Butler, M. (1975) *Jane Austen and the War of Ideas*. Oxford: Oxford University Press.

—— (1981) *Romantics, Rebels and Reactionaries: English Literature and its Background 1760–1830*. Oxford: Oxford University Press.

—— (1993) 'Culture's Medium: The Role of the Review', in S. Curran (ed.) *The Cambridge Companion to British Romanticism*, Cambridge: Cambridge University Press, pp. 120–47.

Byrne, P. (2002) *Jane Austen and the Theatre*. London: Hambledon and London.

Carroll, L. (2003) 'A Consideration of Times and Seasons: Two Jane Austen Adaptations'. *Literature Film Quarterly* 31.3: 169–76.

Cohen, P.M. (1991) *The Daughter's Dilemma: Family Process and the Nineteenth-Century Domestic Novel*. Ann Arbor, Mich.: University of Michigan Press.

Collins, Irene (1994) *Jane Austen and the Clergy*. London: Hambledon and London.

Copeland, E. (1995) *Women Writing about Money: Women's Fiction in England, 1790–1820*. Cambridge: Cambridge University Press.

Copeland, E. and McMaster, J. (eds) (1997) *The Cambridge Companion to Jane Austen*. Cambridge: Cambridge University Press.

Dalton, E. (1995) 'Mourning and Melancholia in *Persuasion*'. *Partisan Review* 62.1 (Winter): 49–59.

Dames, N. (2001) 'Austen's Nostalgics'. *Representations* 73 (Winter): 117–43.

Devlin, D.D. (1975) *Jane Austen and Education*. London: Macmillan.

Doody, M.A. (2001) ' "A Good Memory Is Unpardonable": Self, Love, and the Irrational Irritation of Memory'. *Eighteenth-Century Fiction* 14.1 (October): 67–94.

Douglas, A. (1999) 'Austen's Enclave: Virtue and Modernity'. *Romanticism: A Journal of Romantic Culture and Criticism* 5.2: 147–60.

Duane, A.M. (2001) 'Confusions of Guilt and Complications of Evil: Hysteria and the High Price of Love at Mansfield Park'. *Studies in the Novel* 33.4 (Winter): 402–15.

Duckworth, A.M. (1971) *The Improvement of the Estate: A Study of Jane Austen's Novels*. Baltimore, Md.: Johns Hopkins University Press.

Dussinger, J. (1990) *In the Pride of the Moment: Encounters in Jane Austen's World*. Columbus, Ohio: Ohio State University Press.

Easton, F. (1998) 'The Political Economy of *Mansfield Park*: Fanny Price and the Atlantic Working Class'. *Textual Practice* 12.3 (Winter): 459–88.

Evans, M. (1987) *Jane Austen and the State*. London: Tavistock.

Favret, M. (2000) 'Being True to Jane Austen', in J. Kucich and D.F. Sadoff (eds) *Victorian Afterlife: Postmodern Culture Rewrites the Nineteenth Century*. Minneapolis, Minn: University of Minnesota Press, pp. 64–82.

Fergus, J. (1983) *Jane Austen and the Didactic Novel: 'Northanger Abbey', 'Sense and Sensibility', and 'Pride and Prejudice'*. London: Macmillan.

Ferguson, F. (2000) 'Jane Austen, *Emma*, and the Impact of Form'. *MLQ: Modern Language Quarterly* 61.1: 157–80.

Ferguson, M. (1991) '*Mansfield Park*: Slavery, Colonialism, and Gender'. *Oxford Literary Review* 13: 118–39.

—— (1992) *Subject to Others: British Women Writers and Colonial Slavery, 1670–1834*. London: Routledge.

Ferris, I. (1991) *The Achievement of Literary Authority: Gender, History and the Waverley Novels*. Ithaca, NY: Cornell University Press.

Finch, C. and Bowen, P. (1990) ' "The Tittle-Tattle of Highbury": Gossip and the Free Indirect Style in *Emma*'. *Representations* 31 (Summer): 1–18.

Fleishman, A. (1967) *A Reading of Mansfield Park: An Essay in Critical Synthesis*. Minneapolis, Minn.: University of Minnesota Press.

Fraiman, S. (1993) *Unbecoming Women: British Women Writers and the Novel of Development*. New York: Columbia University Press.

Gallagher, C. (1994) *Nobody's Story: The Vanishing Acts of Women in the Marketplace, 1670–1820*. Oxford: Oxford University Press.

Gallop, D. (1999) 'Jane Austen and the Aristotelian Ethic'. *Philosophy and Literature* 23.1 (April): 96–109.

Galperin, W.H. (1998) 'What Happens when Jane Austen and Frances Burney Enter the Romantic Canon?', in T. Pfau and R.E. Gleckner (eds) *Lessons of Romanticism: A Critical Companion*. Durham, NC: Duke University Press, pp. 376–91.

—— (2000) ' "Let Us Not Desert One Another": Jane Austen and the Romantic Century'. *European Romantic Review* 11.1 (Winter): 35–45.

—— (2003) *The Historical Austen*. Philadelphia, Pa.: University of Philadelphia Press.

Gard, R. (1992) *Jane Austen's Novels: The Art of Clarity*. New Haven, Conn.: Yale University Press.

Gay, P. (2002) *Jane Austen and the Theatre*. Cambridge: Cambridge University Press.

Gaylin, A. (2002) *Eavesdropping in the Novel from Austen to Proust*. Cambridge: Cambridge University Press.

Gibson, P.C. (2000) 'Fewer Weddings and More Funerals: Changes in the Heritage Film', in R. Murphy (ed.) *British Cinema of the 90s*. London: British Film Institute, pp. 115–24.

Gilbert, S. and Gubar, S. (1979) *The Madwoman in the Attic: The Woman Writer and the Nineteenth-Century Imagination*. New Haven, Conn.: Yale University Press.

Goodlad, L.M.E. (2000) 'England's "Glorious 'Middle Way' ": Self-Disciplinary Self-Making and Jane Austen's *Sense and Sensibility*'. *Genre* 33 (Spring): 51–81.

Green, K.S. (1991) *The Courtship Novel 1740–1820: A Feminized Genre*. Lexington, Ky.: University Press of Kentucky.

Greenfield, S.C. (2002) *Mothering Daughters: Novels and the Politics of Family Romance, Frances Burney to Jane Austen*. Detroit, Mich.: Wayne State University Press.

Gross, G.S. (2002) *In a Fast Coach with a Pretty Woman: Jane Austen and Samuel Johnson*. New York: AMS.

Handler, R. and Segal, D. (1990) *Jane Austen and the Fiction of Culture: An Essay on the Narration of Social Realities*. Tucson, Ariz.: University of Arizona Press.

Harding, D.W. ([1940] 1963) 'Regulated Hatred: An Aspect of the Work of Jane Austen', in I. Watt (ed.) *Jane Austen: A Collection of Critical Essays*. Englewood Cliffs, NJ: Prentice Hall, pp. 166–79.

Harris, J. (1989) *Jane Austen's Art of Memory*. Cambridge: Cambridge University Press.

Haslett, M. (2000) *Marxist Literary and Cultural Theory*. New York: St Martin's Press.

Higson, A. (1995) *Waving the Flag: Constructing a National Cinema in Britain*. Oxford: Clarendon.

—— (1996) 'The Heritage Film and British Cinema', in A. Higson (ed.) *Dissolving Views: Key Writings on British Cinema*. London: Cassell, pp. 232–48.

Horowitz, J.B. (1991) *Jane Austen and the Question of Women's Education*. New York: Peter Lang.

Hough, G. (1978) 'Narrative and Dialogue in Jane Austen', in *Selected Essays*. Cambridge: Cambridge University Press, pp. 46–82.

Hudson, G.A. (1999) *Sibling Love and Incest in Jane Austen's Fiction*. Houndsmills: St Martin's Press.

Hunt, L.C. (1988) *A Woman's Portion: Ideology, Culture and the British Female Novel Tradition*. New York: Garland.

James, H. (1985) 'The Lesson of Balzac', in *Literary Criticism: French Writers etc.* New York: Library of America, pp. 115–39.

Johnson, C.L. (1988) *Jane Austen: Women, Politics and the Novel*. Chicago, Ill.: University of Chicago Press.

—— (1995) *Equivocal Beings: Politics, Gender, and Sentimentality in the 1790s. A Study of Wollstonecraft, Radcliffe, Burney, and Austen*. Chicago, Ill.: University of Chicago Press.

Kaplan, D. (1987) 'Female Friendship and Epistolary Form: *Lady Susan* and the Development of Jane Austen's Fiction'. *Criticism* XXIX.2 (Spring): 163–78.

—— (1992) *Jane Austen Among Women*. Baltimore, Md.: Johns Hopkins University Press.

Kaufmann, D. (1992) 'Law and Propriety, *Sense and Sensibility*: Austen on the Cusp of Modernity'. *ELH* 59: 385–408.

Keane, A. (2000) *Women Writers and the English Nation in the 1790s: Romantic Belongings*. Cambridge: Cambridge University Press.

Kelly, G. (1993) *Women, Writing, and Revolution 1790–1827*. Oxford: Oxford University Press.

—— (1997) 'Religion and Politics', in E. Copeland and J. McMaster (eds) *The Cambridge Companion to Jane Austen*. Cambridge: Cambridge University Press, pp. 154–67.

Kettle, A. (1951) *An Introduction to the English Novel*, Vol. I: *To George Eliot*. London: Hutchinson.

Kirkham, M. (1983) *Jane Austen, Feminism and Fiction*. Brighton: Harvester.

Klancher, J. (1987) *The Making of English Reading Audiences 1790–1832*. Madison, Wisc.: University of Wisconsin Press.

Klein, L.E. (1993) 'Gender, Conversation and the Public Sphere', in J. Still and M. Warton (eds) *Textuality and Sexuality: Reading Theories and Practices*. Manchester: Manchester University Press, pp. 100–15.

Knox-Shaw, P. (1998) '*Sense and Sensibility*, Godwin and the Empiricists'. *Cambridge Quarterly* 27.3: 183–208.

—— (1999) '*Northanger Abbey* and the Liberal Historians'. *Essays in Criticism* 49.4 (October): 319–43.

Koppel, G. (1988) *The Religious Dimension in Jane Austen's Novels*. Ann Arbor, Mich.: UMI Research Press.

Korba, S.M. (1997) ' "Improper and Dangerous Distinctions": Female Relationships and Erotic Domination in *Emma*'. *Studies in the Novel* 29.2 (Summer): 139–63.

Kroeber, K. (1971) *Styles in Fictional Structure: The Art of Jane Austen, Charlotte Brontë, and George Eliot*. Princeton, NJ: Princeton University Press.

Lane, M. (1995) *Jane Austen and Food*. London: Hambledon and London.

Langbauer, L. (1990) *Women and Romance: The Consolations of Gender in the English Novel*. Ithaca, NY: Cornell University Press.

Lascelles, M. ([1939] 1995) *Jane Austen and her Art*. Oxford: Oxford University Press.

Leavis, F.R. (1948) *The Great Tradition*. London: Chatto & Windus.

Leavis, Q.D. (2000) *Fiction and the Reading Public*. London: Pimlico.

Lew, J. (1994) ' "The Abominable Traffic": *Mansfield Park* and the Dynamics of Slavery', in B.F. Tobin (ed.) *History, Gender and Eighteenth-Century Literature*. Athens, Ga.: University of Georgia Press, pp. 271–300.

Litz, A.W. (1965) *Jane Austen: A Study in Her Artistic Development*. London: Chatto & Windus.

Lloyd, T. (1999) 'Myths of the Indies: Jane Austen and the British Empire'. *Comparative Criticism* 21: 50–78.

Lodge, D. (1966) *Language of Fiction: Essays in Criticism and Verbal Analysis of the English Novel*. London: Routledge & Kegan Paul.

Looser, D. (ed.) (1995) *Jane Austen and Discourses of Feminism*. Basingstoke: Macmillan.

Lovell, T. (1977) 'Jane Austen and Gentry Society', in Francis Barker *et al.* (eds) *Literature, Society, and the Sociology of Literature*. Colchester: University of Essex, pp. 118–32.

—— (1987) *Consuming Fiction*. London: Verso.

Lynch, D. (1996) 'At Home with Jane Austen', in D. Lynch and W.B. Warner (eds) *Cultural Institutions of the Novel*. Durham, NC: Duke University Press, pp. 159–192.

—— (1998) *The Economy of Character: Novels, Market Culture and the Business of Inner Meaning*. Chicago, Ill.: University of Chicago Press.

—— (ed.) (2000) *Janeites: Austen's Disciples and Devotees*. Princeton, NJ: Princeton University Press.

MacDonagh, O. (1991) *Jane Austen: Real and Imagined Worlds*. New Haven, Conn.: Yale University Press.

Macdonald, G. and Macdonald, A. (2003) *Jane Austen on Screen*. Cambridge: Cambridge University Press.

McDonnell, J. (1984) ' "The Little Spirit of Independence": Sexual Politics and the Bildungsroman in *Mansfield Park*'. *Novel* 17.3 (Spring): 197–214.

MacIntyre, A. (1981) *After Virtue: A Study in Moral Theory*. London: Duckworth.

McMaster, J. (1995) *Jane Austen the Novelist: Essays Past and Present*. London: Macmillan.

—— (1997) 'Class', in E. Copeland and J. McMaster (eds) *The Cambridge Companion to Jane Austen*. Cambridge: Cambridge University Press, pp. 115–30.

McMaster, J. and Stovel, B. (eds) (1996) *Jane Austen's Business: Her World and her Profession*. London: Macmillan.

Mansell, D. (1973) *The Novels of Jane Austen*. London: Macmillan.

Martin, G. (1998) 'Austen and Class'. *Women's Writing 5*.1: 131–44.

Mellor, A. (1993) *Romanticism and Gender*. London: Routledge.

Michaelson, P.H. (2002) *Speaking Volumes: Women, Reading, and Speech in the Age of Austen*. Stanford, Calif.: Stanford University Press.

Michie, E. (2000) 'Austen's Powers: Engaging with Adam Smith in Debates about Wealth and Virtue'. *Novel: A Forum on Fiction 34*.1 (Fall): 5–27.

Miller, D.A. (1981) *Narrative and its Discontents: Problems of Closure in the Traditional Novel*. Princeton, NJ: Princeton University Press.

—— (2003) *Jane Austen, or the Secret of Style*. Princeton NJ: Princeton University Press.

Moler, K. (1968) *Jane Austen's Art of Allusion*. Lincoln, Nebr.: University of Nebraska Press.

Monaghan, D. (1980) *Jane Austen: Structure and Social Vision*. London: Macmillan.

—— (ed.) (1981) *Jane Austen in a Social Context*. London: Macmillan.

Mooneyham, L.G. (1988) *Romance, Language and Education in Jane Austen's Novels*. London: Macmillan.

Moretti, F. (1987) *The Way of the World: The Bildungsroman in European Culture*. London: Verso.

—— (1998) *Altas of the European Novel 1800–1900*. London: Verso.

Morgan, S. (1980) *In the Meantime: Character and Perception in Jane Austen's Fiction*. Chicago, Ill.: University of Chicago Press.

—— (1989) *Sisters in Time: Imagining Gender in Nineteenth-Century British Fiction*. Oxford: Oxford University Press.

Mudrick, M. (1952) *Jane Austen: Irony as Defense and Discovery*. Princeton, NJ: Princeton University Press.

Mullan, J. (1988) *Sentiment and Sociability: The Language of Feeling in the Eighteenth Century*. Oxford: Oxford University Press.

Neill, E. (1999) *The Politics of Jane Austen*. London: Macmillan.

Newton, J.L. (1981) *Women, Power, and Subversion: Social Strategies in British Fiction, 1778–1860*. Athens, Ga.: University of Georgia Press.

North, J. (1999) 'Conservative Austen, Radical Austen: *Sense and Sensibility* from text to screen', in D. Cartmell and I. Whelehan (eds) *Adaptations: From Text to Screen, Screen to Text*. London: Routledge, pp. 38–50.

Odmark, J. (1981) *An Understanding of Jane Austen's Novels: Character, Value, and Ironic Perspective*. Oxford: Blackwell.

Page, N. (1972) *The Language of Jane Austen*. Oxford: Blackwell.

Park, Y.-M. and Rajan, R.S. (eds) (2000) *The Postcolonial Jane Austen*. London: Routledge.

Parker, J.A. (1998) *The Author's Inheritance: Henry Fielding, Jane Austen, and the Establishment of the Novel*. DeKalb, Ill.: Northern Illinois University Press.

Parrill, S. (2002) *Jane Austen on Film and Television: A Critical Study of the Adaptations*. Jefferson, NC: McFarland.

Perera, S. (1991) *Reaches of Empire: The English Novel from Edgeworth to Dickens*. New York: Columbia University Press.

Perkins, M. (1998) *Reshaping the Sexes in Sense and Sensibility*. Charlottesville, Va.: University Press of Virginia.

Phillipps, K.C. (1970) *Jane Austen's English*. London: André Deutsch.

Pidduck, J. (2000) 'Of Windows and Country Walks', in Y.-M. Park and R.S. Rajan (eds) *The Postcolonial Jane Austen*. London: Routledge, pp. 116–38.

Piggott, P. (1979) *The Innocent Diversion: Music in the Life and Writings of Jane Austen*. London: Cleverdon.

Pinch, A. (1996) *Strange Fits of Passion: Epistemologies of Emotion, Hume to Austen*. Stanford, Calif.: Stanford University Press.

Plasa, C. (2001) ' "What Was Done There Is Not to Be Told": *Mansfield Park*'s Colonial Unconscious', in *Textual Politics from Slavery to Postmodernism*. London: Palgrave, pp. 32–59.

Poovey, M. (1984) *The Proper Lady and the Woman Writer: Ideology as Style in the Works of Mary Wollstonecraft, Mary Shelley, and Jane Austen*. Chicago, Ill.: University of Chicago Press.

Pucci, S.R. and Thompson, J. (eds) (2003) *Jane Austen and Co.: Remaking the Past in Contemporary Culture*. Albany, NY: State University of New York Press.

Quinn, V. (2000) 'Loose Reading? Sedgwick, Austen and Critical Practice'. *Textual Practice* 14.2 (Summer): 305–26.

Rasmussen, B. (1993) 'Discovering "A New Way of Reading": Shoshana Felman, Psychoanalysis and *Mansfield Park*', in N. Wood (ed.) *Mansfield Park*. Theory in Practice Series. Buckingham: Open University Press.

Restuccia, F.L. (1994) 'A Black Morning: Kristevan Melancholia in Jane Austen's *Emma*'. *American Imago: Studies in Psychoanalysis and Culture* 51.4 (Winter): 447–69.

Richardson, A. (1994) *Literature, Education and Romanticism: Reading as Social Practice, 1780–1832*. Cambridge: Cambridge University Press.

—— (2001) *British Romanticism and the Science of Mind*. Cambridge: Cambridge University Press.

Rigberg, L.R. (1999) *Jane Austen's Discourse with New Rhetoric*. New York: Peter Lang.

Roberts, W. (1979) *Jane Austen and the French Revolution*. New York: St Martin's Press.

Said, E. (1993) *Culture and Imperialism*. London: Chatto & Windus.

Sales, R. (1994) *Jane Austen and Representations of Regency England*. London: Routledge.

Samuel, R. (1994) *Theatres of Memory*, Vol. I: *Past and Present in Contemporary Culture*. London: Verso.

Schofield, M.A. (ed.) (1986) *Fetter'd or Free? British Women Novelists, 1670–1815*. Athens, Ohio: Ohio University Press.

Sedgwick, E.K. (1991) 'Jane Austen and the Masturbating Girl'. *Critical Inquiry* 17 (Summer): 818–37.

Shaffer, J. (1992) 'Not Subordinate: Empowering Women in the Marriage-Plot. The Novels of Frances Burney, Maria Edgeworth, Jane Austen'. *Criticism: A Quarterly for Literature and the Arts* 34.1 (Winter): 51–73.

Shaw, H.E. (1999) *Narrating Reality: Austen, Scott, Eliot*. Ithaca, NY: Cornell University Press.

Sheen, E. (2000) ' "Where the Garment Gapes": Faithfulness and Promiscuity in the 1995 BBC *Pride and Prejudice*', in R. Giddings and E. Sheen (eds) *The Classic Novel: From Page to Screen*. Manchester: Manchester University Press, pp. 14–30.

Showalter, E. (1977) *A Literature of their Own: British Women Novelists from Brontë to Lessing*. Princeton, NJ: Princeton University Press.

Siskin, C. (1988) *The Historicity of Romantic Discourse*. Oxford: Oxford University Press.

—— (1998) *The Work of Writing: Literature and Social Change, 1700–1830*. Baltimore, Md.: Johns Hopkins University Press.

Smith, L.W. (1983) *Jane Austen and the Drama of Woman*. New York: St Martin's Press.

Sonnet, E. (1999) 'From *Emma* to *Clueless*: Taste, Pleasure and the Scene of History', in D. Cartmell and I. Whelehan (eds) *Adaptations: From Text to Screen, Screen to Text*. London: Routledge, pp. 51–62.

Sorensen, J. (2000) *The Grammar of Empire in Eighteenth-Century British Writing*. Cambridge: Cambridge University Press.

Southam, B.C. (ed.) (1968a) *Jane Austen: The Critical Heritage* [to 1870]. London: Routledge & Kegan Paul.

—— (ed.) (1968b) *Critical Essays on Jane Austen*. London: Routledge & Kegan Paul.

—— (ed.) (1987) *Jane Austen: The Critical Heritage*, Vol. 2: *1870–1940*. London: Routledge & Kegan Paul.

—— (1998) 'The Silence of the Bertrams', in C. Johnson (ed.) *Mansfield Park*. New York: Norton, pp. 493–98.

Spacks, P.M. (1975) *The Female Imagination: A Literary and Psychological Investigation of Women's Writing*. New York: Knopf.

—— (1989) 'Female Resources: Epistles, Plots, and Power', in E.C. Goldsmith (ed.) *Writing the Female Voice*. London: Pinter, pp. 63–76.

—— (1990) *Desire and Truth: Functions of Plot in Eighteenth Century English Novels*. Chicago, Ill., and London: University of Chicago Press.

Spencer, J. (1986) *The Rise of the Woman Novelist: From Aphra Behn to Jane Austen*. Oxford: Blackwell.

Spring, D.A. (1983) 'Interpreters of Jane Austen's Social World', in J. Todd (ed.) *Jane Austen: New Perspectives*. New York: Holmes and Meier, pp. 53–72.

Stewart, M.A. (1993) *Domestic Realities and Imperial Fictions: Jane Austen's Novels in Eighteenth-Century Contexts*. Athens, Ga.: University of Georgia Press.

Stratton, J. (1987) *The Virgin Text: Fiction, Sexuality, and Ideology*. Brighton: Harvester Press.

Sulloway, A. (1989) *Jane Austen and the Province of Womanhood*. Philadelphia, Pa.: University of Philadelphia Press.

Tandon, B. (2003) *Jane Austen and the Morality of Conversation*. London: Anthem.

Tanner, T. (1986) *Jane Austen*. Cambridge, Mass.: Harvard University Press.

Tave, S. (1973) *Some Words of Jane Austen*. Chicago, Ill.: Chicago University Press.

Thompson, J. (1988) *Between Self and World: The Novels of Jane Austen*. University Park, Pa.: Pennsylvania State University Press.

Thompson, J. (1996) *Models of Value: Eighteenth-Century Political Economy and the Novel*. Durham, NC: Duke University Press.

Tobin, B.F. (1990) 'The Moral and Political Economy of Austen's *Emma*'. *Eighteenth-Century Fiction* 2.3 (April): 229–54.

Todd, J. (1986) *Sensibility: An Introduction*. London: Methuen.

Trilling, L. (1967) '*Emma*', in *Beyond Culture: Essays on Literature and Learning*. Harmondsworth: Penguin, pp. 204–25.

—— (1982) 'Why We Read Jane Austen', in D. Trilling (ed.) *The Last Decade: Essays and Reviews 1965–75*. Oxford: Oxford University Press, pp. 204–25.

Troide, L.E. (1994) *The Early Letters and Journals of Fanny Burney*, Vol. III. Oxford: Clarendon Press.

Troost, L. and Greenfield, S. (eds) (1998) *Jane Austen in Hollywood*. Lexington, Ky.: University Press of Kentucky.

Tuite, C. (2002) *Romantic Austen: Sexual Politics and the Literary Canon*. Cambridge: Cambridge University Press.

Turner, C. (1992) *Living by the Pen: Women Writers in the Eighteenth Century*. London: Routledge.

Van Ghent, D. (1953) *The English Novel: Form and Function*. New York: Holt, Rinehart, & Winston.

Wald, G. (2000) '*Clueless* in the Neocolonial World Order', in Y.-M. Park and R.S. Rajan (eds) *The Postcolonial Jane Austen*. London: Routledge, pp. 218–33.

Waldron, M. (1999) *Jane Austen and the Fiction of her Time*. Cambridge: Cambridge University Press.

Wallace, R.K. (1983) *Jane Austen and Mozart: Classical Equilibrium in Fiction and Music*. Athens, Ga.: University of Georgia Press.

Wallace, T.G. (1995) *Jane Austen and Narrative Authority*. New York: St Martin's Press.

Watson, N. (1994) *Revolution and the Form of the British Novel 1790–1825*. Oxford: Oxford University Press.

Watt, I. (1957) *The Rise of the Novel*. London: Chatto & Windus.

—— (ed.) (1963) *Jane Austen: A Collection of Critical Essays*. Englewood Cliffs, NJ: Prentice-Hall.

Williams, M. (1986) *Jane Austen: Six Novels and their Methods*. London: Macmillan.

Williams, R. (1973) *The Country and the City*. London: Chatto & Windus.

Wiltshire, J. (1992) *Jane Austen and the Body: 'The Picture of Health'*. Cambridge: Cambridge University Press.

—— (2001) *Recreating Jane Austen*. Cambridge: Cambridge University Press.

—— (2003) 'Decolonising *Mansfield Park*'. *Essays in Criticism* 53.4 (October): 303–22.

Wooden, S. (2002) ' "You Even Forget Yourself": The Cinematic Construction of Anorexic Women in the 1990s Austen Films'. *Journal of Popular Culture* 36.3 (Fall): 221–35.

Wright, P. (1985) *On Living in an Old Country: The National Past in Contemporary Britain*. London: Verso.

Yeazell, R.B. (1991) *Fictions of Modesty: Women and Courtship in the English Novel*. Chicago, Ill.: Chicago University Press.

Journals and websites

As well as the journals cited above, *Persuasions*, published by the Jane Austen Society of North America (www.jasna.org), is the only journal dedicated to Austen that regularly includes original scholarship and criticism (although it occasionally includes less scholarly Jane worship as well). The American Society of Jane Austen Scholars (facstaff.uww.edu/hipchene/JAusten/home) is a very useful source of links to Austen material of all kinds.

Index

Routledge Guides to Literature

Jane Austen's *Emma*: A Sourcebook

Edited by Paula Byrne

Jane Austen's *Emma* (1815) is at once a comedy of misunderstanding, a razor-sharp analysis of the English class system, and a classic tale of romance and moral growth that has appealed to readers and critics alike.

Taking the form of a sourcebook, this guide to Austen's much-loved novel offers:

- extensive introductory comment on the contexts and many interpretations of the text, from publication to the present
- annotated extracts from key contextual documents, reviews, critical works and the text itself
- cross-references between documents and sections of the guide, in order to suggest links between texts, contexts and criticism
- suggestions for further reading.

Part of the *Routledge Guides to Literature* series, this volume is essential reading for all those beginning detailed study of *Emma* and seeking not only a guide to the novel, but a way through the wealth of contextual and critical material that surrounds Austen's text.

Hb: 0–415–28650–6
Pb: 0–415–28651–4

Available at all good bookshops
For ordering and further information please visit:
www.routledge.com

RELATED TITLES FROM ROUTLEDGE

Routledge Guides to Literature

Jane Austen's *Pride & Prejudice*: A Sourcebook

Edited by Robert Morrison

Jane Austen's *Pride and Prejudice* (1813) is perhaps her most popular novel. A work of comedy, wit, romance, it is also haunted by ironic shadows and dark anxieties as Austen traces the fortunes of central character Elizabeth Bennet.

Taking the form of a sourcebook, this guide to Austen's much-loved novel offers:

- extensive introductory comment on the contexts and many interpretations of the text, from publication to the present
- annotated extracts from key contextual documents, reviews, critical works and the text itself
- cross-references between documents and sections of the guide, in order to suggest links between texts, contexts and criticism
- suggestions for further reading.

Part of the *Routledge Guides to Literature* series, this volume is essential reading for all those beginning detailed study of *Pride and Prejudice* and seeking not only a guide to the novel, but a way through the wealth of contextual and critical material that surrounds Austen's text.

Hb: 0–415–26849–4
Pb: 0–415–26850–8

Available at all good bookshops
For ordering and further information please visit:
www.routledge.com

Routledge Guides to Literature
Thomas Hardy

Geoffrey Harvey

Thomas Hardy found fame as both a major novelist and a supreme poet, whose work reflected the many revolutionary social and intellectual changes of the nineteenth and early-twentieth centuries. One of England's most popular writers, his work is still widely read and enjoyed.

This guide to Hardy's memorable work offers:

- an accessible introduction to the contexts and many interpretations of Hardy's texts, from publication to the present
- an introduction to key critical texts and perspectives on Hardy's life and work, situated within a broader critical history
- cross-references between sections of the guide, in order to suggest links between texts, contexts and criticism
- suggestions for further reading.

Part of the *Routledge Guides to Literature* series, this volume is essential reading for all those beginning detailed study of Hardy and seeking not only a guide to his works, but a way through the wealth of contextual and critical material that surrounds them.

Hb: 0–415–23491–3
Pb: 0–415–23492–1

Available at all good bookshops
For ordering and further information please visit:

www.routledge.com